CW00408614

Heathrow Airport

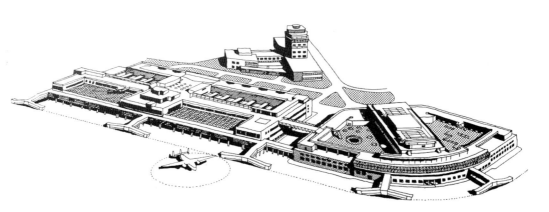

Dedication

This book is dedicated to the memory of a trio of dear friends who worked as press photographers when I came to work as a news reporter at Heathrow Airport (1966–1978):

Steve Arnott (1949–2012)

Gordon Tilling (1931–2011)

and

Tony Hewson (1930–1999)

What a team!

Heathrow Airport

Yesterday, Today and Tomorrow

Alan Gallop

Pen & Sword
AVIATION

First published in Great Britain in 2019
by Pen & Sword Aviation
An imprint of
Pen & Sword Books Ltd
Yorkshire – Philadelphia

ISBN 978 1 52675 918 4

A CIP catalogue record for this book is available from the British Library.

Printed and bound in the UK by T.J. International Ltd, Padstow, Cornwall.

Pen & Sword Books Limited incorporates the imprints of Atlas, Archaeology, Aviation, Discovery, Family History, Fiction, History, Maritime, Military, Military Classics, Politics, Select, Transport, True Crime, Air World, Frontline Publishing, Leo Cooper, Remember When, Seaforth Publishing, The Praetorian Press, Wharncliffe Local History, Wharncliffe Transport, Wharncliffe True Crime and White Owl.

For a complete list of Pen & Sword titles please contact

PEN & SWORD BOOKS LIMITED
47 Church Street, Barnsley, South Yorkshire, S70 2AS, England
E-mail: enquiries@pen-and-sword.co.uk
Website: www.pen-and-sword.co.uk

or

PEN AND SWORD BOOKS
1950 Lawrence Rd, Havertown, PA 19083, USA
E-mail: Uspen-and-sword@casematepublishers.com
Website: www.penandswordbooks.com

Contents

Acknowledgements

This book would have been impossible to write without the help, guidance, comments, contributions and referrals given to me by many people who have played a part in the story of Heathrow Airport.

A postcard from Keith Hayward who started his working life as a 16-year-old school-leaver working for British South American Airways (BSAA) in London and later at Heathrow in 1946 triggered off an incredible trail leading to people who were at the airport on its very first day of operations on 1 January 1946. Thanks to Keith (who at the age of over 90 years young is still working at the airport at the British Airways Archives in a voluntary capacity a couple of days each week), I was put in touch with two other people who flew on that first flight: Mary Cunningham (née Guthrie), the country's first peacetime air stewardess, and Captain Cliff Alabaster, navigator and co-pilot of the BSAA Avro Lancastrian service from Heathrow to Latin America. All three were kind enough to give me their time to recall their airport memories from more than seventy years ago. RIP to both of the latter.

Another set of fascinating memories came from the late John Boulding, MBE, BOAC's former chief investigator of accidents and air safety who lived just 100 steps away from my own home in Surrey. Special thanks as well to three other people who are also no longer with us: Fred Gore, Ray Berry and Flo Kingdon who also freely shared their airport memories.

Thanks, too, to Dennis Martin for providing me with information on the rise and fall of British Eagle; Nicky Carter for material on the villages of Heath Row and Perry Oaks; plus Betty Richardson, Paul Townend, Ted Carpenter, Derek Rylatt, Gordon Pankhurst, Gordon Chubb, Philip Gordon-Marshall, Eric Driver, June Pearce and her brother Dennis Sparks, June Pike, Tony Hesketh-Gardener, Gwen Humphries, Don Parry, Vincent Vere, Tom Marks, Steve Meller, Barry Dix and the late Leslie Green, Stan Stern and Father Peter Knott.

Special thanks to Henry Wilson and Jon Wilkinson at Pen & Sword Books for their belief and commitment to this book. It has been a great pleasure working with you both. Thanks also to Matt Jones and Mat Blurton for seeing the book through the production process.

Finally, love and thanks to my wife, Linda, for her patience and ability to steer me through a multitude of computer problems encountered while writing this and other books. Where would I be without you?

OFFICIAL PROGRAMME.   **PRICE SIXPENCE.**

THE ROYAL AERO CLUB

AVIATION RACE MEETING

(Under the Competition Rules of the Royal Aero Club and the Regulations of the F.A.I.)

AT

WADDON AERODROME, CROYDON.

(By permission of the Air Council.)

Monday, 7th August, 1922.

OFFICIALS OF THE MEETING.

JUDGE:
Lieut.-Col. L. F. BLANDY, D.S.O.

STEWARDS:

Major-General Sir SEFTON BRANCKER, K.C.B., A.F.C.   W. O. MANNING.   Lieut.-Col. F. C. SHELMERDINE.

CLERK OF THE COURSE: HANDICAPPERS: HON. SURGEON:
Lieut.-Col. M. O. DARBY.   Lieut.-Col. W. A. BRISTOW.   Major H. GRAEME ANDERSON.
                              Capt. R. J. GOODMAN CROUCH.

TIMEKEEPERS: PRESS STEWARD: MARSHALS:
F. T. BIDLAKE.   GEOFFREY DORMAN.   J. CAMPBELL.   C. H. GRACE.
J. H. BURLEY.   Capt. L. T. G. MANSELL.   G. WRENCH TOWSE.
                                              Capt. F. R. WALKER.

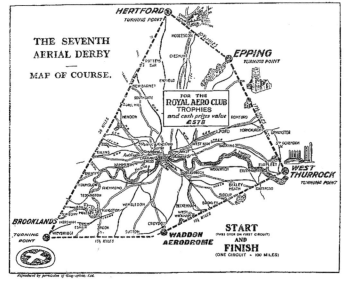

Secretary: HAROLD E. PERRIN, 3, Clifford Street, London, W. 1.   *Assistant Secretary:* B. STEVENSON.

The 1922 Royal Aero Club race meeting was held at Waddon Aerodrome and attracted thou-sands of families; admission sixpence, to include a programme. (*Croydon Archives*)

I have been asked to point out that Heathrow Airport Limited was not involved in the writing, editing or publishing of this book, apart from providing me with valuable background information on their proposed construction of a new runway at the airport. Accordingly, none of the views expressed in this book are those of Heathrow Airport Limited (unless otherwise stated in the written text), which makes no representations or warranties about the accuracy, completeness or suitability for any purpose of the information contained in this story.

Now ladies and gentlemen, boys and girls, it's time to buckle up your seat belts and hold on tight; it could be a bumpy ride ...

Alan Gallop

Chapter 1

Heathrow Fly Past – 1918-1933: How it all Began

During the early years of the twentieth century and long before a group of fields, smallholdings and market gardens sitting on farmland to the west of London became Heathrow Airport, officials from the City of London were determined to create a series of aerodromes dotted around the capital for growing numbers of British businesses wanting to trade with France, Belgium, The Netherlands and Germany.

Successful businesses have always depended on their ability to transport goods and people from one country to another in the fastest possible time. Road, rail and sea transport was all very well but was a slow way of moving certain products, including food and perishables, from Britain to its neighbours on the other side of the Channel and North Sea. Using small biplanes to fly between one grass airstrip near London to another outside of Paris, Brussels or Amsterdam was deigned to be the solution – providing British businesses were prepared to pay a premium price to get their goods and company representatives in the air and on their way from London to continental destinations.

The early years of the First World War rapidly accelerated the progress of aviation faster than the eleven years between the Wright Brothers' first flight in 1903 and 1914. But by the close of the war there were numerous aviators with little to keep them occupied now there were no enemy aircraft to dog fight with over the Western Front. There were also numerous airplanes sitting unused in hangars up and down the country. Early plane makers and aviators were encouraged to push the limits of flight (mostly through flying air shows which attracted thousands of spectators) and others who saw the commercial potential of using aircraft to boost business opportunities.

By 1920 a string of grass airstrips had been positioned around London. They were once used as firing stations from where to shoot down Zeppelins and places where small aircraft could quickly take off and get close enough to airships to score a direct hit. But by 1920 many of the aerodromes had become redundant in peacetime.

To stay in business, airstrips introduced commercial air services to the continent. Two pioneering aerodromes called Waddon and Beddington, located next door to each with just a narrow roadway in between and located near Croydon, to the south of London, were among the first to 'go continental'. Waddon pioneered the first service carrying four passengers to Paris-Le Bourget Aerodrome northwest of the city. It took two and a half hours to cover the journey for a single fare costing £24.00.

A daily service from Hounslow Heath Aerodrome (close to where Heathrow Airport has stood for over 70 years) to Paris-Le Bourget was operated by the Aircraft Transport & Travel Co. using a DH16 aircraft which left on the dot of 12.30 pm each day and took two and a quarter hours to cover the journey. Fares began at £21 and up to four passengers could each carry luggage of up to 15lb, while Instone Air Line at Waddon offered twice-weekly Paris-Le Bourget services for a fare of £12.

A Waddon-Brussels service owned by aircraft manufacturer and operator Handley Page Company using Type O/400 bombers modified for passenger use operated on Mondays, Wednesdays and Fridays, returning from Brussels on Tuesdays, Thursdays and Saturdays. Flights took around three hours and the single fare cost £15 15s.

A regular air service between Hounslow Heath Aerodrome and Amsterdam's Soesterberg Aerodrome also took three hours and the single fare cost £20. It was operated by British Aerial Transport Co., which had major plans to extend its services to other airports both at home and on the continent. However, plans were halted in the early 1920s when the British government decided that travel to and from the colonies and destinations nearer home needed to be made easier, faster and more affordable. The government believed that flight – instead of travel by sea and rail – would also speed up colonial government business and trade that until then was entirely dependent upon ships.

A regular air service between Hounslow Heath Aerodrome and Amsterdam's Soesterberg Aerodrome took three hours and the single fare cost £20.00. It was operated by British Aerial Transport Co. (*Tim Jefkins Collection*)

The government proposed that the four largest airlines operating out of Britain – Instone Air Line, Daimler Airway, Handley Page Air Transport and British Marine Air Navigation – be merged into a single airline to be called Imperial Air Transport Company, flying under the name of Imperial Airways. To encourage the merger the government was prepared to offer a subsidy of £1 million over a ten-year period. The subsidies were to be £137,000 in the first year, diminishing to £32,000 in the tenth year.

The new company was to be based at Croydon Airport (of which Waddon and Beddington airports had been a part) from where Imperial Airways would concentrate on operating to all corners of the British Empire. Croydon – also known as the London Terminal Aerodrome or London Airport – was to become the UK's major international airport during the interwar period and as soon as peace was declared was set to become the country's largest, busiest and most successful international airport.

The first commercial flight to leave Croydon took to the skies on 26 April 1924, when a daily London-Paris-Le Bourget route was opened using a de Havilland DH 34. This route quickly became the busiest in the world. The task of expanding routes between England and the continent from other airports began in the same year with Southampton-Guernsey on 1 May 1924; Croydon-Brussels-Cologne on 3 May; Croydon-Amsterdam on 2 June 1924; and summer services between Croydon-Le Bourget-Basle-Zürich on 17 June 1924.

The first new airliner ordered by Imperial Airways was the Handley Page W8f delivered on 3 November 1924. In the first year of operation the company

Imperial Airways used four-engine Handley Page H.P.42 Heracles aircraft between 1931 and 1939, flying from Croydon Airport to Europe, the Middle East and India. Eight aircraft in the fleet flew 10 million miles without a fatality. (*Science Museum Group*)

The mid-1920s and 1930s marked the truly great days of flying, when passengers wearing tropical clothes would turn up at Croydon on a winter's day, already dressed for sunny destinations. It would take one week or longer to fly to the other side of the world in an Imperial Airways Handley Page 42, equipped to carry twenty to thirty passengers depending on the route. (*Author's Collection*)

carried 11,395 passengers and 212,380 letters. The airport was growing so rapidly that under the provisions of the Croydon Aerodrome Extension Act 1925, the airport had to be greatly enlarged between 1926 and 1928, with a new complex of buildings being constructed including the first purpose-designed airport terminal and control tower, the world's first airport hotel and a set of aircraft hangars. The development cost £267,000 (£14.8 million at today's prices). The airport's terminal building and control tower were completed in 1928, and the old wooden air traffic control and customs building demolished. The new buildings and revised airport layout came into service on 20 January 1928.

In March 1937 British Airways Ltd began operations from Croydon, moving to Heston Aerodrome the following year, and while Imperial Airways served routes across the British Empire, British Airways flew European routes. The two carriers were merged by Neville Chamberlain's government in November 1938 to become British Overseas Airways Corporation (BOAC).

Croydon was closed to commercial airlines during the Second World War to be used by various squadrons of the RAF. Civil aviation returned in February 1946, by which time it was realized that air travel would quickly intensify. The government called for aircraft manufacturers to build larger and faster equipment to meet the needs of a growing demand for air travel. Yet the urban spread of south London and the growth of villages surrounding Croydon had enclosed the airport, leaving no room for further expansion.

To five countries and three of the most important capitals in Europe British Airways fly daily

....Entrusted with the carriage of His Majesty's mails to Scandinavia by day and night, British Airways have gained a notable reputation for speed, comfort and operational efficiency. We would welcome the responsibility of flying you to Paris in 90 minutes, or to Amsterdam, Hamburg, Copenhagen, Malmö and Stockholm in a few hours of comfort. See your travel agent for times of services.

BRITISH AIRWAYS

TERMINAL HOUSE. VICTORIA. LONDON. S.W.1.   Phone SLOANE 0091

In March 1937 British Airways Ltd began operations from Croydon, moving to Heston Aerodrome the following year, and while Imperial Airways served routes across the British Empire, British Airways flew European routes. The two carriers were merged by Neville Chamberlain's government in November 1938 to become British Overseas Airways Corporation (BOAC). (*Croydon Archives*)

In 1952 Croydon Airport was closed as Blackbushe Airport in Hampshire and Northolt Aerodrome in Middlesex could accommodate European flights during the 1950s. The last scheduled flight from Croydon departed at 6.15 pm on 30 September 1959 followed by the last aircraft (a private flight) at 7.45 pm; the airfield officially closed at 10.20 pm. (*Author's Collection*)

In 1952 it was decided that the airport would eventually close as Blackbushe Airport in Hampshire and Northolt Aerodrome in Middlesex could accommodate European flights during the 1950s. However, airlines had their sights on another airport to secure their prosperity: Heathrow.

*   *   *

In the 1930s London's planners and architects had dreams of far more convenient airports than Croydon which would be located in the heart of the capital. A number of visionary ideas were produced by different architects with a view to improving air transport links to and from the UK and making it easier for airlines to bring passengers and cargo right into the capital.

First off the mark was an idea to build an airport on top of London's King's Cross Station. Called London Central Airport, it was to be funded by private equity. Plans were drawn up by architect Charles W. Glover who wrote in 1931 that Croydon Airport was 'inconveniently located for most Londoners, and with the growth of private flying, a central London airport was now needed.' He believed that London-based businessmen needed to be encouraged to fly between meetings, and a central London location would shave forty minutes'

In 1931 plans were drawn up to build an airport – to be called London Central Airport – on the roof of London's King's Cross Station. It was estimated it would cost £5 million and would sit on top of a set of warehousing buildings. A set of concrete runways that looked like spokes in a cart-wheel were planned to be half a mile long and 200ft wide. (Daily Mail *Archives*)

travel time off journeys which currently began in Croydon. 'An airport situated over the sidings at King's Cross is the only suitable site for the development,' claimed Glover.

It would cost £5 million to build the new airport. Its blueprint was based on a hub and spoke design that would sit on top of a new set of large warehouse buildings to be constructed behind the railway station to store airfreight passing through the airport. The freight sheds would offer 75 acres of floor space during a time when freight carried by train was still a major source of railway traffic. Glover also suggested that Covent Garden's market should move from its historic home on the eastern fringes of London's West End between Charing Cross and Drury Lane to a new home on the King's Cross estate.

Glover's sky-high airport would also feature a large bus station for passengers to get around London and transport links to the capital's railway and underground networks. However, to achieve this and make way for the new rooftop airport, hundreds of slum dwellings would have to be demolished and people living in them re-housed in newly-constructed tower blocks. A new road, tentatively named Aerial Way, would be pushed through the former slum estates to link up with Pentonville Road.

The concrete runways themselves – which looked like spokes in a cartwheel – were planned to be half a mile long and up to 200ft wide which Glover noted was 'more than ample for the largest aeroplane, and also provides for a longer run which might be necessary for some types of multi-engine aeroplanes that might be constructed in the future.' In the 1930s London had no skyscrapers, so the approach to and from London Central Airport would be obstacle-free. Airline passengers would travel to the rooftop departures and arrivals area in lifts located in check-in areas on the ground floor station concourse. Aircraft would taxi around the rim of the runway wheel until given clearance to take off. Thanks to the 'spoke' design, the runways would be ingeniously laid out to allow landings and take-offs in eight different directions, depending on the strength of the wind, an aircraft's destination and weight.

The project generated huge amounts of publicity and triggered debates on the floor of the House of Commons. Yet London Central Airport never took off. It was too expensive and it would take years to gain planning permission. It was also dealt a blow by a report just a few months later from the Aerodromes Committee at the Royal Institute of British Architects (RIBA) which advocated state ownership of airports instead of private investors, as Glover had proposed.

* * *

In 1933 the wraps were removed from another improbable plan for an airport located in Central London. The scheme was to construct a large elevated

Plan City Airport Above River Thames

AIRPLANE ELEVATORS
TO HANGAR DECK

LANDING DECK
HANGAR DECK

SECTIONAL VIEW SHOWS ARRANGEMENT OF DECKS

PASSENGER ELEVATOR

BUILDING a monster landing field over the River Thames is now being advocated before officials of the city of London, England, as a means of providing the city with an airport close to its business center. The bridgelike structure, according to one plan put forward, would be high enough to clear the tallest masts of ships and would include an upper deck for landing and a lower deck with hangar space for planes. The diagram above shows details of the project.

By 1933 the wraps had been removed for another airport plan for central London. The scheme called for a large elevated landing strip that would stretch across the Thames upriver from the Houses of Parliament across to London County Council headquarters. It was to be called City Airport but was rejected on the grounds of being too close to historical buildings and liable to making too much noise during Parliamentary sessions. (*The* Engineer)

landing strip, to be called City Airport, which stretched right across the River Thames upriver from the Houses of Parliament and Westminster Bridge on one side and the London County Council headquarters on the Lambeth side.

Four massive steel bridges – or caissons – would span the river supporting a flat concrete roof containing take-off and landing decks long enough for most commercial aircraft in use at that time plus a passenger concourse for travellers. The roof would also contain a control tower and a series of industrial-size elevators capable of transporting aircraft between a series of decks below the concourse to the boarding area. Special elevators for passengers travelling from the street-level check-in area to aircraft at the top were to be located within four of the eight caissons. Two runways were planned, allowing aircraft to take off and land simultaneously. At night the runway roof would be floodlit with arc lamps, allowing aircraft movements to take place at any hour of the day or night.

The elevated runway area would be high enough to clear masts from the tallest ships travelling up and down the river below to and from the Port of London and passing directly underneath the City Airport structure.

The plan, however, was rejected on the grounds that it was too close to buildings of historical importance and liable to make too much noise during parliamentary sessions. It was also ugly and far from pleasing to the eye. It

Future Airport In London's Centre

The ever-increasing delays in travelling between existing airports and city centres, like London and Paris, causes a barrier to fast air travel — even if the passenger goes by 600 m.p.h. jet! The answer is vertical take-off and landing (VTOL) airliners which will bring passengers to the city centres. The possibility of an airport site for these VTOL airliners, at Nine Elms on the South bank of the River Thames in the heart of London, has been studied by Hawker Siddeley Aviation. It would be used for inter-city travel, the major airports being utilised for the long-distance supersonic and airbus jets. The big problem for the city centre airport is defeating engine noise: this has brought about a design study for 'quiet' turbofan lift aircraft with wing-mounted lift pods used only during take-off and landing. Separate jet engines will take over for forward power. We show an impression of such a central airport as it might appear in the future with rail and bus services close at hand for reaching offices and hotels in London. The airport would have two separate take-off and landing pads with exhaust noise suppressors and five loading bays.

Proposed design for a 90-seat short-haul transport with wing-mounted lift pods for vertical take-off and landing. (A) Light-weight jet engines for lift. (B) Engine-driven turbofans which give lift and reduce engine noise by lowering the speed of the exhaust gases. (C) Lift ducts can be closed in forward flight. (D) Separate jet engines for forward power.

AN EAGLE cutaway DRAWING

KEY TO NUMBERED PARTS

(1) Aircraft movement and plotting room. (2) Vertical take-off and landing control tower. (3) Public viewing gallery. (4) Floodlights. (5) Radar scanners. (6) Overbridge from airport offices and communications. (7) Car and coach park. (8) Lift for aircraft refuellers and ground equipment. (9) Take-off exhaust outlets. (10) Exhaust noise suppressors. (11) Take-off pad over the River Thames. (12) Passenger lift raised. (13) Passenger lounge and restaurant. (14) Separate drive in and entrances for passengers and baggage. (15) Main concourse and access to lifts. (16) ... passenger entry to aircraft. (17) Airport apron with five loading bays. (18) Passenger ... (19) Customs and booking office. (20) Existing railway sidings at Nine Elms converted ... services to Victoria and Waterloo Stations. (21) Vertical landing pad with exhaust ... ...ers. (22) Victoria railway bridge. (23) Aircraft after vertical take-off transfer... ...rd flight over the river.

ASHWELL WOOD

A group of businessmen put forward plans in the 1960s to build an airport along the south bank of the Thames at Nine Elms for Vertical Take-Off and Landing (VTOL) aircraft but the idea was scrapped due to the noise made by this type of aircraft. (*The* Eagle)

was suggested that the plan might be considered if it were sited elsewhere on the river, but following a splurge of publicity in the news media, City Airport disappeared from view never to be seen again.

Other plans for aerodromes within London in 1935 included constructing an airport along the south bank of the Thames between London Bridge and

Tower Bridge and there was a later 1945 proposal to construct a cruciform airstrip across the roof of five tall buildings in Liverpool Street. Later still an attempt to build an airport for VTOL (Vertical Take Off and Landing) airliners in London's Nine Elms district on the south bank of the Thames was studied by Hawker Siddeley Aviation which had a special plane on its drawing board designed for inter-city travel between UK and European airports. The idea was to build an airport with separate take-off and landing pads, but the idea was scrapped due to noise from the type of aircraft expected to use it (and produced by Hawker Siddeley), plus the inability to find anyone prepared to invest in the venture. It would not be until 1988 that London was permitted to have an airport within its boundaries when London City Airport opened in the Royal Docks in the London Borough of Newham, 6 miles east of the City of London and east of Canary Wharf, twin centres of London's financial industry and major users of the airport.

Chapter 2

3000 BC–1919: An Historic Fly-Past

'On Hounslow Heath as I rode o'er,
I spied a lawyer riding before.
Kind sir, said I, aren't you afraid
Of Turpin, that mischievous blade?'
                    From an anonymous poem written in 1793

It lies on 4.5 square miles of flat gravel plain between Staines and Hayes in Middlesex and is 14 miles by road from Charing Cross. If the River Thames had not receded from its original bed more than 15,000 years ago to leave on its northern banks a vast flat stretch of gravel subsoil known geologically as the 'Taplow Terrace', Heathrow Airport might never have been built on its present site.

Archaeological research conducted prior to the start of construction work on the airport's Terminal 5 shows that Heathrow has been a 'take-off' point since the Stone Age. Some 5,000 years ago, Druid high priests are understood to have used the site as a spiritual runway to travel to the spirit world or to communicate with ancestors.

Archaeologists discovered that a 2.5-mile-long and 7-metre-wide site stretching from the Terminal 5 site towards where the British Airways' Heathrow maintenance base now stands was once artificially raised 2 metres above the surrounding countryside and flanked by 3-metre-deep ditches. It was almost as if the area had been made ready to receive the arrival of a prehistoric flying machine piloted by Neolithic cavemen working for Jurassic Airways....

There is little doubt that the Heathrow site was once a substantial religious centre used for sacred processions possibly associated with fertility and funeral rituals. During the 1944 construction of Heathrow's runways, remains of a small rectangular building, possibly a Celtic temple with a surrounding colonnade, were uncovered. It was clear from pottery found nearby that this dated from the early Iron Age.

Evidence was also uncovered confirming that Heathrow had been visited by early Roman settlers. The remains of a 300ft² Roman camp, discovered where one of the runways is now located, had probably been one of Caesar's stations after he marched towards the nearby River Thames during his second invasion of Britain in 54 BC in pursuit of Cassivellaunus, the region's earliest known ruler.

Nobody knows how Heathrow – or Hetherewe (fifteenth century), Hetherow and Hitherowe (sixteenth century), Hetherowfeyld and Hedrowe (seventeenth century) and Heath Row (eighteenth century) – got its name. A fourteenth-century document refers to a man named William Atte Hethe, a tenant of some standing whose dwelling later became the site of Heath Cottages, one of several picturesque residential buildings in the village of Heath Row and on the route between Colnbrook and Stanwell. They were demolished in the 1940s to make way for what we know today as Heathrow Airport.

The next known ruler to show interest in the site was King Henry VIII who hunted stag, deer and wild boar on the vast open plains and forests of Hounslow Heath, a large area to the west of London covering thousands of acres of open parkland and oak forests stretching from Brentford to Staines. The king's chief minister, Cardinal Thomas Wolsey, originally paid for a watercourse to be dug from the River Colne at Longford to Hampton Court on a route skirting around what is today the airport's western perimeter. When finally completed in the reign of King Charles I, it would reinforce water supplies to the ornamental waters and fountains of Hampton Court and Bushey Park. Known by a collection of names including the Cardinal's River, the Hampton Court Canal, Queen's River and today as the Longford River, it is still owned by the Crown, managed by the Royal Parks Agency and feeds the same fountains it fed more than 360 years ago.

A second man-made water channel was also built in the reign of Henry VIII to provide power to a water mill in the grounds of Syon House at Isleworth. The Earl of Northumberland bought the river and stately home from King James I in the seventeenth century and the watercourse, known today as the Duke of Northumberland's River, still supplies water to the ornamental lake at Syon Park.

These twin rivers, which originally ran parallel to each other along Heathrow's boundaries, were both diverted along new courses to make way for Terminal 5 and are the airport's oldest visible landmarks.

In the early seventeenth century, a stagecoach journey from London to Bath took three days. Queen Anne had helped re-establish the popularity of Bath as the nearest health resort to London and the only way to get there was by road. By 1784 the journey time had been cut to sixteen hours with relays of horses stationed along the route. The villages of Longford and Colnbrook and their coaching inns shared the boom of the prosperity that followed.

By the early years of Queen Victoria, the settlement and surrounding area of Heath Row – a hamlet at the western end of Hounslow Heath without a

An Exact Reprefentation of MACLAINE the Highwayman Robbing LORD EGLINGTON on Hounflow Heath on the 26th of June 1750.

Heathrow Airport sits on land that was once the hunting grounds of notorious footpads and highwaymen, including Dick Turpin, James MacLaine, Claude Duval, Moll Cutpurse and William 'The Dandy' Page who were active along the Bath Road and hid in small hamlets like Heath Row and Perry Oaks. MacLaine is pictured here in 1750 attempting to relieve Lord Eglington of his money, fine clothes and a blunderbuss. He was later arrested, tried and found guilty and hanged at Tyburn in October 1750. (*Author's Collection*)

church and with a population of less than 100 – was a desolate wasteland occupied by beer houses and flocks of greyhound-like sheep, described by an early observer as 'pitiful and half-starved looking animals subject to rot.' However, thanks to the underlying gravel that provided excellent drainage, the land was extremely fertile, producing enough crops to allow market gardeners and smallholders to take their produce into London by cart to sell and return with wagonloads of free manure supplied by the many horses coming into and out of the city. Londoners were glad to be rid of it. It was then dug into Heath Row's gardens and smallholdings, producing rich and fertile soil which eventually transformed the wasteland into excellent growing and pastureland.

The Bath Road has always catered for travellers and 170 years ago it was lined with coaching inns where passengers, horses and coachmen would rest on their horse-drawn journeys between east and west. A pub named The Magpies, built in 1765, was one such place built to cater for this trade. It still stands today surrounded by modern twenty-first-century coaching inns

– Hiltons, Sheratons, Marriotts and Holiday Inns – catering for passengers travelling between eastern and western continents.

The notorious footpads and highwaymen Dick Turpin, Claude Duval, Moll Cutpurse, Ned Wicks, John Hawkins, George Simpson, John Everett, William Parsons and William 'The Dandy' Page were all active along the Bath Road and hid in small hamlets like Heath Row until a dense cloud of dust on the horizon signalled that another unfortunate mail coach was on its way.

Hangman's gibbets lined roads approaching Hounslow, from which executed malefactors were hung in chains as a warning to passers-by. They did little to deter the violent activities of desperate highwaymen and footpads at large in the area who preyed on passing travellers and merchants.

Highway robbers were eventually put out of business when Hounslow Heath became enclosed, licences refused to publicans known to harbour criminals and mounted police patrols formed to introduce law and order to the area. Stagecoach traffic along the Bath Road further diminished when the Great Western Railway put them out of business in the 1830s. The railway also punctured the lucrative business traditionally enjoyed by the coaching inns along the Hounslow Heath section of the Bath Road, including those in Brentford, Hounslow, Longford and Colnbrook, which lost 80 per cent of their regular trade overnight, plunging many into bankruptcy within the year.

Heathrow Hall was a late-eighteenth-century farmhouse surrounded by land on which wheat, cattle, sheep and pigs were raised. It was owned by one of the several branches of the Philp family who farmed extensively in the area. Heathrow Hall was closed and demolished in 1944. (*Lee Collection*)

By the mid-1930s, Gordon S. Maxwell in his book *Highwayman's Heath* was describing the Heath Row settlement as

> little more than a few cottages and the village pub, 'The Harrow.' There are two fine old farms in this village (Palmer's Farm and Perrott's Farm, both built in the 17th century) both on the right of the road; the first notable for its large stockyard, is Heathrow Hall on the old maps, and the second farm, a little further on, reminds me strongly of one of those delightful old farmsteads met with in the Weald of Kent, minus the oast houses.... In Heath Row are some old cottages which might be in the heart of Devonshire, for their antiquity, their picturesqueness, and lonely situation. Very few people ever see them, for so few go along this road, which leads only, and by a roundabout way, to Stanwell, which is far easier to reach by other routes; no motorist would waste his time on this mere by-road with the arterial horrors so near.

Betty Richardson, who has lived in the Heathrow area all her life, recalls:

> As a schoolgirl I remember watching the airport's development, from market gardens and fields and isolated houses, and a tithe barn – all now gone. With my friends, we would cycle across the fields to Staines from our house at Harmondsworth and sometimes we would go along Tithe Barn Lane – now the site of an airport animal quarantine centre – to

The hamlet of Heath Row was described in the mid-1930s as like cottages found in the heart of Devon 'for their antiquity, their picturesqueness and lonely situation.' Terminal 3 now stands on the site where this picture was taken. (*Lee Collection*)

watch the ducks on some small lakes. It was very quiet and peaceful, a lovely area.

Next to Heath Row was an even smaller hamlet, now occupied by Terminal 5. This was called Perry Oaks, described by Maxwell as

> a few scattered cottages, a delightful old farm and some orchards and meadows … it is hardly a hamlet, even, but it is never-the-less a beautiful spot. Few have ever heard of it, and if you ask the average person if they know it, they look at you as if you were enquiring for a place in Cumberland, or some equally faraway place, instead of one hardly a dozen miles from London. In fact, Perry Oaks, though certainly on the map (and not all of them), is only just so; and therein lies its charm.

In the fourteenth century Perry Oaks was known as Pyrye and Pury and is thought to derive its name from Robert de Pyro, an early tenant farmer. The word Oaks was added later after timber from oak trees growing there was used to repair the Baber Bridge on Hounslow Heath during the reign of King Henry VIII.

Land around Heath Row and Perry Oaks became the site where accurate map-making in England began its life. In 1738 Major General William Roy

Perry Oaks Farm was a large Elizabethan farmhouse with numerous lounges, bedrooms, dining rooms, large picture windows offering views of the surrounding countryside and numerous outbuildings. (*Lee Collection*)

was commissioned to survey part of southern England in order to establish the exact relative positions of the observatories of Greenwich and Paris. Roy spent three months measuring a base line on Hounslow Heath, the first operation of the kind undertaken in England. Work commenced at an area known as King's Arbour, a short distance from Heath Row, where soldiers cleared surrounding ground and guarded Roy's precious instruments.

To ensure accuracy, Roy made his measurements with a steel chain, deal rods and long glass tubes. It took him two years to complete his work from Hounslow Heath to the English Channel and Roy's work became the basis of the General Ordnance Survey of the British Isles. For many years a cannon could be seen at Heath Row, embedded in the ground and enclosed by railings close to the site where 'The Harrow' inn would have provided sustenance to Roy and his men. The weapon marked one end of Roy's base line and a second cannon, 27,404ft away at Hampton Hill, marked the other end. The gun was removed when work commenced in building the first runway.

The Heath Row hamlet continued to be a prosperous place throughout the eighteenth century. In addition to agriculture, the settlement was a thriving centre for trade in lamperns, eel-like creatures with suckers in place of mouths. An observer called Edward Ironside wrote in 1797:

> Hethrow has a very considerable fishery for lamperns, a small kind of lampreys, which are used as bait by the English and Dutch in cod and turbot fishery barges. Large quantities are fetched by the Hollanders during the demand for the fisheries from November to June. The usual price is 6s/- per hogshead; afterwards they are sold for as many pence.

Between the sixteenth and eighteenth centuries, a small number of large barns had been built at Heath Row to store agricultural produce, shelter animals and equipment. One barn had once been part of the Great Barn of Harmondsworth, one of the largest surviving barns from the medieval period and still standing today close to the edge of the world's largest international airport. The cathedral-like timber structure had once included a projecting wing that had been removed when the old manor house nearby was demolished in 1774. Made from oak and standing on sturdy columns, it was re-built at Heath Row, measuring 128ft long, 38ft wide and divided into two floors. A rough roadway running alongside was called Tithe Barn Lane.

At Perry Oaks Farm, just a mile down the lane, stood another large timber-frame barn, which began life in the sixteenth century and by the end of the eighteenth century had been extended to contain seven separate bays.

People living and working at the twin hamlets of Heath Row and Perry Oaks lived in relative contentment until the outbreak of the First World War in

1914. Some local lads went off to fight the war in France and Flanders and, like every other village, town and city in the country, the hamlets had their share of boys who failed to come home. At around 9.15 am on the wet and gloomy morning of 25 August 1919, those working on the land heard a sound in the sky coming from the east and looked up to see a small aeroplane banking around in a westerly direction under the low clouds towards London and the coast. All eyes were focused on the tiny machine – a De Havilland DH 4A – which had taken off from a bumpy grass runway at the former Royal Flying Corps aerodrome 3 miles away on Hounslow Heath and was the first aircraft to appear in the skies above Heath Row.

Ever since the armistice, aerial movements from small aerodromes to the west of London had been reduced to almost nil, but the small De Havilland DH 4A, piloted by Lieutenant Eardley H. Lawford and carrying just one passenger in the single seat behind him – Mr George Stevenson-Reece of the *Evening Standard* newspaper – was making history as pilot of the world's very first international flight. The newspaper had paid 20 guineas for the privilege of being the first journal to go aloft on a peacetime aerial journey between one country and another. The wood and canvas bi-plane was flying 220 miles from

In 1919 a small de Havilland DH 4A, piloted by Lieutenant Eardley H. Lawford and carrying just one passenger made history as Britain's very first international flight. The wood and canvas bi-plane was flying 220 miles from Hounslow Aerodrome to Le Bourget Aerodrome near Paris and Lieutenant Lawford of the new civilian commercial airline company AT&T – Air Transport and Travel – expected to cover the distance in under three hours. (*Tim Jefkins Collection*)

Hounslow Aerodrome to Le Bourget Aerodrome, near Paris, and Lieutenant Lawford of the new civilian commercial airline company, AT&T – Air Transport and Travel – expected to cover the distance in under three hours. In addition to the gentleman from the *Evening Standard*, Lawford was also carrying a cargo of newspapers, a quantity of leather, some Devonshire cream and several braces of grouse destined for the tables of discerning Parisians.

As the small plane disappeared from sight and Heath Row and Perry Oaks farmers returned to their chores in the rain, Stevenson-Reece was penning notes in the tiny makeshift cabin of the tiny aircraft. He wrote:

> The world has watched in astonishment as the confines of our country, protected until now by the waters of the English Channel, have been swept aside by today's daring advance in aerial transport. No longer can these islands of Great Britain assume inaccessibility from other shores as civil aviation adopts the mantle of its military brothers with the commencement of regular air services to the continent.

Once the aircraft had reached an altitude of 1,000ft over London, Lawford admitted that he was having 'a pretty sticky time' flying over the outskirts of the city, hanging on to his compass that was swinging freely above his controls. By the time they were flying over the Crystal Palace at Sydenham 'which showed like a child's toy', the aircraft had reached 2,000ft. Stevenson-Reece continued to scribble notes as he gazed down on London. 'For a moment the Thames appeared like a varnished zinc strip and unexpectedly close,' he wrote. 'Thus, was the course of history changed with the inauguration of a regular London-Paris service and the world's first commercial international civil air service.'

The trailblazing flight took two hours and thirty minutes with Lawford finding his way to the coast by following railway tracks and locating train stations and landmarks along the way. By 2.45 pm that day the plane was back flying over Heath Row's fields again, returning to the aerodrome on Hounslow Heath. 'When you consider that the single journey by train and steamer takes seven hours or slightly more, it is a sufficiently remarkable indication of the speed of aerial transport,' wrote Stevenson-Reece.

Later that day another AT&T aircraft took to the skies over Hounslow Heath, this time carrying four passengers. Mr Holt Thomas, one of the airline's directors, commented:

> If anyone had seriously announced 40 years ago that our businessmen would in a few years be able to have their lunch in London and their tea in Paris and be able to work in the morning at their office, transact business

in Paris and return to London in time for dinner, they would have been
laughed at.

If farmers stacking soaking-wet beetroot and cabbages in the muddy fields
around Heath Row and Perry Oaks that wet August day had time to read the
next day's newspapers, they were probably just as amazed as the rest of the
country. However, they were also glad that their own feet were firmly on the
ground instead of up in the clouds. For them, flying was for the birds…

Chapter 3

1946–49: Professor Abercrombie's Vision

Even in wartime London plans for civil aviation in peacetime were being studied at a high level. Politicians knew that once hostilities were over, there would be a need for commercial air travel by people appointed to get the country back on its feet, restore relations with foreign nations and re-build trade with the rest of the world.

The Port of London Authority lobbied the government for a combined sea and airport to be built south of the Thames near Woolwich. Word came back that they should wait until the return of peace before such a radical idea would be considered.

By 1943, civil servants revisited documents they had put to one side in 1939 and attempted

Professor Patrick Abercrombie, mastermind of the Greater London Plan published in 1944. (*Author's Collection*)

to define London's future growth. In charge of the project was Professor Patrick Abercrombie, a distinguished town planner and vice president of the Royal Institute of British Architects. The need to refocus on a London severely damaged during the blitz was now a major priority for the government and Abercrombie was brought in to mastermind the creation of the Greater London Plan, eventually published in 1944.

In his introduction to the section dealing with civil aviation, Abercrombie wrote:

There is little doubt that air transport will in future play a vastly larger part than it did before the war. Under the stress of warfare, air movements in methods of flying and types of aircraft have been accelerated, inventions have been tested, devices have been perfected, and with the return of peace we may anticipate a greatly increased

A first-edition copy of Abercrombie's Greater London Plan. (*Author's Collection*)

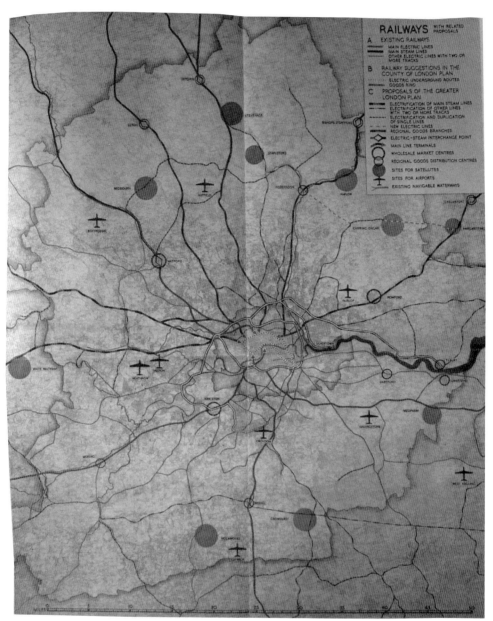

A map of Greater London commissioned by Professor Patrick Abercrombie showing the possible locations for a new airport for London. Heathrow is shown in the centre of the left side of the map next to Heston. (*Author's Collection*)

demand from people who are ready and anxious to travel by air .... But when civil flying becomes permanently established as a normal means of communication and an enormous centre of population is concerned, the planning of a system of airports becomes of first importance.

Abercrombie rejected the idea of a single airport within the boundaries of London itself and – with some foresight – advocated a need 'for a ring of airports from which the centre and the region may be more or less equally accessible. And this question of accessibility by other means than by flying becomes one of the important aspects of the internal communications plan by road and rail.'

The document pondered on the possible use of vertical take-off and landing equipment being used to transport passengers from the ring of airports and landing 'on the flat roofs of some of the great terminal stations.' There was even a plan for BOAC's flying boats – soon to be phased out of operations – to land on some of the large water reservoirs being built to the west of London near Staines, Middlesex. When completed, they would be large enough to allow flying boats to take off and land with ease, but the idea was abandoned because flying boats were slow and the government of the day wanted to encourage manufacture of faster aircraft using traditional runways in the post-war years.

Abercrombie predicted that London needed as many as ten different airports to serve inter-continental and international routes. One of these would be 'an airport of trans-ocean type, which requires extremely careful siting; its demands as to size, etc, are great and it must not be too far out.'

Boldly, Abercrombie stuck his neck out and stated:

> *Now* is the moment for London to prepare a plan for its air terminals, of different types of service, when it is possible to articulate them to the road and rail plan which is being worked out at the same time. As a result, the capital of the Empire will take its rightful place among the cities of the world as one of the greatest centres of civil aviation.

Abercrombie envisaged a single airport

> capable of dealing with distant traffic from all parts of the world. While such an airport should be conveniently near to the centre, it must also be of a size to accommodate the largest aeroplanes. As there is no open space of this order within the built-up area, it will be necessary to find a site further out. Within this area one airport of this character will, it is considered, meet the needs of worldwide traffic; an alternative airport will no doubt be required for use in different weather conditions, but this would be much beyond the area of Greater London.

Fifty-two sites around London were considered, with forty of them rejected as unsuitable for a variety of reasons. Many had been operating as RAF stations and offered possibilities for peacetime use. Top of Abercrombie's list of locations was an area '12 miles west of Victoria Railway Station, on level land with a gravel sub-soil and measuring three and a half miles by three miles.' It was called Heathrow (one of the first times that the two words making up the name of the tiny agricultural hamlet had been joined together to make a single place name).

It is interesting to note that Abercrombie's plan also included land north of the Bath Road because

> it is desirable to provide for possible future needs; it would be unfortunate if a major airport was developed and later had to be abandoned because land in its vicinity had not been kept open; but the portion north of the Bath Road would remain in its present agricultural state, together with various groups of houses on it, for some years to come, if not permanently.

The report noted that

> although the site of this whole airport is on land of first-rate agricultural quality, it is felt that after consideration and thorough weighing up of all the factors, that the sacrifice for the proposed purpose of the part south of the Bath Road is justified. Parts have already suffered impairment of agricultural value through urban encroachments, gravel digging and sludge disposal.

However, he failed to mention that this included 1,300 acres of prime agricultural land farmed by twenty families for many generations.

Abercrombie wanted the airport to be connected to central London via new express roads, 'electric railway to Waterloo and Victoria by means of a short branch to Feltham. A two-mile extension of the tube railway from West Hounslow would also give direct connection with the London Underground system.'

He also suggested that the nearby Grand Union Canal 'provides a means of bringing by barge the large supplies of petrol which will be required, but it may be found desirable to use a pipeline.'

As for the terminal buildings, Abercrombie predicated that they

> will be extensive including control rooms, booking halls, waiting rooms, customs halls, restaurants, hotels, hangars, workshops, repair shops, staff accommodation and canteens, while in addition there will be a railway station, a coach station and car parks. It will also be necessary to provide room for large numbers of the public who may be expected to use the airport. It will be desirable to provide shops, cafes and perhaps a cinema for the entertainment of passengers and their friends awaiting the arrival or departure of planes.

As a final note the professor added: 'Apart from the central area actually occupied by the aerodrome, it is important to prevent any further building development on the surrounding fringe. The existing market gardens on this good fringe land can accordingly be left undisturbed.'

Other airports on Abercrombie's list of possible sites were:

- Heston, Middlesex: 'the future of this existing airport may be mainly in connection with goods traffic. It is near road, rail and canal facilities.'
- Bovingdon, Hertfordshire: 'this site adjoins the express arterial road leading inwards to London and outwards to Birmingham, Lancashire and Carlisle. Weather conditions are more favourable here than any of the other sites.'
- Hatfield, Hertfordshire: 'it has good road and rail facilities. The existing railway line between Hatfield and St. Albans will be duplicated and electrified and will thus afford direct rail communication between the airport and London.'
- Matching, Essex: 'the site will be provided with a spur road about five miles long to the express arterial road, leading inwards towards London and outwards to Cambridge.'
- Fairlop, North-East London: 'the area of the pre-war proposed site would have to be considerably increased. Careful planning will be necessary at the intersection of two express arterial roads to keep them well below the angle of flight from the north-east corner of the airport.'
- Lullingstone, Kent: 'this site, like Heston, may be mainly used in connection with goods traffic.'
- West Malling, Kent: 'this site is near the Maidstone branch (electrified) of the Southern Railway and the main road from London to Folkestone.'
- Gatwick, Sussex: 'the outstanding advantage of this site is its direct connection with the electrified main line of the Southern Railway from London to Brighton. The London to Brighton road (A23) will have to be diverted westwards. The surface drainage of the site may be difficult, as it is only slightly above the River Mole, which has very flat gradient.'
- Croydon, Surrey: 'this existing airport is without rail connection and is surrounded by built-up areas.'

* * *

By 1944, Harold Balfour, a former Royal Flying Corps pilot who had been shot down over Vimy Ridge in 1917, was Under Secretary of State for Air, working closely with Lord Beaverbrook, Prime Minister Churchill's Arms Minister. Throughout the war Balfour had often pondered on what lay in store for civil aviation once peace returned. Like many others, he knew that there would be a huge demand for air transport to and from the London area and over the years

Captain Harold Balfour, MP and Under Secretary for Air and the man 'who hijacked Heathrow for civil aviation.' From *Wings Over Westminster* by Patrick Abercrombie.

had kept close watch on developments taking place at Richard Fairey's private Great West Aerodrome.

At the same time as Professor Abercrombie was drafting his Greater London Plan, Balfour was quietly working behind the scenes to cut through miles of red tape in order to find a suitable site for a major civil airport which could be ready as soon as peace was declared. Balfour was more than familiar with the workings of civil airlines and recognized the pre-war shortcomings of Croydon Airport. He was determined to do something about it.

In his memoirs, *Wings Over Westminster*, Balfour makes a frank admission:

> Almost the last thing I did at the Air Ministry of any importance was to hi-jack for civil aviation the land on which London Airport (Heathrow) stands under the noses of resilient ministerial colleagues. If hi-jack is too strong a term, I plead guilty to the lesser crime of deceiving a Cabinet Committee.

Balfour states that others like him who had studied the needs of post-war civil aviation were aware that surrounding Fairey's grass aerodrome was land ideal for London's main airport. He also knew that any attempt to grab land for civil purposes would mean having to go through long and complicated civil procedures, including a public inquiry. It would also mean that other government ministries, including agriculture and housing, would almost certainly raise objections.

To get around the problem, Balfour worked towards acquiring Fairey's aerodrome and land surrounding it by using emergency wartime powers, allowing him to ride roughshod over almost anything within reason.

Like everyone else, Balfour knew that German defeat was only a matter of time and Churchill's government was deep in planning the next part of the war, including British efforts for the final conquest of Japan alongside American allies.

To win this part of the war, Britain was prepared to supply long-range air transportation of troops and supplies from the UK to the Far East. In the six years since war was declared, aircraft had greatly increased in size and their need for extended landing strips.

Balfour put together a powerful document for Churchill's Cabinet stating that by requisitioning Fairey's private aerodrome and a large area beyond under wartime powers, Britain could create an RAF station from which all of its future needs could operate. Several other bomber airfields in the Home Counties could have done the job just as well, but Balfour was fixed on Fairey's Harmondsworth site.

The Ministry of Civil Aviation, created by Winston Churchill in 1944 to look at peaceful ways of using aeroplanes and airfields and finding something worthwhile for aircraft factories to do after the war, said the new base – to be called RAF Heston – would be used by RAF Transport Command aircraft carrying troops on long routes to the Far East. The Malayan emergency was just getting under way and 13 British infantry battalions had been drafted into the war zone while the Korean conflict involved 40,000 British soldiers.

Balfour's paper was discussed by Churchill and his Cabinet colleagues, who appointed a committee to take the matter forward. Balfour learned that Lord Beaverbrook was to be a committee member and he took the politician and newspaper baron into his confidence as to the real reason he was pressing 'for what we were sure was London's best chance for a great civil airport once the war was over. Beaverbrook played up well.'

As expected, Robert Hudson, the Minister for Agriculture, fiercely objected to sacrificing acres of grade one farmland to aircraft and concrete runways. Aneurin Bevan, Minister of Health with an additional remit covering housing, joined in the protest, claiming that Balfour's plan would take away fringe land earmarked for future housing schemes for the benefit of people bombed out of their London homes.

Balfour made an impassioned speech about the importance of finding a suitable site to help Britain in the next phase of its war effort in the Far East. 'I did not dare to breathe the words "civil aviation",' Balfour recalled. 'I put this right out of my mind so effectively that I really convinced myself of the priority of our case.'

The Cabinet came down on Balfour's side and the Air Ministry duly evicted Fairey Aviation from its aerodrome. Hiroshima killed the next planned stage of the war and the massive site, which Balfour never intended to use for military purposes, passed into his hands.

At around the same time, Churchill created the Civil Aviation Ministry to act separately from the rest of the Aviation Ministry, which would continue to concentrate on military matters until he resigned from office himself on 23 May. The General Election that followed saw the Labour Party topple his government from office, including Beaverbrook and Balfour.

Clement Attlee's new Labour government was keen to win public plaudits as soon as possible and his new Aviation Minister Lord Winster announced that the site originally intended to be an RAF base would pass into civilian use as a new airport for London and construction work and operations would take place simultaneously. He failed to mention that it was likely to cost £25 million: the largest sum ever allocated to a single government-funded project originally intended for military movements and now destined for civil use as soon as practicable.

The farms, market gardens and smallholdings around Heath Row and Perry Oaks in 1944, including Fairey Aviation's large assembly shed and grass landing strip in the centre left. (*Author's Collection*)

The press wanted to know where this new airport might be located, but the Air Ministry insisted on following official wartime advice to civilians for the time being: 'Be like Dad – keep Mum.' The papers sought the opinion of Brigadier General Alfred Critchley, Director General of British Overseas Airways Corporation, whose wartime operations had been severely curtailed and centred on airfields at Whitechurch near Bristol and Hurn Airport, near Bournemouth; a tedious, 100-mile three-hour road journey from London. He told the press that driving from his home in Sunningdale to his office at the Victoria Air Terminal he had discovered 'an excellent site for the future London Airport' but claimed that the Air Ministry could not be persuaded to consider it. He said that his airline's transatlantic services from Hurn were 'particularly impractical' because passengers were forced to by-pass the site on their three-hour-long journeys from London to the south coast, but Critchley declined to name the precise location.

On 31 May 1946 the Air Ministry finally disclosed its plans to Middlesex County Council. Using emergency wartime powers under the Defence of the Realm Act 1939, which prevented an appeal, the government drew up a compulsory purchase order for 2,800 acres of land – including 1,300 acres of prime agricultural land – from the hamlets of Heath Row and Perry Oaks plus Fairey's Great West Aerodrome.

Shortly afterwards the *Middlesex Chronicle*, a local newspaper read by everyone living in the Hounslow and Bath Road area, reported:

> The announcement was made this week of plans for the post-war establishment in south-west Middlesex of the world's largest airport, capable of accommodating the biggest airliners and transport planes likely to be used in the next quarter of a century. The scheme provides for the finest equipment and the port will have a link with London by District Railways. The necessary land covering a wide area in the borough of Heston and Isleworth and urban districts of Feltham, Staines, Hayes and Harlington, Yewsley and West Drayton had, it is understood, been acquired.

Although the location had been reduced to a specific district, the exact site still remained undisclosed. The public was told that 'one of the reasons that led to the sighting of the airport in this district was that it could be done with the minimum disturbance to householders.'

A news blackout was then thrown over the project and it would be almost two years before anything further could be officially disclosed about the world's largest post-war airport scheme taking place in south-west Middlesex, and to be built while the war had still to be won.

Chapter 4

1919–44: The Fairey Flying Machines

'Never take a machine into the air until you are familiar with its controls and instruments; before beginning a landing slide, see that no machines are under you; pilots should carry hankies in a handy position to wipe off goggles; riding on the steps, wings or tail of a machine is prohibited; hedge-hopping will not be tolerated; aviators will not wear spurs while flying; do not trust altitude instruments; if you see another machine near you, get out of its way; don't take a machine into the air unless you are satisfied it will fly; if flying against the wind and you wish to turn and fly with the wind, don't make a sharp turn near the ground – you might crash; it is advisable to carry a good pair of cutting pliers in a position where both pilot and passenger can reach them in case of an accident.'

Flying rules found in the Fairey Aviation hangar at the Great West Aerodrome, Heath Row, 1920

It was assumed that following the pioneering London–Paris flight, Hounslow Heath Aerodrome would become the main airport for London and its surrounding counties, but it was not to be.

AT&T began operating daily weekday services to Paris–Le Bourget using one- and four-seat aircraft depending on demand and business was brisk for the first six months. At weekends it was even possible to take joy-rides over London on fifteen-minute-long hops following the railway line from nearby Feltham up to Waterloo station before turning back over Big Ben and returning above the Thames and down to Teddington before descending to Hounslow Heath again. One passenger even paid AT&T an extra fee to fly him under Tower Bridge and the airline nearly had its wings clipped by the Air Ministry for agreeing to perform the stunt, which was enjoyed by hundreds of onlookers.

However, the bumpy turf covering Hounslow Heath turned into muddy fields during winter months and in January 1920 a Hounslow local newspaper reported:

The use of Hounslow as an airport is to cease, the government has let it be known. The place is not suitable for the purpose because of bad communication with London and is subject to mists. A plateau near Croydon is to be developed. Hounslow is now to be used by the military authorities for the training of cavalry.

Croydon Aerodrome, 10 miles away from Central London, had been in use since 1915 when it was established as part of the Air Defence of London. Military aircraft from Croydon were used to attack raiding Zeppelins in 1916 and enemy aircraft threatening the capital in daylight in 1917. The National Aircraft Factory had also been built on the site and in March 1920 the aerodrome was adopted as the Customs Air Port of London, putting Hounslow Heath out of business and forcing AT&T to move operations to Croydon. The Hounslow Heath site once occupied by the airfield from which the world's first international service was inaugurated is today a mixture of residential streets and industrial properties.

The skies above Hounslow Heath remained silent for the next decade until 1930 when a 46-year-old aero engineer and aircraft-builder called Charles Richard Fairey paid the Reverend Richard Ross, the vicar of Harmondsworth, £15,000 for a 150-acre plot on which to build a private airport to assemble and test aircraft. The site was perfect. The land was flat, with no buildings, trees, railway lines or roads likely to get in the way of aircraft taking off or landing. Fairey's company, manufacturing both private and military aircraft,

Richard Fairey and his wife Frances outside their home in Woodlands Park, Buckingham-shire. (*Author's Collection*)

had been operating from leased premises owned by the Air Ministry at nearby Northolt Aerodrome where runway length and hangar space were limited. Fairey needed a testing site of his own from which to put aeroplanes designed and made at Hayes, Middlesex and Hamble, Hampshire through their paces.

People living at Heath Row, Perry Oaks and along the Bath Road were unhappy when news was leaked that aircraft would soon be buzzing over their hedgerows and rooftops – many of them thatched – creating noise and pollution. However, Fairey assured them that aircraft-building was a slow process: components had to be brought to the site by road for assembly and his company could only produce two aircraft a week. Noise would be kept to a minimum and all aircraft start-ups, take-offs and landings would take place in an area well away from homes.

Fairey finally managed to win local approval by informing residents that once opened, his private airport would host summer events including garden parties for British aviators and flying displays organized by the Royal Aeronautical Society, and they would be able to watch free aerial demonstrations from the comfort of their own garden chairs or bedroom windows. They were also told that a number of VIPs would be attending, including the society's patron, HM The King, no less.

Over the next ten years, Fairey's private airport would be given various names including the Great West Aerodrome, Harmondsworth Aerodrome, and even

One of the most popular planes to be produced by Fairey Aviation before the war was the Fairey Swordfish, photographed here above the flight hangar in 1933. (*Quadrant Picture Library*, Flight International *Collection*)

Heath Row Aerodrome. It was located mid-way between the Bath Road to the north and the Great South West Road (better known as the A30 and opened in 1925) to the south-east. Caines Lane – a quiet and narrow tree-lined road linking the villages of Bedfont and Hatton to Sipson – provided the easterly boundary, while the village of Heath Row plus Heath Row Road, High Tree Lane and the Duke of Northumberland's river marked the western boundaries of Fairey's airport, originally sited where part of Heathrow's runway 27L and some of the airport's busiest taxiways are located today.

In the north-east corner of the site and at the top of Caines Lane, Fairey built what was to become the biggest aircraft hangar of its kind at the time. A company called C.P. Hunter was commissioned to lay down a large stretch of smooth turf along the full length of the site – known as 'Hunterised Greensward' – which would be used as a runway that would be as smooth as a bowling green for take-offs and landings.

The first aircraft to 'christen' the Great West Aerodrome was a new twin-engine long-range bomber built for the RAF and called the Fairey Hendon. The aircraft was delivered in a fleet of lorries from Fairey's aircraft factory in Heaton Chapel, Stockport for final assembly. It took to the skies for the first time on 25 November 1930, with the company's chief test pilot Norman Macmillan at the controls and leader of the design team, D.L. Hollis Williams, as a passenger. The flight, powered by two 525hp Bristol Jupiter engines, was

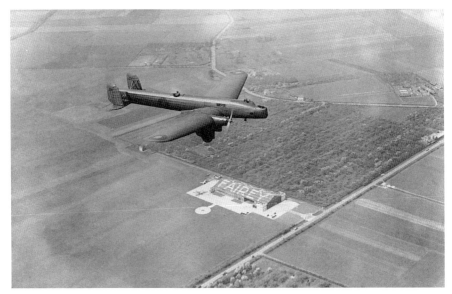

The first aircraft to 'christen' Richard Fairey's Great West Aerodrome was a new twin-engine bomber called the Hendon, built for the RAF. It took to the skies for the first time on 25 November 1930 with the company's chief test pilot, Norman Macmillan, at the controls. (*Author's Collection*)

a total success and another test flight took place the following day. Both flights indicated that modifications needed to be made before the bomber could enter service, but Fairey's new airport had been inaugurated and his latest aircraft tested on site.

The Hendon was the only heavy bomber conceived and built by Fairey Aviation. Fourteen were eventually delivered to the RAF and used extensively until Vickers Wellington and Armstrong-Whitworth Whitley aircraft were ready to leave their production lines.

Local people enjoyed watching the occasional Fairey aircraft soar overhead, until March 1931 when the Hendon prototype overshot the aerodrome, crossed over a road and ended up in an orchard. The accident caused so much damage that the aircraft had to be dismantled and re-built in the giant hangar. Fortunately, there were no injuries to farmers or Fairey people.

In 1935, a junior draughtsman joined Fairey's staff. His name was Peter Masefield and to supplement his small salary he began writing freelance articles for *Aeroplane* magazine. Masefield stayed with the company for two years, going on to become a distinguished war correspondent, flying with the US 8th Bomber Command based in Britain and later an advisor in civil aviation matters to wartime and post-war Cabinets. In later years he would be appointed an executive with leading airlines and aircraft manufacturing

Peter Masefield, who in later life played an important role in the development of British European Airways (BEA), in the design of the Britannia aircraft and from 1965 to 1971 as chairman of the British Airports Authority. In 1939 Masefield was earning £3 10s a week working in the drawing office and wind tunnel of Fairey Aviation at the Great West Aerodrome and spent his entire working life working in and around aviation. (*Author's Collection*)

companies, finishing his career as chairman of the British Airports Authority, owners of Heathrow Airport where his career began thirty years before.

Meanwhile, business was booming at Croydon. A number of small British airlines, including AT&T, were operating flights to Paris, Amsterdam, Rotterdam and Berlin and by 1924 they had merged together to become Imperial Airways. The world's first purpose-built air terminal had opened in 1924 and services were extended to all parts of the British Empire and beyond. Yet not everyone was satisfied, with one passenger describing a flight to Paris as follows: 'They put you in a box, they shut the lid, they splash you all over with oil, you are sick and you're in Paris.'

The mid-1920s and 1930s marked the truly great days of flying, when passengers wearing tropical clothes would turn up at Croydon on a winter's day, already dressed for their sunny destinations. It would take one week or longer to fly to the other side of the world in an Imperial Airways Handley Page 42, equipped to carry twenty to thirty passengers depending on the route.

During the aerial adventure, passengers would be joined by the captain to dine off fine china and drink from crystal cut-glass. On routes to India, Africa, the Far East, Australia and New Zealand, they would stay overnight in special luxury air transit stations in deserts and jungles and while aircraft were refuelled and made ready for the next day's flight, would sleep in comfortable beds, take a bath and enjoy sumptuous meals before flying off on the next stage of their air odyssey to far-flung places coloured pink on the world map. In some desert locations, armed tribesmen on horseback would line landing strips, firing rifles into the air to welcome the arrival of British aircraft or line up carrying burning torches to mark out the landing strip. The art of intercontinental air travel really began at this time, courtesy of Imperial Airways.

* * *

There were dark clouds on the horizon by the mid-1930s. Everyone was talking about war and how any conflict might affect commercial life and the way people lived and worked in Britain. When war was finally declared on 3 September 1939, Croydon was closed to civil aviation to become an RAF fighter station and a major player in the Battle of Britain and the London base for RAF Transport Command.

Over in Westminster, civil servants were preparing to draft a document with the working title of 'A Plan for London' seeking to examine how London might cope with the return of peace and city expansions in the decades that would follow. It would address issues including population, housing, industry, use of land and transport issues. The war brought a temporary end to research for the document, but it reappeared in 1944 and became a major force in

Fairey Aviation, one of the great names in early British aviation. (*Author's Collection*)

identifying numerous things the capital and its surrounding areas would require in peacetime, including sites for civil airports.

At the Great West Aerodrome, Fairey Aviation was busy testing a new single–engine light bomber combat aircraft called the Battle, built to carry a crew of three and up to 1,500lb of bombs. As the early years of the war progressed, increasing numbers of aircraft were brought to Fairey's private airport for assembly and testing as part of the country's massive rearmament programme. Aircraft sections were made at Austin Motors' factory in Birmingham and then rushed down to Harmondsworth, where they were quickly pieced together in the massive hangar before being wheeled

Entrance to Richard Fairey's Great West Aerodrome on what is now Heathrow Airport. (*Author's Collection*)

Thanks–
to the men who flew
Fairey Aircraft to Victory

FAIREY SWORDFISH

FAIREY BATTLE

FAIREY SEAFOX

FAIREY ALBACORE

FAIREY FULMAR

FAIREY BARRACUDA

FAIREY FIREFLY

from the
FAIREY AVIATION
CO. LTD.

THE FAIREY AVIATION CO. LTD., HAYES, MIDDLESEX, ENGLAND

Most of the aircraft used in this 1948 advertisement for Fairey Aviation were either assembled or tested at the Great West Aerodrome. (*Author's Collection*)

out onto the green turf and taken into the air. The first squadron to fly them was No. 63 based at Upwood. The Fairey Battle was not one of the company's most successful planes, but it served the RAF well during the early years of the conflict and the period known as 'the phoney war'.

Fairey wanted to expand his business at the Great West Aerodrome but met with resistance from the Air Ministry. Nobody was prepared to give him a reason why. He argued that he was helping the war effort by churning out aircraft built to RAF specifications and delivered on time. If he could expand his Harmondsworth facilities, Fairey Aviation could increase productivity and deliver twice as many aircraft.

Then in 1944 a bomb was dropped on Richard Fairey's private airport, not by Göring's Luftwaffe, but by the Air Ministry who coldly informed him that he must quit the Harmondsworth site and make way for a new RAF Transport Command airfield – to be shared with the US Air Force – to be used by long-range B-29 'Flying Fortress' aircraft air-lifting troops, reinforcements and supplies to help defeat the Japanese and win the war in the Far East.

The explanation given was an outright lie and it took Fairey Aviation until 1964 to receive £1,600,000 in compensation for being forced to leave its private airfield during its busiest and most productive phase. Richard Fairey died in 1956.

Fairey transferred flight-testing operations to nearby Heston Aerodrome and White Waltham in Berkshire and people living around the Great West Aerodrome held their breath to see what would happen next.

Chapter 5

1945–46: Wimpey's Wonderful Workforce

People living in Heath Row and Perry Oaks feared the worst. Many had noticed increasing numbers of strangers wearing suits and carrying clipboards arriving in the area, walking up and down their normally quiet lanes and making copious notes. Occasionally one of the strangers would drop into The Harrow pub for a pint of beer, but no amount of friendly probing across the bar could coax information about the purpose of their visits. Some thought they had something to do with a sewage disposal works about to be built in fields close to Perry Oaks. Others thought the men had something to do with gravel-raising schemes extracting sand and ballast on fallow land close to their village.

Then official letters began arriving, stating that under emergency wartime powers their homes and gardens, farms and orchards, barns and smallholdings would be acquired by a government compulsory order for military use. Villagers were told they would be compensated at current market rates and the Ministry of Health (working with local councils) was charged with providing assistance, where required, to relocate them elsewhere. Twenty farming families who would be displaced were forced to accept alternative accommodation at higher rents and for many, genuine hardships lay ahead. Compensation was based on 1939 property prices plus 30 per cent. Additional compensation would include payment for crops or produce grown in 1944 and payments based on proof of the previous year's income. Farmers or smallholders unable to produce paperwork confirming sales from crops, fruit, vegetables, livestock or poultry sold in 1943 would have a problem on their hands.

Orders to vacate homes lived in and land worked on for generations were politely worded, yet firm and irrevocable. Within weeks, an army of workmen and their vehicles had moved into the area, felling trees, uprooting bushes and hedgerows, pulling down fences and demolishing homes and barns. Work on wiping the ancient villages of Heath Row and Perry Oaks from the map had begun in earnest and creating the world's longest runway on the same site was about to get under way. There was no going back.

At the same time Fairey Aviation – with a full order book of military aircraft to assemble, test and deliver – had to vacate the Great West Aerodrome and relocate to Heston Airport which proved to have inadequate air traffic control

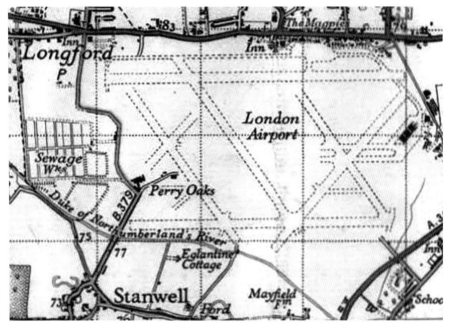

A 1946 map showing an outline of the proposed airport runway layout in-between Longford and the Bath Road to the north and Stanwell to the south. (*Author's Collection*)

facilities for a flight test centre. Two years later the company was forced to relocate again to White Waltham, near Maidenhead. These disruptions cost the company dearly by way of reduced productivity and profits.

Heath Row and Perry Oaks villagers were re-housed in ordinary suburban homes in Heston, Hayes and Harlington. Some went further afield. None of them offered any growing or pasture land. The Ministry of Health, desperate to find accommodation for hundreds who had lost homes in the blitz, had little time for a handful of farmers who through no fault of their own had got in the way of a military airport development. It would be years before they were properly compensated and many claimed they were never paid the sums they had expected.

By May 1944, George Wimpey & Company from Denham, near Uxbridge was a household name in building and civil engineering when it was awarded a contract to construct three runways for the new airport scheme, permitting aircraft to take off and land in any possible wind direction with a 4 mph crosswind. The runways would also enable simultaneous take-offs and landings, allowing them to achieve optimum utilization.

A large workforce was recruited to work around the clock to complete the task, working Monday to Saturday with Sunday being the only day when work stopped. Each man recruited was instructed to remain silent about the work they were engaged to perform. If challenged about their employment around

Wimpey's workmen move onto the former Heath Row site ready to start constructing the first of three airport runways. (*Author's Collection*)

the former Great West Aerodrome, they were to say that they were clearing and preparing the site for a large peacetime housing scheme, and nothing else.

Wimpey's airport army was a motley collection of men. Experienced surveyors, engineers and builders in reserved occupations worked alongside young and inexperienced lads awaiting military 'call-up' and drafted in to work as labourers. Middle-aged and elderly members of the Local Defence Volunteer Force – better known as the Home Guard – who had worked in pre-war building jobs offered their services, while Labour Exchanges across Middlesex sent every available man on their books to help remove for all time the traces of former farms, market gardens and disused gravel pits. A small number of German prisoners of war and Land Army girls were also brought in to help clear the land.

From 6 June 1944 onwards, convoys of buses and lorries daily collected runway gangs from town squares, railway and underground stations and drove them to the giant building site. At the end of the day they drove them back again before collecting another contingent of Wimpey workers to labour on the next shift, working in all weathers by the light of hurricane lamps and headlights from 200 lorries, 40 mechanical excavators, 50 bulldozers and tractor-drawn equipment.

A group photograph of just a few of Wimpey's employees chosen to help build the airport's runways. They look happy to be working at home instead of in uniform on one of the battlefields of Europe. (*Author's Collection*)

Hundreds were housed and fed on the site in a temporary village split into two sections: 'Tintown' made up of Nissen hut-type half-circle-shaped dwellings made from corrugated tin and 'Timbertown' constructed from wood and taking on the appearance of an army barracks. 'Tintown' offered indoor recreational facilities including table-tennis and card tables. A room was included where workers could listen to their favourite radio programmes while enjoying a smoke and a cup of tea. Outside there was a football field and a cricket pitch. A 'Timbertown' hut was turned into a makeshift theatre where films were screened and concert parties performed.

Residents of the twin villages were encouraged to help 'Dig for Victory' and create wartime gardens growing vegetables for the work camp's kitchen. Anyone wanting to drink beer could easily walk or cycle to one of the many pubs in Stanwell, Longford or along the Bath Road, but George Wimpey & Co. did not tolerate drunkenness and anyone returning to the village the worse for wear was immediately sacked. The company argued that many people still lived close to the building site and were exposed to enough disruption during runway-building without having to put up with drunken navvies keeping them awake at all hours of the night.

Work on the runway progressed throughout 1945 when a giant mixer and a huge travelling spreading machine were brought in to produce enough concrete to make a runway 9,000ft long, 300ft wide and 12in thick. (*Author's Collection*)

Runway gangs worked a forty-eight-hour week and were paid £5 16s whatever their trade or profession. Workers signed up by Wimpey until all airport runways were completed – expected to be towards the end of 1946 – were given one week's paid holiday a year.

It was clear from the beginning that laying the east-west runway would present a raft of engineering problems. The area included 120 acres of ponds and disused gravel workings that needed to be drained without flooding the surrounding area. To get around the difficulties a pair of temporary pits was dug at either end of the runway site into which 100 million gallons of water and half a million cubic yards of silt was discharged. At a later stage, a large drainage scheme was incorporated into the plan to collect rainwater that would normally have soaked into the ground but would soon sit on top of a 300ft-wide expanse of concrete runway. The water was directed through 13 miles of 54in concrete piping towards a pair of balancing reservoirs located on either side of the A312 road. More than seventy years later it is still in use as part of a nature reserve dedicated to the conservation of plants and wildlife species surrounding Heathrow Airport.

Wimpey's workmen then had to fill in the former ponds and gravel pits, making sure that the elasticity and resilience of the filled ground was similar to natural surrounding land and ensure the runway would absorb the shocks transmitted by the wheels of thousands of aircraft tyres as they thudded down to land from all parts of the world.

During the first seven months of construction, 2 million tons of earth and gravel were excavated and 36,000ft of multiple ducting for electric cables and 60 miles of wire were laid through the ducts.

When searchlights picked out German bombers in the night sky over Middlesex, the hurricane lamps and vehicle headlights were quickly switched off, leaving a large dark area over which the Luftwaffe found nothing worthy of dropping their deadly cargo. The bombers, however, found plenty to destroy nearby. Residential areas were a key target along with the railway depot at Feltham, just 4 miles away and a prime target thanks to its goods yards and main line running directly into central London. The King George VI reservoir on Staines Moor – to the west of the airport building works – was completed in 1939 but remained unfilled during wartime. Local people claim that a mock-up of Clapham Junction railway station was built on the reservoir's sandy floor to lure enemy bombers away from the real thing. This has never been proved, but the Ministry of Defence still uses the reservoir – now containing millions of gallons of drinking water for Londoners – and it is closed to the general public.

Flying bombs were another hazard and several found their way into the streets and homes of people living in communities around the runway building site, forcing hundreds of families to evacuate their children to safer communities in countryside areas of the Midlands and Northern England. Betty Richardson's dad had other ideas. Betty, from Harmondsworth, recalls:

My parents moved to Harmondsworth from North London at the outbreak of the war. I had two older brothers and had just started going to school. I don't think our parents wanted us to be evacuated so they moved to what they thought would be a safer area. I remember my dad telling me that I would become a country bumpkin.

Betty remembers that during the London blitz 'we could see London burning from our bathroom window and that gives you some idea of how flat the area was (and still is) without all the buildings which have subsequently been erected.'

Work on the runway progressed in 1945 when a giant mixer and a huge travelling spreading machine were brought in to produce enough concrete to make a runway 9,000ft long, 300ft wide and 12in thick. Daily quality tests were conducted to ensure an average strength of over 30 per cent above the standard demanded in the original specification. It took fourteen weeks to mix, spread and compact the concrete runway and half of Wimpey's workforce was laid off during this period when mechanization took over from manpower.

In addition to the runway (known as runway No. 1), a 100ft-wide taxiway and apron also had to be laid adjacent to the Bath Road. As soon as this was completed, men laid off while the concrete-spreading operation got under way were re-engaged to begin clearing the site for two more runways; both 2,000 yards long and 100 yards wide, one running north-east/south-west (runway No. 2) and the second north-west/south-east (runway No. 3).

All three runways were built with a view to being extended as soon as the Air Ministry saw fit to do so; the main one by a further 6,000ft and the two smaller ones by an extra 3,000ft. By mid-July 1945, 1,114,000 square yards of 12in-thick concrete had been laid on the largest civil engineering project ever undertaken in Britain and by Christmas 1945 work on runway No. 1 was complete, No. 2 was 25 per cent completed and No. 3. 80 per cent completed.

Writer Paul Townend was allowed to inspect the runway building site for an article that could only be published once the war was over and the airport in use. He recorded:

Concrete is made by the lorry load in giant mixers at various strategic places on the aerodrome. Watching these mixers, I was reminded of a huge cake-making machine; the ingredients of stone (graded to various sizes), sand, water and cement are loaded like a cake mixture into the tall

A giant concrete-spreader was used to travel forwards and backwards over the runway surface to ensure the material dried evenly. (*Author's Collection*)

Concrete was mixed inside a large mixer using three basic components: water, aggregate (rock, sand or gravel) and Portland cement. Once it had been mixed to the correct consistency, double doors at the base of the mixer opened and released the material down into a waiting lorry underneath. The doors then closed in order to collect the next batch of mixed concrete. (*Author's Collection*)

towers and churned around until the concrete is ready to be disgorged down a chute into a waiting lorry. From there it is driven and dumped in front of the concrete spreaders, astonishing power-driven machines which advance on rails spreading and levelling the piles of concrete as they jerk inexorably forward. On a blistering hot day, a 3,000-yard-long runway presents an amazing sight. Heat waves dance along the shimmering surface, and before the eye has succeeded in reaching the end, the runway has been transformed into a long band of glistening water. This, of course, is only the optical illusion one gets from standing at one end; a pilot's view when he approaches in his aircraft will be totally different.

Many claim that the RAF never used the site later to be known as Heathrow Airport. This is untrue. In 1940 when the Battle of Britain was at its height, Hurricane aircraft from 229 Squadron, based at nearby Northolt, were diverted to Fairey Aviation's grass airstrip for safety while their home base was under threat of enemy attack. In 1945 RAF Lancasters, Halifaxes, DC3s, Ansons and Yorks were also diverted to land and take off from runways still under construction. Although the site received military aircraft, it was never formally adopted as a traditional RAF base, complete with hangars, maintenance sheds and living quarters, although a building intended to be used as a control tower was constructed on the north side of the aerodrome.

By Christmas 1945, enough concrete had been mixed and poured onto the runways to build a new road from London to Edinburgh, a distance of over 400 miles. Now all that was needed was an aeroplane to christen it.

Chapter 6

1 January 1946: Heathrow Takes Off

The first peacetime Christmas for seven years had come and gone and the miserable winter of 1945/46 had wiped away all euphoria of victory from an exhausted Britain.

Rationing was still in force and would still be around for several years more. For thousands of servicemen and women returning to 'Civvy Street' and spending their first Christmas at home for what seemed like an eternity, the prospects for 1946 looked gloomy.

People in West London suburbs opening their curtains and peering out of the window on New Year's Day 1946 witnessed a bitterly cold and grey day with traces of fog left over from the day before. Most could go back to bed and pull eiderdown and candlewick bedspreads over their heads and sleep on for another few hours. Some had stayed up late to welcome in the New Year, but the drunken carousing that had regularly been seen on the last days of the year prior to wartime had yet to return. Beer cost money and there wasn't much of it around on the first day of the first full New Year of peacetime.

Christmas had been a challenge. Turkeys were expensive, chicken was scarce and beef a lavish luxury, assuming you could find someone to buy it from and money to pay for it. Thousands of people scraped together the components of their Christmas from men in sharp suits and suede shoes, hair slicked back with brilliantine and known to the world at large as 'spivs', to themselves as 'entrepreneurs' and to the police as black marketeers – people with the ability to get you anything you couldn't get for yourself, for a price and without coupons.

Products bought over the counter were expensive to anyone fresh out of uniform. A pack of ten Churchman's No. 1 cigarettes would set you back 1s 3d in 1946 (the equivalent of £2.42 in 2018), 1oz of pipe tobacco started at 2s 8d (£5.16 at today's prices) and new rubber hot-water bottles, back on sale again now the factory had reverted to manufacturing its original products after the government had requisitioned it to make rubber dinghies for the navy, cost half a crown (2s 6d, or £4.84 today).

Post-Christmas sales sold 'Utility' dress coats reduced from £11 to 22s but nylon stockings still cost 1s 6d (£2.90) *and* four precious clothing coupons. If you were rich and could afford a new car, a 1.5 litre Jaguar saloon would

With only a few days to go before the first flight took off from the new runway, workmen, their tools and piles of sand still clutter the taxiway before everything stopped for Christmas 1945. (*Author's Collection*)

set you back £535 (£20,722). Non-millionaires could buy a used Austin 7 for £85 (£3,292 today) or a Coventry Eagle for £27 10s (£1,065).* New or old, rich or poor, car salesmen were hardly enjoying brisk business in the winter of 1945/46. Decent furniture, carpets, toys, bicycles or prams hadn't been seen in shop windows for years, or so it seemed.

To forget their immediate post-war troubles, people sought entertainment: dancing at the Palais, Locarno or Victory ballrooms or going to the 'flicks' to see a newsreel, a second feature (usually a western) and then laugh at Bob Hope and Bing Crosby in *Road to Utopia* or thrill to Cornel Wilde in *A Thousand and One Nights*; exciting, humorous, escapist fantasy entertainment designed to help folks forget their New Year domestic blues.

Now that the war was over things were changing for the people of London and its suburbs. For those not called up for active service or working in reserved occupations, civilian work in wartime had been relatively easy to find but not brilliantly paid. In the spring of 1944, just as thousands of children were being evacuated to the country to escape Hitler's flying bombs, hundreds of men were recruited to begin laying concrete for a triangular pattern of runways that would form part of a massive new development for the RAF. The triangular configuration would allow aircraft to take off in any wind direction.

By the end of 1945, one of the runways was completed but signals that the war was ending meant that the RAF would no longer need a massive new

---

* I am obliged to The Cost of Living – www.thedesignlab.co.uk – for calculating 1946 inflation adjusted prices for 2019 amounts.

base on the outskirts of its bruised and battered capital and would instead send soldiers into battle by sea from British ports. By a roundabout route the aerodrome moved from military to civilian use and was designated 'the world's largest airport' and 'the country's largest post-war building scheme', and on the first day of the New Year of 1946 it was ready to be used.

* * *

Ruislip teenager Keith Hayward was up early on that New Year's Day. The 16-year-old had gone to bed early the night before at his parents' home because he didn't want to oversleep and be late for his very first job in London.

Because it was a bank holiday, transport into central London was restricted to a limited service, although it had been ages since trains and buses had operated to any kind of timetable. It was cold and dark as the lad made his way past houses with curtains still tightly drawn towards Ruislip's underground station and the Piccadilly line that would take him to Green Park and the offices of British South American Airways (BSAA) at 19 Grafton Street, London W1.

With his company issue greatcoat pulled tightly around his shoulders and his smart new uniform neatly pressed by his mother the night before, Keith couldn't believe his luck as he sat in the almost empty train rattling its way towards London. Just a few weeks before, he had been an aircraft-mad student at Harrow County School and a member of the Air Training Corps. Now, following a rousing talk to young lads about the new peacetime utopia that awaited Britain given by the legendary head of the RAF's Pathfinder Force, Air Vice Marshal Donald Bennett, CB, CBE, DSO, Keith was now about to work for the man himself. Bennett had been appointed chief executive of a new airline, which that day would make the first flight from London's new Heathrow Airport, and Keith would be part of the team travelling to the airport later that day to witness the historic departure as one of BSAA's newest and youngest trainee traffic officers.

He had already 'done his bit' for the flight before Christmas, rushing around London to the Passport Office and various South American embassies fixing documents and visas for crew members and flight engineers who would today be flying down to South America on the company's first departure: the very first flight from the new airport.

* * *

Mary Guthrie stayed in bed a little longer that morning. The 24-year-old former Air Transport Auxiliary pilot would be driving herself to Heathrow that day from her mother's flat in Basil Street, Knightsbridge and she didn't

Aircraftwoman 2nd Class Mary Guthrie – British South American Airways first in-flight stewardess and first to fly with the airline to Latin America – was a member of the wartime Women's Auxiliary Air Force (WAAF), the female auxiliary of the Royal Air Force. Mary flew Fairchild 24 and Spitfire aircraft between RAF bases. 'They were good days, very exciting and I remember them with affection,' said Mary in 2005. (*Mary Cunningham Collection*)

need to be there until later in the morning. She hoped she could remember the directions she had been given through London's streets and out of town towards the Bath Road running alongside the massive building site from which she would be taking off to South America at lunchtime that day. It was all very exciting.

By 1 January 1946 and to her great surprise, Mary had become one of London's best-known 'faces' after her photograph had appeared in national newspapers telling readers that the

> blue-eyed, fair-haired former nurse will step on board the Lancastrian airliner 'Star Light' as first hostess of British South American Airways. But because the words 'hostess' and stewardesses are officially disliked, she will take her title from the 'Star' class of airliners and be known as a 'Star Girl'.

Mary had been well-trained for the demanding job ahead of her; two whole days of training. She had landed the job by accident while visiting BSAA's offices to talk to someone about a navigation course and had been pointed in the direction of an airline executive who asked if she knew anything about nursing ('Yes'), had any military training ('Yes, sir') and could speak any foreign languages ('*Oui, oui*'). Now, after two days learning how to prepare hot meals from frozen food – known as 'frood' – at Joe Lyons' Corner House, Marble Arch, here she was driving towards an airport still under construction to become 'Britain's first post-war air hostess'.

Patchy fog still clung to the fields as she headed out of West London's built-up areas and towards smallholdings and market gardens surrounding the building site where a small plane looking more like a bomber was waiting to take passengers and crew on board. In the boot of her car was the suitcase she had carefully packed the night before. It contained her new woollen swimsuit, which she hoped to christen in the warm waters of the Río de la Plata (River Plate) at least once before returning to freezing Britain in nineteen days' time after a round trip of 14,400 miles.

As she approached Harlington, the words her stepfather had spoken over the Christmas holidays rang in her ear: 'I don't approve of this job you've been offered, Mary. You're likely to be captured by white slavers in South America and we'll never see you again. Buenos Aires is no place for a young girl.'

The mist was clearing now, but it was still bitterly cold as Mary turned left at The Magpies pub and into an area containing a two-storey square block building with a smaller structure on top, which looked like a cube-shaped greenhouse but which she immediately recognized as an RAF-style control tower. A row of other temporary prefabricated buildings, large tin sheds and ex-military caravans stood to one side and Mary parked her car in front of one of them. As she removed her suitcase from the boot, she could see the Avro Lancastrian on which she would soon be queen of the tiny galley in front of the passenger cabin and squashed between a pair of metal wing spars. She knew it would be an exhausting flight across the Atlantic and the Serra do Espinhaço (Espinhaço Mountains) to exotic South America. Someone had told her it might take thirty hours, and there would be no time for sleeping.

* * *

At some stage during his six-year service in the RAF, Wing Commander Robert Clifford 'Cliff' Alabaster, DSO and Bar and DFC and Bar, from Willesden, North London had mentioned to a friend that the next three decades would be a pretty interesting period for aviation, never thinking that he would be part of that exciting future.

On New Year's Eve 1945, the wing commander – better-known to RAF pals as 'Alibe' and pronounced 'Ally-bee' – had enjoyed a couple of celebratory drinks at home in Wembley before turning in to bed for a good night's rest, the last sleep he would enjoy for almost two days.

Passing a few New Year party stragglers on their way home to bed, Alibe headed in the direction of 19 Grafton Street and the top floor of the building where he had started a special school for ex-RAF pilots and navigators wanting to join a civil airline once the war was over.

Under the peacetime 'command' of his former Pathfinder Force boss, Air Vice Marshal Donald Bennett, Cliff had started the school at which airmen spent seven hours each day sitting at trestle tables in a purpose-built classroom and were taught how to fly civilian airliners for BSAA. By October 1945 more master bomber pilots had signed up with the airline than remained in the immediate post-war RAF.

During the war this elite corps of air crew with high navigational ability flew at the head of thousands of Lancaster and Mosquito bombing sorties to targets in Berlin and the Ruhr. They flew at altitudes of just a few hundred feet among balloons and flak to accurately pinpoint enemy targets with coloured flares that allowed the main bombing force to achieve more accurate bomb drops. Between 1943 and 1944, the Pathfinders made a vital contribution to the success of Britain's bombing offensive against Germany and to the D-Day preparations.

Now 60 per cent of BSAA's crew were former Pathfinders looking for new flying roles in post-war life, including Alibe, an experienced navigator and pilot. Working for their old boss and alongside RAF chums seemed like a safe bet in the uncertain world of civilian life. Ground staff attached to the Pathfinders were also drafted into the new airline in managerial and administrative jobs and 19 Grafton Street was more like an RAF station with staff still wearing their military uniforms and doors marked 'Wing Commander X' and 'Squadron Leader Y'.

Alibe would have liked a cup of tea in the basement canteen the airline shared with staff working for the fashionable ladies' hairdresser Mr Teasy-Weasy (Raymond Bessone), whose stylish salon had opened next door. However, it was a bank holiday and the canteen was closed, so he made his way to the ground floor where a group of excited staff, including the company's youngest and newest staff member, Keith Hayward, had gathered to board a special bus transporting them to the airport to witness their new company's first departure.

Several others boarding the staff bus that day would be travelling on the Lancastrian – registration G-AGWG – which the company had christened 'Star Light'. It was one of fourteen Lancastrians British South American Airways would operate during its short lifespan. Built by A. V. Roe & Co (Avro) at Woodford, Greater Manchester, the design was a modified version of the famous four-engine wartime Lancaster heavy bomber. Gun turrets and other military fittings had been removed and an extended nose section fitted to carry freight and passenger luggage. Four Rolls-Royce Merlin engines powered the plane, which BOAC had been operating successfully on long-haul 'Kangaroo Routes' from Bournemouth to the Far East and Australia for the last year.

Fitted with up to thirteen single seats staggered on both sides of the aircraft, the converted bombers were designed as a 'stop-gap' commercial aircraft while British plane-makers worked furiously to produce new passenger airliners for peacetime flying. They were far from perfect, with a tiny galley located between the Lancastrian's main spar, meaning that Mary Guthrie would have to clamber over the large angular metal girder every time she had to serve meals to her passengers and collect empty trays. Passengers sitting at the front would also have to negotiate the same angular metal spars as the crew whenever they needed to use the tiny and primitive chemical toilet at the rear of the aircraft. The Lancastrians were also unpressurized, noisy and forced to fly at low altitudes in all weathers across South America's great mountain ranges which blocked out all radio communications. BOAC flying crews used to travelling in luxurious flying boats were not impressed with the Lancastrians, and when asked to test-fly one of the aircraft a pilot wrote in his report: 'Unsuitable as an airliner but, with a few modifications, will make an efficient bomber aircraft.'

'Star Light' would soon be joined by other BSAA Lancastrians also carrying the 'Star' name along the front nose section: 'Star Dust', 'Star Land', 'Star Glow' and so on.

In addition to Alibe, also travelling on the bank holiday staff bus was Air Vice Marshal Bennett himself, the Australian-born former Imperial Airways flying boat captain and mastermind behind the RAF Pathfinder force. Bennett would be in command of the flight and for the journey he had taken his best

Air Vice Marshal Donald Clifford Tyndall Bennett, CB, CBE, DSO (14 September 1910–15 September 1986) was an Australian aviation pioneer and bomber pilot who rose to be the youngest air vice marshal in the Royal Air Force. He led the 'Pathfinder Force' (No. 8 Group RAF) from 1942 to the end of the Second World War in 1945. He was described as 'one of the most brilliant technical airmen of his generation: an outstanding pilot, a superb navigator who was also capable of stripping a wireless set or overhauling an engine.' (*Australian Memorial*)

pin-stripe 'civvy' suit, a 'civilianized' version of his RAF greatcoat and a new black Homburg hat out of the wardrobe. Alibe would be in the seat next to Bennett as first officer, navigating the Lancastrian over some of the world's longest water crossings, often by stars in the night sky and frequently popping up into the aircraft's Perspex astrodome to get a star fix with his sextant.

Other bus passengers booked to fly that day included the airline's Chairman, John Booth, former bomber pilot Wing Commander Douglas 'Crackers' Cracknell, DSO, DFC and Bar (first officer), First Radio Officer J. McGillivray, Second Radio Officer R.W. Chandler, First Engineer T. Campbell and Second Engineer G.S. Rees.

* * *

As the bus cruised to a halt at the edge of the airport taxiway, the passengers could see a large crowd gathered on the apron around 'Star Light'. Three large saloon cars with newsreel cameras mounted on top were positioned beneath one of the wings and a posse of pressmen armed with cameras and notebooks stamped their feet on the concrete and blew on cupped hands in an attempt to keep warm. Earlier that morning, reporters, photographers and newsreel cameramen had been taken on a joy-ride around the new airport in a DC3 'Dakota' to give them a better idea of the great length and width of Heathrow's runways and the airport's general layout.

Alibe saw that the Lancastrian's front nose-cone section was open and assorted boxes and parcels were being passed from a lorry to men at the top of a wooden tower with a ladder running up one side. It looked more like something used in a medieval siege than a simple aircraft loading device which had been hastily assembled days before and built high enough to allow ground staff to load goods into the forward freight compartment.

No sooner had staff climbed from the bus than a black motorcade swept onto the apron and stopped a few feet away from 'Star Light'. A driver from one of the cars quickly jumped out and ran around the vehicle to open the back door, out of which climbed two men: one a small middle-aged man wearing a Homburg hat, thick black overcoat and round spectacles, and the other a man dressed in similar clothing but about 6in taller. They obviously recognized Bennett and the men walked towards each other, warmly shook hands, wished each other a Happy New Year and agreed that it was, indeed, a very cold day. The smaller man was Lord Winster, Minister for Civil Aviation, who just a few days before Christmas had bowed to pressure and agreed to take the wraps from Britain's new showpiece airport to allow Bennett to operate a series of 'proving flights' to South America on behalf of the British government. The taller man was Ivor Thomas, MP, and Parliamentary Secretary at the Ministry

Minister of Civil Aviation Lord Winster (centre at microphone) bids Godspeed to passengers and crew travelling on the first flight to leave London's new airport, Heath Row on 1 January 1946. Air Vice Marshal Donald Bennett, Chief Executive of British South American Airways and captain of the first flight – an Avro Lancastrian called 'Star Light' – stands to his left. John Booth, the new airline's chairman, stands between Lord Winster and Bennett. Standing to Bennett's left is Captain D.A. Cracknell (navigator) and 'Star Girl' Mary Guthrie. Captain Cliff Alabaster (first officer) stands to Lord Winster's right (hands crossed in front of him). (*Keith Hayward Collection*)

of Aviation who was joined on the tarmac by Sir William Hildred, Director General of Civil Aviation.

The men were desperate to counter negative media stories about the new airport, its cost (estimated in 1946 at £25 million, or £968.333 million in today's money), when it might open for business and how successful it might – or might not – be. Anxious to demonstrate that his ministry was keen to get on with things, Lord Winster let Bennett launch his fledgling airline from the airport on exactly the same day that it passed from military to civil aviation ownership. Not only would it provide newspapers and newsreels with a great home-grown story on an otherwise 'slow news day', it would also win his Ministry full marks for initiative in allowing a new British airline to use the airport's only runway in service within days of being completed.

* * *

Those flying in 'Star Light' that day surrendered their luggage before Ministry of Aviation officials shepherded the freezing crowd into a large informal group under the Lancastrian's starboard wing. The group included government officials, a handful of passengers travelling on board to Buenos Aires, BSAA staff, their wives, a few airport staff who had been recruited to work in the control building, a delegation of construction workers engaged in building the second runway and an army of pressmen impatient to get on with the story. Three microphones had been positioned on the apron – one for each newsreel company – and at 11.45 am, the crowd was brought to order.

With hands thrust deeply into his overcoat pockets, Lord Winster told the crowd in a carefully modulated voice and without the aid of a prepared speech:

> I think it's a happy omen for the flight that yesterday's fog has cleared away and Air Vice Marshal Bennett, who leads the flight, will take off in fine, bright, clear weather. To me this aeroplane with its beautiful name, 'Star Light', is a symbol of the determination of our country to regain our place in the markets of the world and to use the air as a means of cultivating good relations with other nations and cultivating with them the arts of peace. During the war Air Marshal Bennett pioneered the transatlantic delivery of aircraft. Today he starts off on another pioneering

A BSAA Avro Lancastrian prepares for take-off from Heath Row Airport in 1947. Note the square-shaped brick building in the background. This was the airport's first control tower and originally built to RAF specifications when the airport was originally designed as RAF Heston. (*Cliff Alabaster Collection*)

job and this flight is the first step towards the establishment of a swift and regular British air service to South America. Air Vice Marshal Bennett, and all who fly with him today, are truly ambassadors, representing the spirit and determination of this country to play the same leading part in the air that it has always played at sea. I wish them all Godspeed and a pleasant and successful journey.

There was a round of genuine applause before Bennett was invited to say a few words:

We are about to take off on our first flight and about to do so with a fast four-engine airliner of proven quality. It has those things that are necessary for an airline: safety, speed and comfort. Our service will start within a few weeks, immediately following this proving flight. We hope to offer the peoples of this country and South America a service of which we will be proud and they will be happy to use. On this, the first day of 1946, we propose to take the first practical steps in getting that going.

There was more applause and cries of 'hear-hear' which were broken by the sounds of an air-raid siren, no longer used to announce the terrifying arrival of Luftwaffe bombers overhead but now used by peacetime factories across the

Mary Guthrie is the last to board the first flight to depart from Heath Row. Thanks to her photograph appearing in national newspapers, Mary Guthrie had become a household name by 1 January 1946. (*Mary Cunningham Collection*)

country to signal that 12 o'clock midday had arrived; time for lunch, and today time for the first official departure from the capital's new airport.

The siren also signalled that it was time for Mary Guthrie to climb up the Lancastrian's steps to welcome her boss, his crew and BSAA's first passengers on board. In total, Mary would have eighteen people (including herself) to look after on the thirty-hour flight: ten passengers and eight crew. Press photographers, however, had other ideas. They wanted 'just one more shot, Mary', but Mary had a job to do and quickly ran up the steps where the aircraft door was already open to admit the airline's first flyers.

First to board were BSAA's fare-paying passengers who had each paid £190 2s (£7,363 in today's money) to fly one-way to Montevideo or £192 6s (£7,448) for the single fare to Buenos Aires. Flying in those days was truly for the wealthy. Mary's passenger manifest told her that travelling on the plane would be Signor Falcao, the Brazilian Consul General in London; Colonel Stirling Wylie, British Military Attaché in Uruguay; Mr Donald Edwards, a BBC foreign correspondent and Signor and Signora Marroquim, a Brazilian couple who had spent Christmas in London and were now returning home to Buenos Aires. Also on board were five BSAA staff who would be 'dropped off' along the 7,200-mile journey to South America to represent the new carrier

There was not a lot of room to roam around inside the passenger cabin of BSAA's Avro Lancastrian 'Star Light', but it did include comfortable seating with a drop-down table on the rear of the seat in front and brightly-decorated curtains at the window. (*Cliff Alabaster Collection*)

BSAA Avro Lancastrian 'Star Watch' starts its engines at Heath Row before another long flight down to Latin America. (*Cliff Alabaster Collection*)

as country managers including Lisbon, Bathurst (Gambia), Natal (on Brazil's eastern Atlantic seaboard), Rio de Janeiro, Montevideo and Buenos Aires.

Next up the steps were Alibe, Crackers and Bennett, the latter leaning out to shake hands with scores of colleagues wanting to give the famous Pathfinder and skipper of Heathrow's first departure their personal good wishes.

It was time to depart and as soon as Bennett, Alibe and their crew had quickly gone through their pre-flight checks and Mary had made sure that each passenger was settled and their seat belt buckled, 'Star Light' was ready to taxi out towards the airport's brand-new 3,000-yard runway. A small Union Jack flag that had been poking out of the cockpit window was taken inside as the Lancastrian accelerated and its nose wheel lifted 1,000 yards along the runway, using just one-third of its length. As it rose further into the air, it banked towards the south and soon disappeared into low cloud covering Middlesex.

'Fly With the Stars' says a BSAA advertisement in a December 1947 business publication. (*Author's Collection*)

DECEMBER 6, 1946

Fly with the Stars
to
South America
Central America
and
The West Indies

Regular Services for
PASSENGERS, FREIGHT and MAIL
as follows:
Tuesdays and Fridays to LISBON, DAKAR, NATAL, RIO DE JANEIRO, MONTEVIDEO and BUENOS AIRES.
Saturdays to LISBON, DAKAR, NATAL, RIO DE JANEIRO.
Wednesdays to SANTIAGO.
Mondays to AZORES, BERMUDA, JAMAICA and CARACAS.

For further information apply to
LEADING AGENCIES, or to
BRITISH SOUTH AMERICAN AIRWAYS
19, GRAFTON STREET, LONDON W.1.

'By Lancastrian to Australia': a 1946 trade advertisement promoting the merits of the 'civilianized' former Lancaster bomber turned into a passenger airliner. Thirty were built and sold to air-lines operating long-haul services in the UK and Australia. Flying time from London to Sydney was forty-nine hours. Today the route can be covered in twenty-one hours and thirty-five minutes. (*Author's Collection*)

No sooner had 'Star Light' disappeared into the early afternoon murk than the world's newest airport was officially closed again, to re-open eighteen days later when the Lancastrian returned from its long journey over cities, oceans and mountains. It would be nearly five months before it was 'officially' declared open.

The crowds dispersed, many to board buses taking them to witness how work was progressing on the second runway, now 80 per cent completed, and gaze at the enormous concrete-mixing and pouring machines used to create them. Afterwards, they would return to one of the temporary buildings along the Bath Road to enjoy a buffet lunch hosted by Lord Winster.

Young Keith Hayward was not invited to the party. After all, he was only a 16-year-old new starter in the topsy-turvy world of peacetime civil aviation, yet thrilled to be part of the history that had been made that day. He had also been given permission to go home early, where his mum had promised to have his New Year tea waiting for him on the table back in Ruislip.

The manufacturer of a spark plug company who supplied equipment to the Avro Lancastrian used on the airport's first day first flight used the opportunity to promote his firm to 1946 readers of aviation magazines. (*Author's Collection*)

Chapter 7

1945–46: Enter the Pathfinders

O ne morning shortly before Christmas 1945, Air Vice Marshal Donald Bennett, CB, CBE, DSO was driving from his home in Farnham Royal, Buckinghamshire to the offices of his newly-formed company, British South American Airways, in Grafton Street, Mayfair. His route usually took him along the Bath Road in the direction of Hounslow and Hammersmith and past the site where a new airport originally built for the RAF and now destined for civil use was taking shape.

Instead of driving past the site, Bennett, who in his early thirties had been the RAF's youngest air vice marshal, swung into the building site and asked to speak to Wimpey's chief foreman. After a few moments Mr Steer, the building company's resident engineer, appeared from one of the many building huts lining the Bath Road.

Captain Cliff 'Alibe' Alabaster in 2004 with a model of a Lancastrian bomber on which the commercial version – known as the Lancastrian – was based. Cliff was a crew member on the first service from Heathrow. (*Author's Collection*)

Cliff 'Alibe' Alabaster, who worked alongside Bennett in the RAF's famous wartime No. 8 'Pathfinder' Group and was now running the navigational school for BSAA at Grafton Street, takes up the story:

Bennett had ended his RAF career and been appointed Chief Executive for a new airline which planned to operate services from the UK to South America. He had to deal with people at the Air Ministry who didn't have half of his experience and knowledge and were getting in the way of him starting up the new airline. So, he by-passed them. On the day before we were due to take delivery of our first Lancastrian airliner from Avro's factory in Waddington, Lincolnshire, he called into the airport building site and had a quiet word with someone from Wimpey and told him that he wanted to land a Lancastrian there the following day. He asked if they could move all of their building barrels and equipment off of the runway and out of the way. I don't think for a moment that he had to grease any palms because Bennett was – how shall I put it? – careful with his money.

So sure enough, next day he landed the Lancastrian at the airport and tucked it away in a corner before going up to the Air Ministry to discuss the new passenger proving flight BSAA had been licensed to operate from the UK to South America. The Air Ministry demanded to know what proving flight and what passengers he was talking about. They told him that if he wanted to fly passengers he could only do it from Hurn (Bournemouth) Airport from where BOAC was conducting long-haul operations. Bennett said he would do no such thing and was going to fly from the new airport at Heathrow. They told him it was impossible and still incomplete, covered in building equipment. Bennett informed them that he had already landed there and that's where his plane was parked ready for its first operational flight. And because he'd already landed there he might as well take off from there. The Air Ministry was aghast because, of course, they knew nothing about it. But Bennett got his way. That's how he always got his way, by being one step ahead of everyone else and going straight to the top. He didn't care who he had to climb over to get his own way.

* * *

Following the end of the war, Lord Beaverbrook had been influential in creating three new state-owned airline corporations: British Overseas Airways Corporation (BOAC) serving Commonwealth, Far East and North American destinations; British European Airways (BEA) flying short-haul European and UK domestic routes; and British South American Airways (BSAA) operating to Latin America.

BSAA had originally planned to trade under the name of British Latin American Airways. Founded by a consortium of private shipping companies under the leadership of business tycoon John Booth (of the Booth Steamship Company), the company was funded with a start-up capital of £1 million. Bennett, who had briefly flirted with politics as Liberal MP for Middlesbrough after leaving the RAF in 1945 and lost his seat at the General Election shortly afterwards, needed a high-profile job and he liked the idea of being in charge of a new British airline.

The same election that had ousted Bennett from his parliamentary seat also booted out Churchill's Conservative government to make way for Attlee's Labour Party and plans for nationalizing just about everything in the country, including airlines.

There were rumours that Australian-born Bennett was to be offered the job of governor general of his home country, but Bennett wanted a job that would keep him in the air and in charge of a major British organization with international prospects.

BOAC, however, had other ideas. As the country's flag-carrying airline, it felt it was entitled to have the South American routes to itself and had, in fact, already operated its own proving flight to Buenos Aires using an Avro Lancastrian flying from its main operational base at Hurn, near Bournemouth; a three-hour drive from London. Air Minister Lord Winster called an airline showdown with BOAC which was represented by its Director General, Brigadier General Alfred Critchley while John Booth and Bennett appeared for BSAA.

Critchley claimed that his company was ready to begin regular flights to South America within three months and as soon as it had taken delivery of new aircraft. Bennett responded that he was ready to start flying almost immediately. He had paid Avro £30,000 for each of the twelve Lancastrians that were almost ready for delivery and in the advanced stages of being converted from 20,000lb payload bombers into comfortable passenger airliners with thirteen reclining seats. He informed Lord Winster that he had already recruited more than forty ex-Pathfinder crews to his new airline's staff, including twelve captains and fifteen first officers, and he had personally negotiated bi-lateral route agreements with Brazil, Argentina and Uruguay.

The BOAC chairman accused Bennett and Booth of having nowhere to base their aircraft, warning them that BOAC was using every inch of space at Hurn. 'Surely, you can spare one hangar for BSAA?' protested Lord Winster, but Bennett informed the meeting that he had already made his own 'very satisfactory arrangements'. Asked to provide details, he told Lord Winster that he had created a maintenance base at an airfield on the outskirts of London under the direction of Group Captain Sarsby, ex-chief engineer of the

Pathfinder Force who knew every inch and rivet on a Lancaster. When Winster asked for the name of the airfield, Bennett replied that he would rather not reveal its name in front of Critchley 'because he will do everything he can to stop me.'

After the meeting was adjourned and Critchley had left the building, Bennett told Lord Winster that the chairman of Wimpey & Company was a fellow Australian who had loaned him four small buildings at London's new airport taking shape to the west of the capital and had been given use of its runways. Maintenance and hangars were located at Hawker Aircraft's private airport at Langley, near Slough just 4 miles away from the new airport still awaiting hangars, a completed control tower and passenger facilities.

Lord Winster told Bennett and Booth that the new airport was to be named Heathrow Airport after one of the small villages that had disappeared under the bulldozers to make way for the runway. Although the RAF still – technically – owned the airport, there were pressures to turn the site over to the Ministry of Civil Aviation (a new division of the Air Ministry) for commercial use. 'How soon?' asked Bennett. 'How soon would you like it?' replied Winster, with a smile. 'How about January 1?' Bennett replied quickly. 'Good God,' said Winster, 'that's only a couple of weeks away!'

There had been much discussion on what to name Britain's new airport. There was speculation that it would be given a unique name and 'Britainfield' was widely tipped. Other possible names included 'London International', and names in honour of British personalities from the past including William Shakespeare, King George VI and Winston Churchill. Churchill himself favoured naming the airport 'Swintonfield' after the Rt. Hon. Sir Philip Cunliffe-Lister, the first Earl of Swinton, a Conservative politician appointed by Stanley Baldwin to become Britain's first Secretary of State for Air and in charge of the Air Ministry. As a politician he was responsible for urging the government to speed up production of Spitfires and Mosquito aircraft which Churchill later said helped to shorten the war. Swinton was highly regarded by the RAF and people working in both military and civil aviation before and during wartime. The earl, however, was a very modest man and politely declined the invitation to have an airport named after him, so in order to keep the peace and get on with naming Britain's new international airport, it was christened after the small hamlet which now lay under concrete and asphalt but was still a vivid memory for people who once lived there. It was named Heathrow Airport. But not for long.

* * *

Aeroplane magazine, 11 January 1946:

Whoever thought of introducing the press to Heathrow and staging a coincident departure of a British South American Airways proving flight to South America on January 1, the day on which the Air Ministry handed over Heathrow to the Ministry of Civil Aviation should be sent straight to the top of the class. It made it possible for Lord Winster to say in his ceremonial speech that his Ministry 'gets on with things'. It gave him the opportunity to allay fears of the daily press that all was not well with Heathrow; and it gave him the chance of showing that he was making use of the nucleus organisation built up by Messrs Booth and Bennett to get the British South American Airways service started. Full marks, therefore, to the Ministry of Civil Aviation for its initiative and for the opportunity of seeing London's embryonic airport, and an airliner using it, soon after the first runway was completed. Bennett has actually used it before, so it was not the first take-off. Anything else we say on the subject of Heathrow, therefore, must not be allowed to detract from this fully merited praise and the excellent press which the occasion received.

The magazine then went on to probe into the airport's construction and layout 'and here the picture is not as propitious as the hopeful augury suggested by the departure of "Star Light", the BSAA Lancastrian to South America.' It criticized the lack of airport buildings, stating that

at present there is a small temporary central building which could accommodate only a very limited number of radio, meteorological, operations and other essential personnel. The number of aircraft handled will be limited accordingly. As for customs, immigration, passenger rooms and facilities, offices, freight sheds, maintenance hangars, technical stores and all the other requirements of a civil airport, there is nothing but a few huts at present to serve this purpose. Obviously temporary buildings will have to be built if, as is apparently planned, the airport is to be put into service gradually as and when each of the three runways is completed. All three runways should be finished in June.

The magazine attacked the proximity of the airport's taxi track to the Great West Road and a future need to spread airport buildings along the road instead of locating them in one key area. It predicted that either the 12in-thick taxiway would be dug up and relocated or the Great West Road diverted.

The magazine then mentioned 'the unholy union' between the military and civil authorities regarding the airport's creation, stating:

It seems clear that the original idea for developing this site was with the object of making it the major civil airport for London. The political difficulty of allocating millions of pounds on a civil vote in wartime had to be circumvented, a position we are convinced could, and should, have been openly faced and overcome. The only way to get the money allocated was on a military vote. That is why the explanation is now put out that Heathrow was built for Transport Command and the Japanese War; as if there were not hundreds of perfectly good runway aerodromes all over England for this purpose! Why choose one of the few places in this country suitable for the main London Airport?

* * *

Sixteen days after 'Star Light's' historic departure from Heathrow (which some newspapers still referred to as Heath Row), the BSAA Lancastrian returned to London, and the media were again out in force to welcome its crew home, including the country's best-known air hostess and 'Star Girl', Mary Guthrie. The following story from the *Daily Express* dated Wednesday, 16 January 1946 with the headline 'I Had £25 But Could Have Spent £2,500 – Ocean Hostess Sees Glamour Shops' by the paper's air correspondent Basil Cardew provides wonderful insight into Britain's post-war needs and aspirations:

The world's first trans-ocean air hostess, Miss Mary Guthrie, of Knightsbridge, SW, stepped on to the Heath Row tarmac at 1.15 pm yesterday with bananas, tangerines, pineapples, cream cakes and a still damp swimsuit in her suit case. She had collected these and also a tropical

On her return to London from South America Mary brought back a pair of pineapples and several pairs of ladies' stockings, 'things you just couldn't buy in London because of rationing,' remembered Mary. (*Mary Cunningham Collection*)

bronze on the first all British airline flight to Buenos Aires – a 14,400-mile trip that started only a fortnight ago.

She attended to the passengers disembarking from 'Star Light' before telling the story of this milestone flight for British air transport. Captained by AVM Donald Bennett, the Pathfinder ace, the Lancastrian arrived from Lisbon after an up-to-the-minute journey from South America in which a record was set up between London and Rio de Janeiro in the flying time of 28 hours 18 minutes.

Even the American airlines have not employed hostesses on long sea crossings, so it was news to find out how Miss Guthrie, a 24-year-old former ATA pilot got along and she said: 'I had four swims – one in West Africa and the others at Rio, Montevideo and Buenos Aires. We flew from winter to the glamour of high summer in South America. As it was a proving flight we did not go fast and I have lost some sleep, but I had to be on duty at night. The South Americans were very pleased to see a British plane with a British crew on the new air service. I suppose it's because we did so much in the war that the whole crew were to find such genuine joy on our arrival. And the shops – they were a dream. I saw everything that a woman has wanted in England for the last six years of war – piles of fully fashioned silk stockings at 16s a pair, nail varnish, evening gowns, stacks of toeless shoes and even the two-way stretch girdles that are never seen here. I was allowed £25 for the trip but I could have spent £2,500. Most things are expensive compared with pre-war prices here.'

AVM Bennett said they had now got some sort of organization for the airline at every stop. He confirmed that 'Star Light' had achieved speeds of 240 mph – the fastest cruising speed of any airliner. 'We have started up first and we intend to keep British aviation right ahead on the British–South American run,' he said.

Chapter 8

1946: Tented Terminals and 'Piddle Pennies'

Three weeks after 'Star Light' had inaugurated the world's newest airport, newspaper stories began appearing about advanced plans to expand Heathrow. The *Middlesex Chronicle* reported the story on 19 January 1946 with the page one headline 'Heathrow Airport to Double Its Size'.

The story claimed that a Bill would shortly be introduced through Parliament identifying land and houses it planned to purchase to aid the airport's next phase of development, allowing expansion to spill across the Bath Road and increase Heathrow's size from 1,500 acres to 4,000 acres.

'People living in East Bedfont, Cranford, Stanwell, Sipson, Harmondsworth and Harlington – areas all affected by the proposed extensions – have been much alarmed in recent weeks by rumours and London newspapers report of proposed wholesale demolitions of houses, historical monuments, etc,' the paper reported.

A *Middlesex Chronicle* reporter who made inquiries at the Ministry of Civil Aviation learned that although Sipson village 'is doomed by the proposed development', it was hoped to save about one-third of Harlington, including its historical church and sixteenth-century Dawley Manor Farm, once owned by the Earl of Tankerville.

Asked about the total number of houses likely to be demolished, the paper learned that the number would be about 1,000. An official told the paper: 'We have done our best to avoid demolition of houses and historical monuments, but of course some will have to go. Over 100 alternative plans were examined and an enormous amount of care taken.'

Readers were told that the expansion plan would be spread over seven to ten years 'and the majority of people affected will be able to retain possession of their houses for the major portion of that time, although a few individual houses on the Bath Road might have to go before then.' Parts of the ancient village of Stanwell on the airport's south-west side were expected to be affected and its historic church likely to be demolished. Large numbers of new houses would be constructed in Harlington 'to provide accommodation for airport officials and employees.'

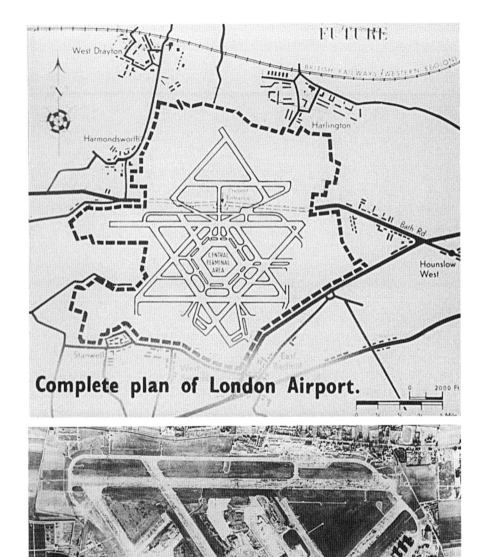

'A complete plan of London Airport' originally produced in June 1946 shows how the Ministry of Civil Aviation planned to expand the airport's boundaries north and south of its existing site to create new runways and taxiways. (*Author's Collection*)

A 1946 aerial shot of Heath Row Airport, renamed 'London Airport' the following year, 'because it is easier for foreigners to pronounce' according to Minister for Civil Aviation Lord Winster. Only one runway has been completed and the remaining two came into use early in 1947. The Bath Road can be seen running along the bottom left-hand corner of the photograph. (*Author's Collection*)

Communities around the airport held their breath and feared the worst. More than seventy years later, many of the same communities are still holding their breath as similar plans to those first mooted in 1946 resurface like a ghost from the past.

* * *

BSAA operated five more 'proving' flights to South America between February and March 1946 and Mary Guthrie was the 'Star Girl' in charge of three of them. The airport was 'officially opened' to airline traffic on 25 March, by which time work on the 38ft-high control tower, originally built for the RAF, had been completed and a series of prefabricated huts constructed alongside to accommodate meteorological, teleprinter and radio operational staff.

Other buildings were of a less permanent kind; in fact, casual observers unaware that an airport had been built might be forgiven for thinking that they were looking at an army outpost or Bedouin encampment. A tented village had been thrown up next to the main apron near the Bath Road using ex-military brown marquees that would double as waiting rooms and arrival and

The airport's first buildings took casual observers by surprise and they could be forgiven for thinking that they were looking at a Bedouin encampment, a circus or an army outpost. Ex-military marquees were used as temporary terminals in 1946. Duckboards were laid down so that passengers would not sink into the mud as they walked out to waiting aircraft. Outside were three bright red telephone boxes, a 'pillar box' posting box and a mobile post office. (*Author's Collection*)

departure terminals for the remainder of the year until more permanent – yet still temporary – buildings were ready for use.

The 'waiting room' marquee, complete with windows overlooking the apron, was equipped with long rolls of coconut matting on uneven floors made from clinker and sand. It contained comfortable armchairs and settees (many of which were stolen during the dead of night), and small tables with vases of fresh flowers. Passengers could buy tea from a small refreshment stall at one end, while those wishing to send telegrams could use facilities provided by Western Union which operated from a dining-room table along one side of the marquee.

Passengers knew when it was time to depart because take-off times would be chalked on a giant blackboard purchased from a local school. Airline staff would also call across the marquee to passengers asking them to assemble before being escorted out across the duckboards to their waiting aircraft. Passengers filed past customs and immigration officers who occasionally inspected luggage on wooden tables. A cardboard sign indicated which items were to be declared and likely to incur a tax payment.

Inside 'terminal' marquees passengers could relax in comfortable chairs, buy tobacco and newspapers from the newest branch of W.H. Smith & Sons, send a telegram from a Western Union cable station and find out about arriving and departing flights from information chalked on a blackboard. (*Author's Collection*)

The Bricklayers pub just across the Bath Road from the tented terminals provided valuable refreshment for passengers in need of a pint or who were delayed by fog. In 1954 the pub was re-named the Air Hostess and was demolished in 1988. (*Author's Collection*)

Another marquee contained more armchairs and tables, a cashier and the newest branch of booksellers W.H. Smith & Sons that had moved to London Airport from Strawberry Hill station in Twickenham. Ted Carpenter, who was assistant district sales promoter at the time, recalls that the bookstall was painted green. 'I was paid £6 a week – and no commission – at the time,' Ted recalled in 1996. 'The floor of the bookstall used to get soggy underfoot at times, despite a covering of coconut matting.'

The marquee shop was so popular that it generated more than £2,000 in sales between July and December 1946 and more than £6,000 during the same period the following year, making it one of the company's most successful – and smallest – sales outlets. In addition to books, newspapers and magazines, it also sold cigarettes and tobacco and sales were split between 'print and smokes'.

When it rained, the marquees leaked and dozens of buckets and bowls had to be brought in to catch water seeping into the 'terminal'. To reach aircraft parked on the apron, passengers walked over wooden duckboards, which protected their shoes from a sea of mud that existed underneath. The boards extended from the marquees to the concrete apron.

There was no heating in the marquees and it was often cold as well as damp, but Britain had only recently come through six years of wartime discomfort and a 'blitz spirit' still prevailed across the country, which made allowances for

People looking for a job at London's new airport only had to call over the fence and someone would come out to handle their inquiry. Almost half the jobs going at the airport were filled in this way. (*Author's Collection*)

an airport still going through its birth pangs. When the weather was warm, the canvas marquee walls could be removed to allow a cool breeze to blow through. Fire buckets full of water and sand were positioned outside every entrance and exit in the event of a careless match, cigarette or cigar butt setting the 'terminal' on fire.

Outside the marquees were three bright red telephone boxes, a post box and mobile post office. Dozens of former RAF mobile caravans doubled as staff offices for airlines, customs, immigration and retail employees.

Airport toilet facilities were primitive, to say the least, but there was one flushing toilet located in a police guardroom tucked away between two marquees. If terminal porters spotted a wealthy-looking passenger, they would direct them towards the flushing toilet and more often than not be rewarded with a tip for their trouble. Porters called this little perk their 'piddle pennies'.

To transatlantic visitors, everything looked a mess. They called it 'Tent City' and couldn't believe how primitive London's new airport looked. Back home they had 'real airports – like La Guardia – with real buildings which had bars and restaurants, car parks and viewing areas.' British travellers were content to wait. Lord Winster had told them that London would eventually have the best airport in the world, and they believed him. Like everything else in post-war Britain, it would come … eventually.

* * *

The date that Heathrow 'officially opened' is covered in confusion. BSAA's Lancastrian 'Star Light' with Bennett, Alibe and Crackers up front and young Mary Guthrie looking after passengers at the back had been the first departure on 1 January 1946. Five more 'proving' flights operated by BSAA had followed. Yet, despite the nationwide publicity that this service generated in newspapers and newsreels in both Britain and South America, it was always regarded as a trial run and never an 'official' service, despite the fact that passengers paid to travel on the flights.

On 28 May 1946 another Lancastrian took off into heavy skies over Heathrow – G-AGLS – operated jointly by BOAC and the Australian airline Qantas. This was known as the 'Kangaroo Service' and BOAC claimed that passengers flying down under that day were the airport's 'first fare-paying passengers to depart from the airport.' The airline had originally inaugurated the service from Hurn four months earlier and established a record flying time for the journey: forty-nine hours. It would be carrying just six passengers, who would sleep in special bunks installed for the long route and sit in armchairs positioned next to a table and a window. The flight would also be the airline's first from Heathrow, from which it now planned to operate after winding down Hurn operations.

On 28 May 1946 another Lancastrian took off into heavy skies over Heathrow – G-AGLS – operated jointly by BOAC and Australian airline Qantas. This was known as the 'Kangaroo Service' and BOAC claimed that passengers flying down under that day were the airport's 'first fare-paying passengers to depart from the airport'. Had they not heard about the Lancastrian that took off on 1 January 1946? (*Author's Collection*)

The BOAC-Qantas flight carried just six passengers on the journey who would sleep in special bunks installed for the long route and sit in armchairs positioned next to a table and a window. The flight would also be the airline's first from Heathrow, from which it now planned to operate after winding down operations at Hurn. (*Author's Collection*)

In March 1946 the Latin American airline Panair do Brasil received its first Lockheed 049 Constellation and became the first airline outside the United States to operate this aircraft. The first flight took off on 27 April 1946 from Rio de Janeiro to Recife, Dakar, Lisbon, Paris and Heathrow where it became the first foreign international airline to land in the newly-inaugurated airport a full month before it was 'officially' opened.

On its first 'official day' of operations, three rival airlines raced across the world hoping to be 'first' to land at Heathrow. Pan American's Constellation service, 'London Clipper', appeared in the skies above Heathrow after a fourteen-hour flight from New York's La Guardia airport at the same time as American Overseas Airways Constellation 'Flagship Great Britain' from the same city announced its arrival in London air space. Then a third aircraft requested permission to land: the BOAC-Qantas Lancastrian returning to Britain from Australia and arriving in the air traffic zone two hours earlier than planned thanks to strong tailwinds. It had covered the 12,000-mile journey in sixty-three hours and fifteen minutes. All three airlines had been operating from Hurn while European carriers operated from Croydon, which the RAF had handed back for civilian use earlier in the year. BOAC's flying boat fleet continued to fly to Africa and the Far East from its Poole base.

In March 1946 the Latin American airline Panair do Brasil received its first Lockheed 049 Constellation and became the first airline outside the United States to operate this aircraft. The first flight took off on 27 April 1946 from Rio de Janeiro to Recife, Dakar, Lisbon, Paris and London Airport where it became the first foreign international airline to land at the newly-inaugurated airport a full month before it was 'officially' opened. (*Author's Collection*)

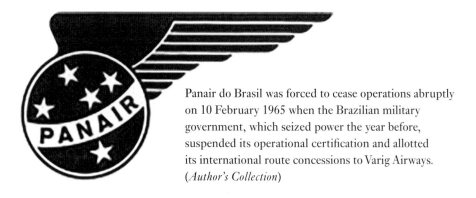

Panair do Brasil was forced to cease operations abruptly on 10 February 1965 when the Brazilian military government, which seized power the year before, suspended its operational certification and allotted its international route concessions to Varig Airways. (*Author's Collection*)

Which would first be allowed to land and lay claim to the title of being 'first commercial airline' to land at Heathrow? Would it be one of the American airlines, in recognition of that country's support for Britain during the recent war and acknowledgement of the United States' achievement in civil aviation with the development of the sleek triple-tail plane Lockheed Constellation?

The race was won by Pan American (just!), but both Constellations were allowed to taxi onto the apron, switch off their engines and discharge their passengers at the same time. To save face, both airlines were given the distinction of being 'first overseas airline' to land at London's new airport.

On seeing the ex-army marquees waiting to welcome arriving passengers, an American was heard to remark: 'Say, what time does the circus start?' On seeing airport staff scurrying around in their brown overalls, many foreign

On its first 'official day' of operations two rival American airlines raced across the world hoping to be 'first' to land at Heathrow. Pan American's Constellation 'London Clipper' appeared in the skies above Heathrow after a fourteen-hour flight from New York at the same time as American Overseas Airways Constellation 'Flagship Great Britain' from the same city an-nounced its arrival in London airspace. Which airline was the winner? (*Author's Collection*)

passengers thought that German prisoners of war had been drafted in to help out at Britain's new airport.

Readers may choose their own preferred airport opening date: 1 January, 28 May or 31 May 1946. Air Vice Marshal Bennett went through the rest of his life claiming that his 'Star Light' Lancastrian had been the airport's first service. BOAC – now British Airways – claims 28 May as the airport's opening date, while Heathrow's owner, BAA plc, claims 31 May as its 'May Day', even though by that time at least thirteen aircraft had either taken off or landed at the new airport that used surplus brown military tents for terminals.

* * *

Waiting to greet passengers on 31 May was Lord Winster with a delegation of parliamentarians and air attachés from all countries whose airlines were expected to use the airport. An impressive array of aircraft lined the tarmac for the VIPs to inspect and demonstration flights took place using a BOAC DC3 and an RAF York; aircraft that would become regular users of the airport in the months to come.

Winster knew that waiting pressmen wanted another good story about the airport, and he had one for them. He told the media that he planned to alter the airport's name from Heathrow to London Airport 'because the name Heathrow is extremely difficult for many foreigners to pronounce.' It would be another twenty years before the name Heathrow returned as the airport's official name.

Winster had more information to convey:

Because the airport will be the first piece of England on which thousands of foreign visitors will land, I attach great importance to the design of the terminal buildings, which will be among the finest of their kind in the country. The lay-out of the airport will also be improved so as to be capable of handling 160 aircraft movements an hour in good weather and 120 in bad.

He told the media that he envisaged the airport eventually having six runways made up of three parallel pairs arranged around a central terminal building. The two runways still to be completed would be ready for use in June 1946 and he expected them to be capable of handling the world's largest aircraft, including the Bristol Brabazon, a giant British-designed passenger aircraft still in the early planning stages.

Winster said that the tents and mobile caravans would soon disappear, to be replaced by more substantial buildings which would in themselves also be temporary 'because they will be superseded at a later date by permanent buildings in the centre of the airport, between the triangular runways.' He told the media that 'access to these buildings would be by way of a tunnel extending from near the Staines Road entrance to near the Bath Road entrance.'

He also stated that

> both the Minister of Transport and I are fully alive to the necessity of developing access to the airport. Rail transport is being examined in conjunction with the main railways and the London Passenger Transport Board. For airport employees, access will be provided by extending the Underground Railway beyond Hounslow West and the airport itself.

It would be another twenty-five years before the London Underground finally pulled into the airport, first with a link to Hatton Cross and in 1977 into the newly-built Heathrow Central Station.

Winster also confirmed that further airport extensions were planned 'but there will be no substantial demolition of houses or other property before 1950. One of the reasons for siting the airport in this district was that it could be done with a minimum of disturbance to householders.'

Plans published three weeks later triggered off mass alarm in communities surrounding 'London Airport'. As suggested in Professor Abercrombie's original vision, they showed the airport extending north of the Bath Road towards Harlington and West Drayton. The villages of Poyle and Sipson would be engulfed and the airport extended south-east to where Terminal 4 now stands. It was estimated that up to 1,200 houses would be demolished, more than 11,000 people displaced and a massive project undertaken to re-house families elsewhere in south-west Middlesex. The airport was expected to provide employment for up to 10,000 people in the next few years and there was talk of a new airport satellite town being built exclusively for the personnel. The Ministry of Civil Aviation predicted that 1,450 staff would work for the organization by the end of the year, rising to 8,000 in 1950 and 10,000 by 1954.

* * *

The airport had now become a major news-gathering centre. Media stories about airport developments, airlines and passengers resulted in regular visits from air correspondents attached to London-based publications, which in turn gave birth to a resident news-reporting and photographic agency, working day and night to feed stories to daily and evening newspapers.

The agency was run by Squadron Leader William 'Bill' Brenard, a larger-than-life winner of a Distinguished Flying Cross, whose father Bob had founded the original news-reporting operation at Croydon Airport before the war.

Using one of the former military caravans as his newsroom and darkroom, Brenard Air News Service – Brenard's for short – was at the airport from the beginning. In appearance Brenard himself looked like Frans Hals' portrait of the Laughing Cavalier, complete with a large round and open face, Van Dyke beard, twirling moustaches and an obvious zest for life. Like the painted cavalier, Brenard could laugh up a storm; a loud and generous 'Har! Har!! Har!!!' of a laugh that could be heard outside his caravan-newsroom and across the airport's aprons. In the early days he came to his 'office' still wearing his RAF flying jacket and quickly won new friends, many of them former armed forces personnel like himself to whom he gave jobs as reporters and photographers. He remained one of the airport's best-known personalities until his death in the early 1980s.

One of Brenard's early reporters, Ray Berry, recalls the airport and Brenard's early days:

Bill Brenard was like a cross between the Laughing Cavalier and Orson Welles, a larger-than-life man who you could hear coming in your direction from half a mile away. Bill ran Brenard Air News Service, London Airport's news and photographic agency for over half a century and was an icon during the airport's early years. (*Brenard Press*)

My first impression of London Airport was of nothing but a vast expanse of mist. From the top of my number 81 bus on the Bath Road, there wasn't a single aircraft to be seen, but my view hardly extended beyond the concrete of the north side parking apron. The immediate foreground seemed to be smothered by row upon row of camouflaged vehicles, military and RAF caravans. At their centre stood a handful of prefabricated, single-storey buildings like barrack blocks with flat roofs. This, I discovered a few days later, had recently succeeded the muddy brown tents, which had served as the airport passenger terminal for most of the past twelve months.

The caravans I had glimpsed from the bus were the temporary offices of airlines, other services and private companies. One was the head office of Brenard's. It resembled a khaki-painted box-shaped removal van on an army truck chassis, with two similar size 'winged' annexes. The annexes were served by single doors directly from the centre van, which was accessed through a similar door at the rear. This central office, some 15ft long x 6ft in width, became a 'news room'. One of the annexes served as a copy room and the other, draped in wartime blackout material, as a dark room for the company's two photographers.

Two fitted desks were provided on opposite walls in the newsroom with three or four folding chairs. Two more chairs were available in each annexe, which also boasted long, portable folding tables. The maximum number of people to be accommodated overall comfortably would not have been more than six. The average was usually three.

In summer the temperature inside the central caravan was unpleasant, to put it heatedly. The entrance and/or annexe doors often had to be left ajar as the main windows (in the roof) were fitted, wired glass frames. The annexes, on the other hand, allowed wind to blow in from most points of the compass summer or winter, as here the walls consisted only of heavy, opaque green canvas draped between the floors and the ceilings. The prime source of winter heating was three paraffin oil burners (Aladdin Valor stoves) supplemented occasionally by unofficial low-wattage electric heaters. No one, as far as I can recall, ever took responsibility for trimming the wicks of the stoves, so the fumes were frequently suffocating in their intensity. And, of course, we all smoked incessantly.

The floors, too, were cold to the feet, as there was nothing between them and the ground, about 2ft below. Coconut matting helped slightly in the news room, but the lino in the annexes was always icy to the touch.

I met Bill Brenard within 15 minutes of my 'interview' with his then news editor just inside the caravan. He crashed through the door wearing both his RAF sheepskin flying jacket and calf-length fur boots, which he proceeded to kick across the floor. First impression was that he was abrupt and apparently didn't suffer fools gladly. But when in answer to one question, I concluded by addressing him as 'sir' he laughed and then snapped back 'and don't call me "sir".'

Bill Brenard's news agency made a major contribution to the success of London Airport by keeping it in the public eye for the next fifty years. There was little that went on at the airport that Brenard's didn't know about. Here is a selection of some of Brenard's early news stories from London Airport, each one packed with the kind of facts, figures and gossip post-war newspaper-readers expected and which eventually made the airport the second most important news-gathering centre in Britain after Westminster:

3 June 1946: The first British land plane (rather than sea plane) service between London and New York, competing with two American airlines over the world's most profitable route, is to start on the first of next month. On that day a BOAC Constellation – one of five built in California

The Lockheed Constellation ('Connie') was a propeller-driven, four-engine airliner built by Lockheed Corporation between 1943 and 1958 at Burbank, California. As the first pressurized airliner in widespread use, the Constellation helped to usher in affordable and comfortable air travel with dozens of airlines including BOAC and TWA. (*Brenard Press*)

for £1 million – will take 40 passengers, a crew of five and three stewards from London Airport to La Guardia Airport, New York in under 20 hours. Calls will be made at Eire and Newfoundland on the 3,445-mile trip. Fares will be £93 single, £168 return (£5 7s per hour). The new British service – the first since flying boats were withdrawn in March – will run twice weekly. Within a fortnight there will be tri-weekly services, speeding up to four per week and then daily. Flying at 20,000ft 'above the weather' the four-engine 8,800hp planes will have cabins 'pressurised' at 8,000ft. Hot and cold meals will be served on board at 300 mph.

5 June 1946: The eight tons of peaches brought into London Airport from France on Monday sold at Covent Garden yesterday from 6d to 1s 3d each wholesale. Shop prices are at least double. The best English peaches cost 5s to 10s each and a wholesaler said yesterday that French fruit cannot be compared with the best of English. 'They are smaller, have large stones, less flesh and coarse skins,' he said.

2 July 1946: At 13 minutes past 10 tonight, BOAC's new Constellation aircraft left London Airport to open BOAC's regular commercial service between London and New York. At 10 o'clock the 42-seat aircraft had only 22 seats filled and of those three were occupied by non-paying priority government passengers, including Lord Knollys, BOAC's Chairman. In the 20 empty seats were rugs, pillows and newspapers. Excuse for the wasted space was: 'Because of headwinds, which sometimes reach 70 mph on the east-west run, additional petrol

has to be carried for safety reasons. So, we decided to take only 22 passengers. At 11 pm an American Overseas Airways Constellation took off from the same 3,000-yard airstrip with 39 passengers bound for New York. Total for the BOAC trip tonight will amount to £1,679; for the American Constellation $3,697.

4 July 1946: Three bags full of women's model clothes containing everything from swimsuits to evening gowns complete with matching accessories lay on the floor of the customs tent at London Airport this morning. Three girls, whose clothes they are, are sitting in their rooms at a London hotel wearing garments borrowed from a fourth. And on the question of whether or not the girls and the clothes will get together again today depends on whether one of the girls, Jean French from New York, tennis star and model, will go to France to take part in the national tournament next week. Whether the three girls, professional models who put on a 'flight of fancy' show in a transatlantic Clipper yesterday, will put on the show again for television picture page programmes today remains to be seen. Will three of the girls keep their promise to show off their fashions to English designers and go to Paris next week? Or will they take the next plane back to New York today? The girls, Jean French, Joy Fog and Frances Dyer with their chaperone, Eveline Wade, brought over 55lb of luggage each – about £250 of clothes, accessories and cosmetics, given to them by American designers and business houses. Explained Miss Wade: 'The clothes the girls have been displaying are not new and belong to the girls personally. We brought them over just to show British and French dress houses our ideas for autumn fashions and we meant to buy some fashion creations over here to take back with us.' Customs estimate of duty payable is £350.

5 July 1946: A proposal to reduce the air fare from London to New York from £93 15s to £81 5s may mean that it will be cheaper to fly the Atlantic than to sail by liner. Airline operators believe that the £81 5s single fare will mean more than a saving of £8 15s on the £90 passage by sea. There is no tipping on the Atlantic air routes and at least two days of travel are saved.

On 11 July all airlines – including BOAC – using the gleaming new Constellation aircraft were forced to withdraw them from services following a fire on board a Trans World Airlines model which crashed at Reading, Pennsylvania. BOAC's Lancastrians and Liberators, which had been taken out of long-haul service, were rapidly pulled out of their mothballs and reintroduced. However, the Lancastrians only carried twelve passengers and the Constellations air-lifted twenty-five, forcing the airline to operate twice as many aircraft – using twice

On 11 July 1946 all airlines – including BOAC – using the gleaming new Constellation air-craft were forced to withdraw them from services following a fire on board a Trans World Airlines model which crashed at Reading, Pennsylvania. (*Author's Collection*)

the amount of fuel – until the American planes were reintroduced in the middle of August.

By the end of September more than twelve airline companies were using London Airport. All three runways were in use and although it would be years before the airport was complete (and more than seventy years later is still under construction), regular users were impressed with the speed with which the new semi-permanent passenger buildings and offices were taking shape under the supervision of airport manager Mr R.C. Pugh.

* * *

The first terminal was ready by the end of 1946: a building constructed using materials used in constructing post-war prefabricated houses. It was not perfect, but larger, wider, warmer, more spacious, comfortable, colourful, friendlier and more bustling than the marquees. It was inspired by American airline terminals, which offered individual airline desks, seating areas, cafés and shops, although it would be April 1947 before a licence could be obtained to open a bar from which to sell alcohol.

Airport reporter Ray Berry remembers those early airport buildings:

The airport's passenger buildings were primarily single-storey prefabricated structures with mainly flat roofs. The walls were made of asbestos-based fibre panels held in a skeleton of preformed reinforced concrete pillars. But the Ministry of Civil Aviation did their gallant best to brighten up the ersatz appearance with gallons of liberally and frequently applied salmon pink, biscuit beige and dove grey gloss paint on the interiors. One welcome touch in these potentially scruffy 'lounges' was the hundreds of square yards of carpeting on the concrete floors.

Before the end of the year BOAC had transferred the remainder of its Middle and Far Eastern services from Hurn to London Airport and all of the airline's Lancastrians, Yorks – another aircraft from Avro's Manchester aircraft works – DC3s and Liberators became familiar to staff working there and increasing numbers of passengers using it.

Aircraft manufacturers on both sides of the Atlantic were busy courting both BSAA and BOAC in the hope of selling their new long-range civil aircraft for peacetime fleets. Air Vice Marshal Bennett would not consider equipment built by an American or any other 'foreign' manufacturer. He was determined that his fleet would be all-British through and through and in addition to his ex-RAF Lancastrians (some of which he purchased from Avro at knock-down prices and would eventually number fourteen), he bought a fleet of Avro Yorks, a high-winged and noisy monoplane that could carry up to thirty passengers. The first few Yorks each came with a £40,000 price tag, but Avro subsequently dropped its prices when they failed to sell as well as the company had hoped.

Now that the war was over, Britain could resume designing and manufacturing commercial aircraft. A wartime agreement with the US government resulted in Britain concentrating its efforts on building military aircraft while America supplied transport aircraft. Although the agreement was successful, it gave the Americans a head start on designing and producing passenger planes that could be used in peacetime. By 1946, the DC3, a military passenger and cargo plane, had been adapted for commercial use along with the four-engine DC3 'Skymaster' and the Constellation. However, Britain had civil aircraft on the drawing board, if not in the skies…

While BOAC and other foreign airlines agreed to purchase some American aircraft, Avro's future depended on the success of its new 'Tudor', a fully-pressurized commercial passenger plane commissioned by the Ministry of Supply in wartime and now rapidly taking shape at the company's factory near Manchester. The Tudor was a four-engine low-wing monoplane able to carry thirty-two passengers and a crew of four. Bennett liked the plane and Avro looked to BSAA to help make their first post-war passenger plane a success. After putting a Tudor prototype through its paces, BOAC demanded major modifications to the aircraft and began losing interest in bringing it into the fleet. Bennett took the same aircraft on his own trials and flew it around the Caribbean, later stating that this was the perfect plane for his airline and he

While BOAC and other foreign airlines agreed to purchase some American aircraft, Air Vice Marshal Bennett of BSAA purchased the British-built Avro Tudor for his fleet. (*Author's Collection*)

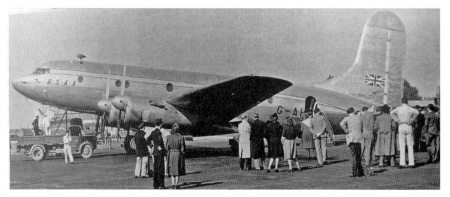

By sea, and by land, Britain has led in transport development since Tudor days. Now, by air, a 'Tudor' leads again . . .

a superplane by **AVRO**

THE AVRO TUDOR II

failed to see why BOAC had rejected it. He ordered six enlarged versions of the aircraft, which would be known as the 'Tudor IV'.

By November 1946, the Ministry of Civil Aviation began receiving the first complaints about aircraft noise at London Airport from local residents. All correspondents received the following pompous reply:

> With the development of air traffic, which is proceeding rapidly, it is regretted that it is not possible to encourage any hope that the arrivals and departures at London Airport could arbitrarily be restricted to particular hours, solely on the grounds that some local inconvenience be caused to residents by aircraft arriving or leaving the airport during those hours when the residents may usually be sleeping.

Noise complaints still continue to pour in to Heathrow, and every other commercial airport in the country.

BSAA Avro Tudor IV 'Star Lion' prepares to board passengers on its inaugural flight from London. (*Keith Hayward Collection*)

During the same month, the airport experienced its first industrial unrest when lorry drivers working for Wimpey & Co. came out on strike 'because of alleged dictatorial attitudes (by the company's management) and non-union membership' by two foremen. Wimpey said that the strike was settled amicably following joint negotiations between a strike committee and management 'and further negotiations would proceed through the official machinery which had proved so successful during the two and a half years in which construction at the airport had proceeded.' More – many, many more – industrial disputes at Heathrow would follow this little local difficulty in the seventy years that followed.

On 30 November 1946 a Christmas party was given for 250 children whose parents worked at the airport. They stood on the tarmac to greet Father Christmas, who arrived in a Lancastrian 'Christmas Special' carrying toys donated by nine airlines operating to and from London Airport. Children were told that Santa Claus had arrived a few days early 'owing to tail winds'. Airlines announced that they planned to serve Christmas dinners to all passengers travelling on December 25: soup, roast turkey, creamed potatoes, Brussels sprouts and peas, Christmas pudding, mince pies and whipped cream. The food was prepared in new 'in-flight' kitchens opened at the airport and would then be re-heated on board aircraft.

London Airport came to the end of its first year, stating that 63,151 passengers and 2,386 tons of air cargo had been handled travelling to and from eighteen destinations on 2,046 aircraft movements. Only one of the three British state airlines using the airport had made a profit that year: BSAA.

The prospects for 1947 looked better than good ...

Chapter 9

1947–49: Taking Part in Something Worthwhile

The cost of creating London Airport and running it during its first year was so high that it would be years before the government recouped its £25 million investment. It needed more airlines, more passengers, more freight, more commercial tenants and more 'side shows' to help generate revenue. In 1947 a Ministry of Civil Aviation employee was prepared to predict the direction British airports needed to follow to be profitable. Under the headline 'Dance and Swim at the Airport', the *Daily Express* carried the following story on 3 October:

> Dance halls, swimming pools, band concerts and joy flights are being planned for state airports to give them a holiday atmosphere – and to slash operating losses which are now more than 50 per cent. The architect of the brighter airports scheme is 50-year-old, £1,330-a-year Director of Amenities to the Ministry of Civil Aviation. 'Courtesy is my number one priority,' he says. He has plans for shops – including hairdressers – restaurants and even classrooms for children. Mr Scott expects the 'side shows' to pay for 40 per cent of an airport's total operating costs.

More than seventy years later, most of Mr Scott's predictions have been realized decades ago. Hotels surrounding today's Heathrow Airport provide the swimming pools, music and dancing, while the airport itself is now one of Britain's leading retail centres, with most of the country's best-known shops operating branches in the terminals. Rents paid by the retail and catering sectors generate millions of pounds for the airport owner, Heathrow Airport Holdings Limited. Airports today must be profitable if they are to survive, and thanks to Mr Scott's foresight back in 1947, London's major gateway to and from the world is the most profitable thanks to its 'side-show' contributions.

However, Scott's ideas about joy flights at London Airport were short-lived. By 1947 the airport had become a magnet for visitors wanting to see aircraft landing and taking off. A day trip to the airport was a treat, a chance to rub shoulders with passengers checking in for flights to exciting destinations. Day-trippers were forbidden to enter the departure buildings, but many found a way to rub shoulders with passengers posing as their friends and planning to

For 20s (£1) it was possible to take a joy ride 'around the houses' from London Airport in an eight-seat wooden-built Dragon Rapide operated by Island Air Services (later re-named Birkett Air Services) which promised passengers aerial views of famous London landmarks, weather permitting. (*Brenard Press*)

wave them off at departure gates. This little plan often worked among adult airport day-trippers but carried little weight with hundreds of children drawn to London Airport during school holidays who were duly ejected into the open-air public enclosure.

However, there was a way of experiencing a passenger's-eye view of London and its new airport without having a passport or an air ticket. Mr Scott's suggestion that fun flights might be a way of generating revenue for airports resulted in a short-lived but popular scheme that existed between 1947 and 1952 when a small company called Island Air Services

During the war Monique Agazarian flew alongside Mary Guthrie in the Women's Auxiliary Air Force. After the war she joined Island Air Services as a pilot on short flights around Britain and to the continent. She also operated 'joy ride' flights from London Airport over the city and above Windsor, often accompanied by her bull terrier Spike. (*Brenard Press*)

(later re-named Birkett Air Services) offered thirty-minute 'flights around the houses' in eight-seat Dragon Rapide wooden bi-planes.

A larger-than-life lady called Monique Agazarian ran the company. The daughter of an Armenian-born businessman, like Mary Guthrie who had been a wartime Air Transport Auxiliary pilot, Monique was famous for flying a Spitfire at low level down Piccadilly on VE Day.

She charged 12s 6d for a fifteen-minute circuit of the airport – including a fly-past over Windsor Castle – and £1 for an hour-long journey over London and its docks. Always accompanying the passengers was Monique's bulldog Spike who posed for hundreds of passengers sitting in the pilot's seat. Monique's aerial trips were enormously popular with families and a treat in her Dragon Rapide made a wonderful – if expensive – birthday present. Monique was probably responsible for converting many boys away from wanting to be train drivers to becoming pilots when they grew up.

Sadly, the cost of a joy-ride in Monique's Dragon Rapide was too high for many people. Derek Rylatt remembers:

As a small boy I remember being taken to the airport which was surrounded by grasslands virtually to the horizon in those days. I recall there were various displays and marquees everywhere, the purposes of which were lost on a young child. The Dragon Rapide offered pleasure flights and I recall being disappointed at not being able to take a flight as the fare of 12s 6d was a small fortune in those days.

The DH.89 Dragon Rapide was a 1930s short-haul biplane. Capable of accommodating six to eight passengers, it proved an economical and durable craft especially for short joy rides, despite its relatively primitive plywood construction. (*IWM Duxford*)

Later Monique organized weekend gambling jaunts from London Airport to Deauville and Le Touquet (£4 return) and business was brisk until the day her Dragon Rapide got caught up in taxiway turbulence caused by the engines of a Constellation and, being a wooden aircraft, it blew over causing several injuries. By that time the airport was becoming busy throughout the day and the Ministry of Civil Aviation called a halt to joy-riding. Monique, by now married to a BEA pilot flying from Northolt Airport, began a charter operation flying flowers from the Scilly Islands. When London Airport became too expensive to use as a base, she moved operations to Ramsgate Aerodrome in Kent and reintroduced joy-riding with limited success.

* * *

Overseeing the rapid growth of London Airport was Air Marshal Sir John D'Albiac, 53, who was given the title of 'Airport Commandant' and a brief to oversee all air traffic control, communications and general management duties. A former officer with the Royal Marine Artillery, D'Albiac was an observer during the First World War and sighted an enemy submarine near Ostend, making the first attack on a submarine from a British aircraft. The next war found him in Greece in charge of 80 British aircraft that had to face 800 German and 300 Italian machines. He was later posted to Ceylon at the time of the attempted Japanese invasion, which was repulsed by planes under D'Albiac's command. After that the Japanese never returned to that part of the Indian Ocean in any force.

A straight-backed authoritarian and now remembered by former airport reporter Ray Berry as 'one of nature's gentlemen', D'Albiac would run London Airport with his own 'air of authority' and military style for the next ten years. He was expected to 'live on the job' in a special detached house with a garden, still referred to by some airport old-timers as 'the commandant's house', at the junction of Caines Lane and the Bath Road.

One of D'Albiac's first jobs was to oversee major changes to Heathrow's runway layout. The RAF-style runway triangle had been working well ever since the airport opened,

Overseeing the rapid growth of London Airport was the popular Air Marshal Sir John D'Albiac, 53, who was given the title of 'Airport Commandant' and a brief to oversee all air traffic control, communications and general management duties, all of which he did extremely well. (*Elliot & Fry*)

but the Ministry of Civil Aviation quickly recognized that more runway capacity was needed and plans were devised to create six concrete runways incorporating the original triangle. Each runway would be extended to 1.75 miles and form the pattern of a six-pointed star, allowing parallel take-offs and landings. During runway alterations the plan was slightly modified, limiting the number of runways to five and converting the sixth into a taxiway.

D'Albiac was also part of a team tasked with masterminding the next stage of the airport's development: planning the design and construction of a major airport city, complete with terminal buildings, a control tower, offices and a public viewing area all located in the centre of the runway complex and linked to main roads leading to the airport by the tunnel first mentioned by Lord Winster in 1946.

* * *

There had been only one disaster at the airport since it had opened. Early in 1947, a nervous foreign passenger who had just arrived in London became distressed after being closely questioned by customs officers about how long he planned to stay in the country. They wanted to know if he carried enough money to support himself while in Britain, and they wanted to see his return ticket. The man decided to try to make a run for it, dashed onto the airport apron and right into the revolving propeller of an aircraft about to depart. Scores of passengers looked on in horror, unable to stop the poor man from meeting his untimely end in such a grim fashion.

The first major incident at the airport involved a Douglas DC-3C owned by the Belgian airline Sabena (similar to the one photographed here) which crashed in fog on 2 March 1948. Of the twenty-two people on board, twenty were killed, most of whom had British nationality. (*Author's Collection*)

There were other close shaves – known at the airport as 'near misses' – in which air crew had either misunderstood or failed to understand instructions from the Control Tower. Fortunately, air disasters had been avoided. This was to change shortly after 9.00 pm on 2 March 1948 when a DC3 from the Belgian airline Sabena and flying to London from Brussels crashed on landing and burst into flames. Of the twenty-two passengers and crew, all but two were killed.

The aircraft landed in a nosedive on the grass. There was an explosion and the aircraft burst into flames. Visibility was poor due to fog, and rescue squads worked to put out the fire and save lives using portable searchlights and vehicle headlamps. The heat was so intense that fire-fighters were unable to get close enough to the crashed plane to make any further rescues.

The pilot had been warned about the foggy weather by radio while flying over the British coast and told that visibility was reduced to 20 yards. The aircraft was 'talked down' until it was just a few feet away from the runway. What happened next was never ascertained. One theory stated that as the DC3 had touched down, the port wheel had buckled causing the aircraft to lurch to one side and hit the ground, fracturing the main tank and starting a fire.

The crew of 3 were Belgian and of the 19 passengers, 14 were British, 2 were Italian, 1 was Russian, 1 from Poland and the other a Cuban.

A bizarre story surrounds this tragic air crash. Several fire-fighters and members of the police rescue squad battling to save lives that night claimed that a man wearing a pin-striped suit, bowler hat and carrying a briefcase and rolled umbrella was seen at the crash site. In the noise, heat and confusion, he was given little attention and it was assumed he was some sort of airport official. Nobody saw him arrive or leave. On several later occasions, and also in foggy weather, control tower staff were alerted to something small moving out on the runway and several claimed to have seen a man in a pin-striped suit and bowler hat, carrying a briefcase and rolled umbrella who disappeared just as quickly as he appeared. Although the last reported sighting was in the late 1960s, some airport operational staff still talk about the spectre.

* * *

By 1947, everybody wanted to work at London Airport and landing a job was not difficult, especially for ex-servicemen and women. Gordon Pankhurst, who by 1977 had become superintendent of Terminal 3, recalled:

In those days Heathrow was surrounded by fields and farms. I was in the police force at the time and one day just happened to be cycling past the new airfield. I shouted to an ex-RAF type to ask if there were any jobs going, and I've been here ever since.

Another airport veteran was Leslie Green, a former Heathrow general manager, who joined the Ministry of Civil Aviation in 1946. Speaking in 1977, he remembered the airport's early years as 'great days, a time when everyone pulled together and helped each other.' According to Leslie,

> the war had everything to do with it. We had all come through a great deal together. Everyone had lost someone close, had their home flattened by a bomb or been posted overseas for years at a time. We were all different people, but thanks to the war, we had something in common – the wartime experience. That's what made the airport work in its earliest pioneering days. It was the blitz spirit. If anyone was ever in trouble, everyone rallied round to help them out of it. Everyone knew everyone else and had great respect for each other. Staff addressed their bosses as 'sir' in much the same way as they would have done in the armed forces. We even snapped to attention when someone senior approached us and some of us even saluted. For many airport staff, it had been their habit to do so for several years, so carrying this over into civilian life came quite naturally to many of us.
>
> When Sir John D'Albiac came into the terminal just about everyone snapped to attention and he would walk down the length of the building turning left and right, telling us to 'carry on, carry on'. We all knew that we were taking part in something worthwhile. Every one of us was aware that air travel was the future, and anyone who worked at London Airport in the late 1940s was a witness to this each day. The place just grew before your eyes.

Stan Stern, a well-known airport personality in the 1970s and head of travel company Airport Assistance, recalls a twin-engine plane trying to smash the London-Paris air record in 1946 in a Lancastrian fitted with jet engines. 'A little way down the road from the runway was a well-kept market garden full of flowers in full bloom,' recalled Stan. 'As the plane turned to move down the runway, the blast from the jet engine reduced the garden to a brown scalded patch. Not a flower left.' Still, the plane achieved the distance in fifty-five minutes and later went on to knock thirteen minutes from the record a few days later, by which time a large fence had been erected in front of the market garden ...

Gordon Chubb from Weybridge, Surrey recalls what it was like to arrive at London Airport as a passenger. He writes:

> I find it difficult to convey to present-day travellers the basic nature of early post-war civilian air travel and its ground facilities and how completely

domestic they were in scale. In January 1949 I arrived at London Airport from Nairobi on an ex-United States Air Force Skymaster operated by an airline called Skyways. This was a War Office charter flight via Khartoum and Tripoli. Having disembarked on the runway we walked to the concrete prefabricated buildings. It took but ten minutes to pass between officials sitting on Dickens-like high stools who dealt with immigration and foreign currency controls. The last official then invited each passenger to leave by a small door in the wall behind his desk. On stepping through the door and closing it in the normal way, one turned around to find oneself almost alone in a tiny car park directly on the Bath Road. That was it! One was back home in an unpainted, battered, post-war London to become, once again, one of its proud citizens dressed, for the most part, in equally drab and threadbare clothes.

Philip Gordon-Marshall recalls the airport's fire services during the late 1940s:

We only had two sets of fire appliances. One was kept in a Nissen hut, which was the fire station, while the other stood out on the tarmac. The crash crews, dressed in full uniform, used to get jolly hot waiting there (the sun really used to beat down in those days). So, Doug Lovegrove, sensible man that he was, thought it would be a good idea to take his trousers off. There he stood, overalls off, trousers off, just about to put his overalls back on – when the alarm bell rang! This meant that Doug had to climb up through the flap in the cabin roof to direct the hose – all of which he did in his underpants.

* * *

By September 1947, the first of BSAA's Tudor IV aircraft – 'Star Lion' – was ready to enter commercial service following a goodwill passenger-carrying proving flight to South America. Air Vice Marshal Bennett planned to replace the noisy Lancastrians and cumbersome Yorks with the new thirty-two-seat planes.

Bennett had been unlucky with his aircraft. In August 1946 a Lancastrian had crashed in the Gambia without any fatalities. The following month a York crashed at the same airport and twenty-four passengers died. Another York crashed in Senegal with six fatalities, followed by the Lancastrian 'Star Dust' which crashed in the Andes Mountains in August 1947. It would be more than fifty years before its wreckage was found. The following month another Lancastrian hit a radio mast in Bermuda and although there were no fatalities, the aircraft had to be written off. Then on 14 November 1947 'Star Light', the plane that had made history by becoming the first service from London Airport, crash-landed in Bermuda after its undercarriage collapsed. There were no deaths, but yet another BSAA aircraft had bitten the dust and was now unusable.

After piloting the new Tudor IV back to London Airport, Bennett declared that the Tudor would be economical to operate, allow his company to run at a profit and that 'from a passenger point of view the greatest improvement in the Tudor is the increased silence which, I think is greater than comparable aircraft currently in use. I am delighted with the Tudor from a technical point of view and can see nothing wrong with it.'

In October Tudor IV 'Star Tiger' commenced flying from London Airport to Bermuda following a fanfare of publicity at the airport. Twelve weeks later the aircraft disappeared without trace over the sea north-east of Bermuda. No wreckage was ever sighted or discovered. Lord Nathan – who had replaced Lord Winster as Minister for Civil Aviation – ordered the Tudors to be grounded while a full inquiry took place.

The *Daily Express* invited Bennett to comment on the decision and the former Pathfinder chief took advantage of the opportunity to criticize the people running Britain's civil aviation interests. Under the banner headline 'I Contest Lord Nathan's Grounding of Tudor IV', Bennett told air correspondent Basil Cardew:

> There are two outstanding forces at work in civil aviation in Britain today. In the first category are those who are openly anti-British in aviation. In the second those who entered it either for selfish reasons or for other reasons – but are totally ignorant of aviation.
>
> These two categories are more influential than the professionals and those who have given their lives to it.

Bennett went on to attack the way in which the government had interfered with how the state-owned airlines were run 'to such a degree that it has become increasingly difficult for an airline executive to be held responsible for the results he achieves.' He criticized the government for preventing airlines from dealing directly with aircraft manufacturers and Lord Nathan's decision to ground the new aeroplanes, stating that it was he who should make such decisions:

> I very deeply regret, therefore, that I should have been ordered to withdraw the Tudor IV from service, thereby inferring a lack of confidence in this type of airliner ... I have no lack of confidence in the airliner, nor in the ability of British aviation in general to achieve the success which British temperament and ability are bound to win if given the freedom.

On 10 February 1948, the board of BSAA terminated Bennett's appointment as chief executive owing to 'differences of opinion over matters of policy'. In a page one story, Bennett said:

I have today had the proudest honour of my life. I have been sacked for speaking my own mind. I granted an interview to a newspaper correspondent at which I expressed views concerning the obvious ills of British civil aviation in general, and concerning recent interference with the management by the Minister for Civil Aviation. It is because of this article that I have been forced to discontinue my appointment. I have been forced to take this course for exercising what I consider to be a right – namely freedom of speech.

Lord Nathan claimed Bennett's dismissal was

Just over one year after flying the first service out of Heathrow, Air Vice Marshal Donald Bennett was fired from his job as chief executive of BSAA after a 'difference of opinion' with his airline's board over the Tudor IV aircraft. (Daily Express)

not an isolated incident of its kind, but the culmination of a long series of differences between the airline's Board and its Chief Executive; that the Board had accordingly lost confidence in him, deciding that they had no option but to dispense with his services, that having refused the Board's suggestion that he should tender his resignation, it had been obliged to dismiss him and were making him a gratuitous payment of £4,500 in compensation for loss of office.

There was talk of pay increases for BSAA staff to counter rumours of mass resignations from the airline by Bennett's Pathfinder colleagues, but nobody walked out. Cliff Alabaster remembers:

Many of us were not surprised when Bennett finally left the airline. We knew that something, or someone, had to give and were not surprised when the Chairman, John Booth said that the management was unable to support Bennett after what he had publicly said about them.

I personally felt let down by Bennett and his behaviour when he left the company. I was in charge of navigation for BSAA and worked closely with him. When he took issue with people at the Ministry of Civil Aviation, he told them he didn't care what they thought – this is what I say. He was very strong-willed and wouldn't give in to these people. He was often disrespectful to them. Sometimes I would pop into his office and ask how things were going and he would start on about 'these idiots at the Ministry'. He would demand that they came to see him. He refused to go and see them.

Don Bennett never came around to say goodbye to us. He didn't write to anyone, either. After he had left, I met him from time to time at various reunions, once on the tenth anniversary of the first flight in 1956 and again in subsequent years. The last time I saw him was at the fortieth anniversary reunion. I learned of his death while I was away sailing in the Channel Islands and although I missed his funeral, I went to his memorial service in St Clements Danes Church.

Bennett accepted an invitation to contest a forthcoming by-election at North Croydon for the Liberal Party, declaring that he 'would fight to the utmost against Socialist strangulation which has squeezed the spirit and strength of the people, restricting our production and impairing our trading efforts.' He was beaten by the Conservative candidate, going back into civil aviation with his own private airline and using Tudor IVs to fly over 1,000 sorties during the Berlin Airlift.

In March 1949 the government announced that BSAA would merge with BOAC. A statement said the merger

is necessitated by the fact that the ban on Tudor IVs leave BSAA with York aircraft only, which are not competitive and the obvious way of keeping BSAA routes in operation is to turn to BOAC, a complete merger with which (besides achieving efficiency and economy in other directions) will enable both corporations' services to be organised with a minimum of aircraft.

Keith Hayward recalls: 'It was a sad day indeed for the BSAA staff, where *esprit de corps* was a matter of justifiable pride.'

The merger finally went through on 26 July 1949; three years and seven months after BSAA operated the first flight from London's new airport, now being used by 394,000 passengers travelling on 36,675 flights and with a throughput of 12,629 tons of freight.

Chapter 10

1950s: Silver Wings to Paris and Flying on the 'Never-Never'

arly in 1951, Britain's most influential weekly news magazine, *Picture Post*, sent writer Brian Dowling to report on what was happening out at London Airport. 'From whichever way you approach it, as a passenger, or a friend of a passenger, or just as a normal curious person, London Airport is a ragbag of fantasy,' wrote Dowling, adding:

Everything is larger than life, and disturbing, though not unpleasantly so. There's its size; its impermanency, contrasted with its grandiose plans for the future; its huge working population, of whom so few seem likely to be connected with flying; the intricacies of its administration; its romance, deriving from the actual business of flying, and clashing all along the line with the airline companies' determination to sell flying as matter-of-factly as soap; its constant traffic of celebrities, surrounded by popping flashbulbs; its inherited nautical flavour, in whose context the jargon of practical flying is a constant irritation; everything about it appears as a jumbled mass of impressions which refuse to jell in the mind.

Picture Post was a photojournalistic magazine published between 1938 and 1957. It is considered a pioneering example of photojournalism and was an immediate success, selling 1,700,000 copies a week after only two months. The February 1951 edition devoted most of its content to a feature on London Airport and quickly sold out. (*Author's Collection*)

Picture Post described the airport's early shanty-town buildings as

tatty and mud-stained – the airport continually expands in a wen of temporary prefabs, above which aircraft rudders loom like ship superstructures in docks. Buildings push up like mothballs and disappear just as quickly; and even the newest ones are doomed to a very short life. Old houses, too, on the outskirts of the field, are suffering the fate of vanished Heath Row, and their shells, with old strips of wallpaper hanging from the walls, are perhaps the nearest thing to a symbol which London Airport has to show. Their steady destruction gives the feeling that here were those undisciplined and unorganised boxes where soft people, chockfull of 'human error' used to live; while the future only belongs to the great impersonal hangars, where perfect machines can live in perfect functional surroundings.

As far as passengers were concerned, Dowling reported that

from the time when they hear the surrealist request to 'kindly take leave of your friends in the lounge and follow the green light' to the time when the aircraft door clangs to, departing passengers are jollied along by personable receptionists. There's a formula for each movement, a set of detailed, unambiguous instructions for every action.

Those who remain, either waiting for friends or for aircraft, are left under discreet supervision in the lounge, where they can ask questions and buy buttered buns or 'genuine antiques' to their heart's content. But all this careful insulation from shock, all these attempts to make them believe that the whole thing's a matter of course – the public will always see them as the smile on the face of the tiger. The uniforms that flit through the lounge on undeclared business, the bearded pilots in sober blue and mechanics dressed in birdman zoot-suits, the stealthily prowling newsmen who go to the airport each day as other men go to the office; such things don't pass unnoticed. They prove to the layman that flying still has its own mystique, that those who actually work it are initiators of a cult. And why shouldn't the layman believe it? It's nonsense to say that travelling through the air in a flying machine is merely the result of intelligent application of scientific laws. When, on a bright summer's day, a silver shell leaves the ground with a furious thunder of engines, not one of the 10,000 who watch from the public enclosure will deny there's magic in it. Even an engineer will sometimes look thoughtful. And whatever they do to London Airport, with steel and concrete and arty décor, they'll no more take the glamour from it than they could from a goods-yard at night.

* * *

The world's largest (at the time) civil airliner, the 130-ton Bristol Brabazon I, made its maiden flight from the Bristol Aeroplane Company's base at Filton on 4 September 1949. It remained in the air for twenty-seven minutes, flying at an altitude of 4,000ft at a speed of 160 mph. Brabazon was intended to be the great silver hope of Britain's commercial plane-making industry and publicity produced by the Bristol company announced that the luxury aircraft had been 'designed specifically as a trans-oceanic airliner to provide fast travel for a large number of passengers at one time and primarily intended for BOAC non-stop London–New York services and as such will set standards in comfort and amenities hitherto unknown in the history of air transport.' It had cost British taxpayers £12 million which the government thought was a good investment and bound to re-coup its costs within five years. It was dubbed – by its manufacturer – as 'the Queen Elizabeth of the air'.

Everything about Brabazon was big. At 177ft long, it was only 54ft shorter than one of today's A380 Airbus jets, but its 230ft-long wingspan was 9ft wider than an A380. It would have a 25ft-diameter fuselage with upper and lower decks and was three times higher than a double-decker bus. It would have sleeping berths, a dining room, a cinema for thirty-seven people and 'stand-up' cocktail bars and comfortable in-flight lounges. It was held together by 1.5 million rivets. There would be plenty of room for each passenger: 200 cubic feet per traveller; about twice the interior room of a car. Leg-room would not be a problem and the seats, which would recline into full-length beds, would allow passengers to lie down and sleep as the plane rumbled its way across the North Atlantic's night skies.

However, Brabazon's passenger capacity was small and only 50 to 60 passengers could travel in the big bird, compared to between 555 and 853 passengers (depending on the seating configuration) in one of today's A380s. It would also take twelve hours to cross the Atlantic to New York, roughly the same time taken by BOAC's American-built Constellations. Today the journey can be made in around seven hours.

Like many commercial airport and aeroplane initiatives in the late 1940 and early 1950s, Brabazon was conceived during wartime to meet anticipated British post-war aviation requirements. The committee in charge of investigating the future needs of Britain's civilian airliner market met under the leadership of Lord Brabazon of Tara, after whom the country's new airliner, expected to take the world by storm, was named.

However, Brabazon was not only big; it was also ugly, slow and noisy. After witnessing a fly-past at the 1949 Farnborough Air Show, BOAC had serious misgivings about purchasing a plane that would clearly fail to meet its needs. The airline needed an aircraft that could carry more passengers in a faster, quieter and more fuel-efficient machine and Brabazon did not provide the

ROTOL

PROPELLERS ON THE BRABAZON I.

ROTOL LIMITED GLOUCESTER ENGLAND

solution. Nevertheless, the government put pressure on the airline which had no option but to at least consider bringing a fleet of Brabazons into service to operate on prestigious London Airport-New York blue ribbon routes.

BOAC and the Bristol Aeroplane Company both agreed that Brabazon needed extensive modifications and a second version – Brabazon Mk II – rolled out for its maiden flight in September 1949 and in June 1950 made its London Airport debut.

Prime Minister Clement Attlee would be the first VIP to fly from the airport in the massive plane alongside twenty MPs as it made a series of take-off and landing displays for the benefit of potential customers, local residents concerned about the noise it was reported to make, and thousands of tourists expected to flock to the airport to view Brabazon.

Yet there was a snag. Although Brabazon was perfectly airworthy having flown for 130 hours and had appeared at the 1950 Farnborough Air Show just a few days before, nobody at the Bristol Aeroplane Company had thought to obtain a passenger certificate allowing Mr Attlee and his fellow politicians to take a joy-ride around London Airport. The flight was permitted to go ahead, but without the PM and his chums.

Brabazon appeared in the skies over London Airport on the afternoon of 15 June 1950 with Bristol Aeroplane's chief test pilot Captain Bill Pegg at the controls. Captain Cliff Alabaster was at work in his office next to the Bath Road and heard it approaching:

> I went outside to take a look as it arrived. It seemed to be travelling very slowly; so slowly in fact that I thought it was going to drop out of the sky. I suppose that was because it was much larger than other planes we were used to seeing and flying at the airport. It was noisy, too. Brabazon was a cumbersome old bird and I knew that no airlines would ever take it into their fleets. It was built to show the world what British aircraft technology was all about, but it became the white elephant that nobody wanted.

John Balding was on his way to work at BOAC engineering from his home in Hayes

Opposite: The 130-ton Bristol Brabazon was designed to be the saviour of the post-war British commercial aircraft industry, but the massive 177ft-long airliner was a huge failure. Nevertheless, thousands of curious spectators descended onto London Airport to catch a close-up during Brabazon's one and only visit. Some stylish advertising designs were used to help sell Brabazon to aircraft buyers, but there were no takers for the giant plane. (*Author's Collection*)

when I heard this racket in the sky and looked up and saw the Brabazon. It was a massive piece of engineering with lots of power. But it wasn't going anywhere. It just seemed to hang there in the sky over London Airport. No wonder it was a failure. It went nowhere – and very slowly, too.

On 16 June 1950, the *Daily Express* reported:

More than 4,000 people waited at London Airport last night for a trip round the 130-ton Bristol Brabazon, the world's largest airliner. They paid 6d to enter the public enclosure, then queued for seats in coaches at 1s per head. The coaches were allowed within 50ft of the floodlit Brabazon, guarded by 49 policemen. No one was allowed within touching distance.

The following day Brabazon made three practice take-offs and landings with Captain Bill Pegg at the controls. Thousands of people in the public enclosure along the Bath Road watched it lumber and roar its way down the runway and slowly rise into the air. Each time the plane landed, Captain Pegg reversed the eight Centaurus 18-cylinder engines which braked the giant airliner to a standstill.

The airport had expected 50,000 people to turn up, but in the end 13,361 spectators paid sixpence to view Brabazon and most of them forked out an extra shilling to climb into the bus to view the big bird up close before it flew back to Filton for further modifications.

By the beginning of 1951, there were still no orders in place for Brabazon and BOAC had clearly lost all interest in the aircraft, knowing that something better and more economical was on drawing boards of other British aeroplane manufacturers. Bristol took their big bird – now looking more like a dodo – to the Paris air show where Captain Pegg took off again to put it through its paces in the hope of landing some orders. There were none.

Brabazon stood unused and neglected in a massive hangar at Filton for the next two years. Occasionally engineers tinkered around with the plane until they were told to put down their spanners for good in February 1952. In September 1953, Duncan Sandys, Attlee's Minister of Supply, told Parliament that the government had decided that 'further expenditure on the Brabazon project could not be justified' and had given directions that the plane should be dismantled. He said that the project, although costly, had made 'a most valuable contribution towards the progress of British aviation', despite the fact that £6.5 million had been spent on the project compared to the original estimate of £4 million.

The Bristol Brabazon was not a total failure. At least half of the investment poured into the project, including vast hangars and a runway extension at Filton, allowed Bristol to use its expanded facilities for other aircraft. Designers, plane-makers and engineers who had worked on Brabazon had all learned new techniques that were used on other aircraft and a few years later the Bristol Britannia, one of the world's most successful propeller-driven airliners – and known as 'the whispering giant' – rolled out of the same hangar. A few years later, another aircraft would emerge from the same structure, developed as a partnership between England and France. It would be known to the world as Concorde.

* * *

By 1951 it was becoming cheaper to fly across the English Channel and the Atlantic Ocean from London Airport. British European Airways (BEA) was formed as a state-owned airline in 1946 and had originally operated from Northolt Airport. It transferred part of its operations to London Airport in 1950 and by 1954 when Northolt was handed back to the RAF, had carried 3 million passengers and was operating more than 100 aircraft.

Following the arrival of BEA, London Airport's passenger figures rose to 796,000 by the end of 1951, the first time that the airport recorded more travellers than Northolt. The airport was now on a roll that would continue for the next seventy years and beyond.

Prime routes from London Airport were competitive. The London–Paris sector was one of the most popular and BEA battled it out with Air France for their market share. In December 1951 both airlines announced they were cutting London–Paris fares by up to 40 per cent from £8 10s single and £15 6s return to £5 10s 6d single and £9 19s return. BEA's thirty-six-seat Vikings and Air France's thirty-three-seat Languedoc 161s would operate the services.

At the same time BOAC and ten other airlines flying across the Atlantic announced that they, too, were slashing fares between London Airport and New York in order to make flying more affordable. BOAC reduced fares from £141 2s single to £96 9s.

A 'fly now, pay later' scheme was launched by BOAC and BEA in line with other post-war hire purchase schemes sweeping the country and allowing people to obtain furniture and cars through a system better known as 'buying on the never-never'; a never-ending trail of regular payments which never ended from one year to the next. The airline scheme allowed passengers to purchase tickets for any service and pay in instalments, providing the total transaction exceeded £20. Airlines asked for 10 per cent of the full air fare up front and the balance paid off in monthly instalments over a period of between six to twenty-one months depending on the final cost.

British airlines copied their American rivals and produced smart advertising in the daily press to attract customers. Pride of BEA's routes was its daily 'Silver Wing' London-Paris service using Elizabethan high-wing monoplanes, which offered cocktails and a full lunch on board the eighty-minute flight. Also pictured is an advertisement promoting return air fares with BEA from London to Paris from £9 15s, another assuring passengers that 'BOAC takes good care of you' and a popular advert promising travellers that 'experienced passengers fly British', with BOAC of course. (*Author's Collection*)

The hire purchase air fare scheme made a major contribution to BEA and BOAC's passenger-carrying figures in 1953. Together, London Airport's two busiest airlines accounted for 96.3 per cent of all British-owned scheduled services. BEA carried 1.6 million passengers of domestic and short-haul European routes, while BOAC carried 289,239 passengers on its long-haul services. British independent airlines carried 238,673 travellers.

Pride of BEA's routes was its daily 'Silver Wing' London-Paris service which offered cocktails and a full lunch on board the eighty-minute flight. Following the demise of BSAA in 1949, Keith Hayward was transferred to BOAC and by 1951 moved to BEA at London Airport. He remembers:

I was pleased to work for BEA because it meant that I got to work alongside a beautiful high-wing monoplane called the Elizabethan, one of my favourite aircraft. The cabin was quite spacious with room for only 47 passengers who enjoyed a superb lunch on the short crossing across to Paris. Sometimes they even slowed the flight down in order to have more time to serve the meal.

We had a famous senior traffic officer called 'Bim' Kent whose job was to make sure the service got away on time every lunchtime. He was a military type who used to shout at us young fellows to make us move quicker and not delay the flight. We had to salute the aircraft away in those days. The plane flew a little pennant above the cockpit and as it taxied away, staff working on the tarmac had to stop what they were doing, line up, snap to attention and salute it. The Captain would acknowledge it through the cockpit window and then haul in the pennant. This was a BEA flagship service calling for a great deal of attention to detail and a bit of ceremony as they departed. In cold and wet winter weather this

BEA ground staff on tarmac duty were required to snap to attention and salute the departure of the daily 'Silver Wing' service to Paris. (*Keith Hayward Collection*)

could be a challenge as we still had to stand to attention while fumes from high-octane piston engines, rainwater and de-icing fluid blew in our faces. The passengers probably wouldn't have been aware of it, but we certainly were!

In those days we also used huge and primitive walkie-talkie sets which were strapped to our backs. The batteries would often leak, leaving a nasty burn mark in our company issue raincoats, which had to be replaced regularly. They also carried a tall aerial on top and if you had to go on board the aircraft for any reason before departure and forgot about the aerial, there was every chance of ripping out a piece of the ceiling.

I once went on board a Silver Wing service no more than a minute before departure because there was one passenger short and I needed to count heads. As I was doing this, the Captain suddenly burst into the passenger cabin furiously demanding to know what was going on. I told him what I was doing and he told me that if I wasn't finished in one minute he was going to take off with me on board. Fortunately, I had miscounted the passengers and was out of the aircraft and down the steps before you could say Jack Robinson. Those Captains really knew how to rule the roost. There had to be a good reason for an aircraft not leaving on time. There was a leeway of three minutes and after that nobody – not even a young lad like me – was going to stand in the way of the flight departing. He meant it, too. If I hadn't shot down the steps he would have taken off with me on board. It was their military mindset still at work.

Eric Driver, who used to work for a small British airline called Starways, recalls that airline passengers in the 1950s could sometimes be just as awkward as today's travellers:

There was an occasion when a passenger in a DC3 was a little the worse for wear and started to grope the hostess, who quickly called the Captain. 'Are you going to behave and keep your hands to yourself?' the Captain asked. 'Yesshir,' said the passenger. So, the DC3 got under way and started to taxi out towards the runway. Suddenly, we noticed it was making its way towards a vacant stand, the door opened and the passenger was unceremoniously booted out of the aircraft. The door was shut and the DC3 continued its taxiing, leaving a rather puzzled passenger standing in the middle of nowhere!

On another occasion a Starways aircraft was taxiing out to take off without a passenger who had failed to check in for his flight:

An Esso Petroleum advertisement from the 1950s shows a range of aircraft used by BEA at London Airport. (*Author's Collection*)

'A few minutes later we received a call from our friends over at BEA asking us if we were missing a certain passenger,' Eric remembers. 'We asked them how they knew such a thing and they told us they had picked him up walking around the tarmac and were bringing him to us. Once he was delivered, we asked him what he'd been thinking of, walking around a busy airport tarmac. "Well," he said, "I knew I was running late, so I thought I would head off towards the taxiway to wave the aircraft down as it taxied past."'

* * *

While Paris-bound passengers bolted down their lunch on BEA's Silver Wing service, passengers flying on BOAC's overnight New York service from London Airport were getting ready for a more leisurely aerial experience.

By 1951 three airlines operated the 3,500-mile blue ribbon Atlantic route: BOAC, Pan American and Trans World Airlines (TWA). BOAC's luxurious 'Monarch' service was described as 'the last word in luxury air travel'. Using the 'double-decked spaciousness' of pressurized Boeing Stratocruiser aircraft – a fifty-seat American-built bulbous aircraft powered by four propeller-driven engines – the Monarch service was famous for its in-flight 'extras'. These included seven-course champagne dinners served from a trolley brought to passengers' seats by white-jacketed stewards. During the meal, the captain would visit the cabin to chat with passengers and explain the progress of their flight. After coffee and liqueurs in the lower deck lounge, passengers settled for the night in either their reclining seat or retired to the privacy of a comfortable full-size berth 'available for a little extra' (£8 19s extra). As the aircraft approached the last stage of its journey, breakfast in bed was offered.

Advertisements promised passengers opportunities to 'meet congenial companions in the lower deck lounge with its well-stocked bar. Three stewards and a stewardess are available to please you. There will be a complimentary "Speedbird Overnight Bag" for every passenger, an Elizabeth Arden beauty kit for every lady.'

BOAC sold the flight for 'a little over £140, roughly the same as a first-class steamer fare, but the passage is four days faster than the fastest ocean liner' and

The stylish way to fly across the Atlantic in the 1950s was with BOAC on its 'Monarch' service, described as 'the last word in luxury air travel'. During the flight in an American-built Stratocruiser, passengers enjoyed seven-course champagne dinners and slept in full-size beds available 'for a little extra'. (*Author's Collection*)

BOAC and Pan American competed for transatlantic passengers using comfortable Boeing Stratocruisers for flights between London Airport and New York's Idlewild Airport. (*Author's Collection*)

it launched their famous slogan used for the next two decades: 'BOAC takes good care of you.'

Stratocruiser crews were known within BOAC as the 'Atlantic Barons', an elite group able to command the best salaries in the business for flying what was regarded as the toughest route of all across the Atlantic, calling for pilots with the most experience and skill when crossing vast stretches of ocean.

* * *

On 31 January 1952 HM King George VI and Queen Elizabeth travelled to London Airport to wave goodbye to their daughter Princess Elizabeth and her husband Philip, Duke of Edinburgh, travelling on the first leg of a five-month tour of Commonwealth countries. They planned to visit Kenya, Ceylon, Australia and New Zealand, travelling on the BOAC Argonaut airliner 'Atalanta'.

It was a cold day, but hundreds of airport staff, passengers and onlookers turned out to see their king and raise a

31 January 1952: HM King George VI and Queen Elizabeth travelled to London Airport to wave goodbye to their daughter Princess Elizabeth and her husband Prince Philip, Duke of Edinburgh, travelling on the first leg of a five-month Commonwealth tour. They travelled on the BOAC Argonaut 'Atalanta'. (*Barry Dix Collection*)

cheer for his young daughter and her dashing husband. Surgeons had already removed one of the king's lungs four months earlier after finding a malignant tumour (he had been a heavy cigarette-smoker all his life). He looked pale and drawn as he walked bareheaded across the windswept tarmac with his daughter and son-in-law, muffled in a heavy greatcoat, his hands thrust firmly into his overcoat pockets.

The duke shook hands with the king and was first to climb the steps into the Argonaut. Princess Elizabeth followed her husband and at the aircraft door turned and waved to her father. It would be the last time she saw him alive.

The king returned to his wife in the terminal and together they came out of the Royal Lounge as the Argonaut began to taxi out towards the runway. They watched it as it gathered speed, rose into the air and soon became a small speck on the distant horizon before going back inside. This would be the king's final public appearance since he had reluctantly come to the throne in 1936 following the abdication of his brother, Edward VIII.

Six days later, at an exclusive forest hunting lodge near Nyeri in the foothills of Mount Kenya, Princess Elizabeth was told that her father had

On 7 February 1952 BOAC Argonaut 'Atalanta' returned to London Airport from Entebbe with Princess Elizabeth following the death of her father. She set foot on British soil as queen for the first time at London Airport on a site now covered by a large hotel. Waiting on the tarmac to greet their new monarch were Prime Minister Sir Winston Churchill, Foreign Secretary Anthony Eden and Opposition Leader Clement Attlee. (*Brenard Press*)

died of coronary thrombosis during the early hours of the morning. Plans were immediately made for her return home and the young royal couple were rushed to Entebbe, Uganda to where the crew of BOAC Argonaut 'Atalanta' was on its way to collect the young princess who would soon be their queen.

The aircraft took off from Entebbe in a storm and completed the 4,444-mile journey in nineteen hours and forty-three minutes. It included a short stop in El Adem in Libya for refuelling and a change of crew. During the journey the crew maintained regular contact with BOAC's operations room at London Airport by wireless telegraphy. The RAF and Royal Navy had taken precautions all along the route in case an emergency arose.

Over Sevenoaks at 4.06 pm on 7 February 1952, the Argonaut descended to 4,000ft and began its approach to London Airport where the 'Atalanta' touched down in England at 4.19 pm. A small group was waiting on the tarmac, heads bare and wearing black overcoats and armbands. They included Prime Minister Winston Churchill, his Foreign Minister Anthony Eden and Opposition Leader Clement Attlee. They bowed their heads as the door of the Argonaut opened and Princess Elizabeth began to walk down the steps. As her feet touched the tarmac, they looked up to greet their new queen.

The exact place where Princess Elizabeth first set foot on British soil at London Airport as the uncrowned Queen Elizabeth II is now the site of the Heathrow Renaissance Hotel's Brasserie Restaurant, where a striking wall plaque marks the historic spot. The large hotel, with the Bath Road at its front side and a busy airport perimeter road behind it, had once been part of the north side airport tarmac. A special metal plaque commemorating the historic flight was later fitted on the inside door of BOAC's Argonaut 'Atalanta'. The plane was scrapped more than half a century ago. Whatever happened to the plaque?

* * *

By June 1953 and the queen's coronation, travelling to London Airport for the day to watch great airliners from all over the world take off and land was *the* favourite occupation for Londoners. The visitors' enclosure was expanded, a small funfair complete with a roundabout, slide, miniature train journey around a circular track and donkey rides had been installed, along with a children's sandpit and mock-up of an aircraft doorway where visitors could be photographed appearing to be departing or arriving from an exciting aeroplane trip.

A commentator was recruited at weekends and holidays to stand on the control tower balcony and tell visitors through his loudspeaker what was happening out on the runways. Aerodrome control offices housed in the 'glass

Soon after opening, a small viewing area was created for visitors fascinated by arriving and departing aircraft. It soon became London's most visited attraction, outrivalling Windsor Castle, Madame Tussauds and the Tower of London. Seating was provided as close to aircraft as it was possible to get. There were tea tents, donkey rides, a small funfair and sand pits for the children. What more could a family expect from a day out at London Airport? (*Author's Collection*)

June Pike (née Bibby) and Roger Haynes from Staines, Middlesex pretend to arrive from somewhere glamorous on a mock-up of a BOAC aircraft in the public enclosure at London Airport. However, a photograph like this only works when your dad gets the camera angle right and masks out the buildings in the background. (*June Pike*)

More visitors came to view aircraft movements at London Airport in the 1950s than the number of travellers passing through it. Seating was provided close to aircraft parking areas, special guides to the airport and aeroplanes were produced priced at one shilling each and cartoons began appearing featuring characters getting into all kinds of trouble in and around planes. (*Author's Collection*)

house' at the top of the runway fed information to the commentator who relayed it on to the crowds below with the enthusiasm of a cinema newsreel narrator. In 1953, 527,000 people came to London Airport to watch aeroplanes take off and land.

There was also a refreshment bar, which began life – like so many airport buildings – in a marquee. Betty Richardson from Heston got a weekend job working in the refreshment station located on the Bath Road. She remembers:

The whole of the north side consisted of prefab-type huts and marquees. I particularly remember the small fancy cakes that were delivered on baker's trays and would be surrounded by wasps. We had to quickly cover the tray with an empty one and when we served a customer, had to carefully put a hand in and grab a cake, hoping all the time that a wasp hadn't chomped at the icing. Eventually we were given sandwich bags – a new invention – to wrap the fancies in. I can still see the expressions on customers' faces as they looked with approval at fancy cakes beneath a cellophane-type wrapping (rationing was still in force, so fancy cakes were a real luxury).

We served hot tea made in an urn and there was a deposit charge on every cup and saucer – something like 1s 6d. It was self-service with a lady at the end of the counter totting up the prices in her head and using an old-fashioned till. Crockery was washed up in a tin bath behind the scenes. We served ice cream kept in a 'fridge in small drums. The drums would be taken out as required but we had to ensure that most of the ice cream could be sold as once taken out and thawed, it could not be re-frozen. Sandwiches were made by ladies in the kitchen and bagged up, just like the cakes. It was all very basic but hygiene was always observed.

People flocked to the airport to see aeroplanes at that time and I enjoyed

Edna Sparks worked in the airport's first official staff canteen, 'a pre-fabricated building with a very utility interior.' Part of her duties was going to other areas of the airport with refreshments for staff. She is pictured here with other catering staff (in front at the bottom of aircraft steps) standing in front of an Avro York. (*Dennis Sparks and June Pearce*)

working there. In those days people would even stop along the Bath Road, brew tea on a small paraffin stove and picnic on the green grass verges. Imagine doing that today!

The mother of June Pearce from Northolt worked in the airport's first official staff canteen. Edna Sparks was employed in

> a pre-fabricated building with a very utility interior. Part of my mother's duties was going to other areas of the airport with refreshments for staff and she moved around in a van. During the Berlin Airlift in the late 1940s she used to go out to the planes on the tarmac and assist in handing over supplies to crews. Sometimes my brother Dennis and I would go to work with our mother and help out with some of the chores, clearing tables and washing up. There were no dishwashers then. Our reward, if we were lucky, would be a cream cake or a most wonderful apple fritter all hot and tossed in sugar. What a treat that was after all the rationing we had endured during the war and were still experiencing at that time.

Airport reporter Ray Berry remembers that during the late 1940s it was often difficult for many airport staff to find somewhere to eat:

> Just outside the Bath Road entrance was 'Ben's', a small café (the sort of place we call a 'greasy spoon' these days, but I think someone must have stolen his) where you could get hot snacks. Alongside was his café extension with rows of cast-iron tables and a variety of stools and chairs under a corrugated tin roof, which made conversation impossible and leaked constantly in the rain.
>
> On the other side of the road was the proudly-named 'Heathrow Restaurant', a chintzy tea-room with a mock gentility which boasted a fixed 'lunchtime' for a never-varying menu of shepherd's pie and two veg, sausage and mash, and so on. And on the Bath Road, of course, there were three pubs: the Bricklayers' Arms (later renamed the Air Hostess), the Three Magpies and the Old Magpies, both of which boasted highwayman Dick Turpin as a former regular.
>
> Within the airport, an early company called Airwork Ltd provided a staff snack bar adjoining the old terminal building and called the 'Green Dragon', located in a long, low corrugated iron Nissen hut. Later this same Nissen hut became a conference room hosting press events for a host of VIPs, including a venue for Laurence Olivier and Vivien Leigh to say goodbye to Marilyn Monroe and Arthur Miller on completion of her film *The Prince and the Showgirl* in 1957.

Waddon Aerodrome and its neighbour Beddington Aerodrome were located next to each other with just a narrow road in-between and located near to Croydon, to the south of London. Both aerodromes were famous for their aviation race meetings and flying circus acts. (*Croydon Archives*)

Croydon Airport, also known as the London Terminal Aerodrome or London Airport, was the UK's major international airport during the inter-war period. At the launch of the first international air services after the First World War, it was developed as Britain's main airport. After the Second World War, it was replaced by London Airport (Heathrow). (*Author's Collection*)

A British South American
Airways luggage sticker. Today
unused and original BSAA
stickers change hands for top
prices. (*Author's Collection*)

On 29 September 1957, a
TWA Constellation flew from
Los Angeles to London in
eighteen hours and thirty-two
minutes. Today the flight takes
around eleven hours and ten
minutes to cover the same
journey. (*Author's Collection*)

British airlines copied their American rivals and produced smart advertising in the press to attract customers. Pride of BEA's routes was its daily 'Silver Wing' London-Paris service using Elizabethan high-wing monoplanes, which offered cocktails and a full lunch on board the eighty-minute flight. Also pictured is an advertisement assuring passengers that 'BOAC takes good care of you'. (*Author's Collection*)

Heathrow's iconic control tower in the 1970s. (*Brenard Press*)

It was a sad sight for many Heathrow staff when the wreckers moved in to smash the old control tower in the central area to pieces after fifty-eight years of service. The new Terminal 2 is pictured rising behind. (*David Dyson Photography*)

In 1955 London Airport was awarded the coveted London Architecture Medal for the overall design of buildings in the new central area. (*Author's Collection*)

For sixpence you could buy a full-colour brochure telling you everything you needed to know about new buildings at London Airport. Hundreds of aircraft enthusiasts bought a copy and many still own them today. (*Author's Collection*)

David Shepherd (1931–2017) was a British artist and conservationist. On a snowy Christmas Eve in 1955 he had been given permission by London Airport managers to draw some sketches of tarmac activity which he would later work up into a finished painting at home in Frensham, Surrey. It was a freezing cold evening but Shepherd carried on sketching as long as his frozen fingers would allow. The result is a fascinating picture of airline staff doing their best to get passengers to and from their aircraft in a blizzard with aircraft running their engines to stop them freezing and passengers carefully making their way down aircraft steps in case they slipped on the wet snow. (*David Shepherd Collection*)

Colourful airline posters from America's TWA and BOAC. (*Author's Collection*)

For very particular people…B.O.A.C. of course

World's finest airliners…Britannias, DC-7Cs and Stratocruisers

Here drawn up on the tarmac at London Airport are airliners belonging to the three most splendid fleets in the world—*all of them B.O.A.C.!*

The revolutionary B.O.A.C. *Britannia (right)* has already won universal acclaim as the world's fastest, smoothest and most spacious jet-prop airliner. On the *left* of the picture, you see B.O.A.C.'s magnificently fast new DC-7C, first airliner to link the Old World with the New by regular non-stop flights. In the *centre* is the famous B.O.A.C. double-deck *Stratocruiser*—now sumptuously redesigned to offer you such *spaciousness* and luxury as never before. Always fly B.O.A.C.—world leader in air travel!

BRITANNIA services to South Africa, the East and Australia, to Hong Kong and Japan, soon to U.S.A.

DC-7C services to New York, Boston, San Francisco, Detroit, Chicago and Montreal.

STRATOCRUISER "Monarch" services London—New York direct. Other services to Canada; to Bermuda, Bahamas and the Caribbean; also to West Africa.

Consult your local B.O.A.C. Appointed Travel Agent or any B.O.A.C. office.

World leader in air travel

B·O·A·C
takes good care of you

Remember—it costs no more to fly by B.O.A.C.

BRITISH OVERSEAS AIRWAYS CORPORATION WITH S.A.A., C.A.A., QANTAS AND TEAL

BOAC used 'smartly-dressed people' to indicate the kind of clothing it expected passengers to wear when they flew with the airline. The photograph was taken at the airline's maintenance centre on the airport's eastern side. (*Author's Collection*)

In November 1963 BOAC introduced the British-made VC10 into its fleet and began phasing out Comets and Britannias on its Eastern and African routes. The aircraft turned out to be one of the noisiest commercial aircraft ever built. (*Author's Collection*)

A Stratocruiser airliner being refuelled at London Airport, where supplies of Esso Aviation fuels, lubricants and special products are available at any hour of day or night.

It pays to say **ESSO**

FOR ALL PETROLEUM PRODUCTS

ESSO PETROLEUM COMPANY, LIMITED, 36 QUEEN ANNE'S GATE, LONDON, S.W.1

Esso Petroleum proudly boasted that it supplied fuel to airlines using Boeing Stratocruiser aircraft on routes to and from London. (*Author's Collection*)

In March 1970 the airport was shut down for the first time in twenty-four years when its firemen – employed by the airport authority – walked out over a dispute about shift allowances and working conditions. It is illegal for an airport to operate without a full complement of fire officers on hand to deal with an emergency, and aircraft sat on the tarmac unable to move for two days. No incoming planes could land either, costing airlines thousands of pounds in lost revenue. Collectively the airlines put Heathrow's management under pressure to resolve the dispute, and following a mass meeting of firemen the airport's owners were forced into reaching a compromise with firemen and allowing the airport to re-open. It took days to clear the backlog of delayed flights and passengers.

The queen formally unveiled the underground link between Hatton Cross and Heathrow Central on 16 December 1977 when Heathrow became the first airport in the world to offer a rapid rail link to a capital city centre. Heathrow to Piccadilly could be achieved in around thirty-five minutes. Her Majesty travelled to the new station by Tube from Hatton Cross – designated a 'Royal Train' for the three-minute journey – which broke a ceremonial tape as it came to a standstill on the westbound platform. It arrived four minutes late. (*Author's Collection*)

Terminal 4 was designed to accommodate twenty of the world's largest aircraft at one time and allow arriving and departing passengers to be totally segregated from each other. Areas around the terminal and on the opposite side of the road were carefully landscaped with a small series of undulating hills designed to reduce noise levels created by aircraft and motor traffic using the building. The hills separated the terminal and its roadways from part of the small community of Bedfont which almost ran up to the side of the new building. (*Ray Berry Collection*)

Pan American World Airways, originally founded as Pan American Airways but commonly known as Pan Am, was the principal and largest international air carrier in the United States from 1927 until its collapse on 4 December 1991. Here is a Pan Am flight captured leaving Heathrow for New York ten years earlier in 1981. (*Brenard Press*)

By March 2005 and two and a half years into construction, work on Terminal 5 was more than 50 per cent completed and ahead of schedule. More than 4,000 workers were employed on the site, many engaged in raising the terminal's massive 'wave-style' roof structure into place. When put into use in 2008, this spectacular single-span structure provided passengers and staff with a bright and airy environment.

The Boeing 747 dominated the airline passenger and cargo world for more than three decades until the Airbus A380, seating between 555 and 840 passengers, came into commercial operation at Heathrow in 2006.

Friday, 25 October 2003 was a sad day in Heathrow's long history. It was the day that millions of people were about to lose a friend and they turned out in their thousands to say goodbye…to Concorde. (*Tony Parker*)

Heathrow's elegant new control tower – which went into service in 2006 – is located at the western end of the airport's existing central terminal area and stands 87 metres tall, taking on the appearance of a giant lighthouse. Dwarfing Nelson's Column, it gives controllers unrivalled views across the entire airport and west London. The glass cab at the top is more than five storeys tall, weighing over 860 tonnes. The tower was built in pieces before being towed to its site on three massive flatbed transporter lorries. A 25m-tall section was jacked up to a height of 12m to allow a prefabricated mast section to be slotted in underneath until the building was completed and settled into its foundations. (*NATS*)

Before the old Terminal 2 was demolished, notices in the windows told passengers that a new terminal was soon coming their way. (*The Author*)

The new terminal, originally named Heathrow East Terminal, occupies the sites where the previous Terminal 2 and the Queen's Building stood. It was designed by the firm of Luis Vidal+Architects and opened on 4 June 2014. (*Heathrow Airport Limited*)

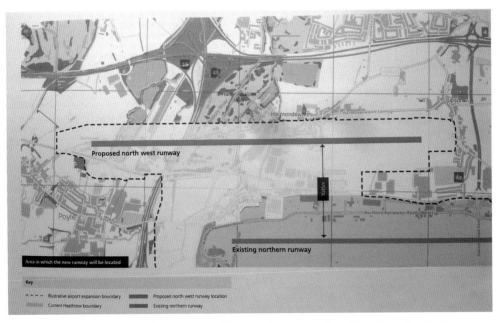

In a world full of uncertainties, one thing is clear regarding Heathrow's third runway project: it will be located to the north-west of the airport's two existing runways between Sipson in the east, Colnbrook in the west and Harmondsworth in the north. Plans to decide the exact position of the runway and its precise length have yet to be finalized. (*Airport Expansion Consultation Document, January 2018*)

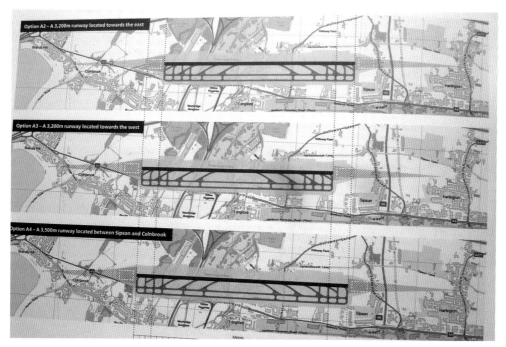

Three possible runway options along the Sipson–Colnbrook–Harmondsworth locations. Top: a 3,200m runway located towards the east. Centre: a 3,200m runway located towards the west. Bottom: a 3,500m runway located between Sipson and Colnbrook. (*Airport Expansion Consultation Document, January 2018*)

How the new runway might look from the air: an artist's impression. (*Airport Expansion Consultation Document, January 2018*)

I'm not aware that continuing official wartime rationing (as opposed to general food shortages) affected public catering to any great extent, any more than it had from 1939–45, though I may have been fooled by the abilities and efficiency of professional caterers. Or perhaps the wartime black market was still active – and equally efficient.

Keith Hayward remembers:

Airport conditions during the late 1940s and early 1950s were often bleak, but the famous 'Ben's Café' was heaven-sent. It took the form of an old lean-to with a tent extension and it sustained us all. But 'Ben's' was just superb and it continued until they demolished it to make way for the tunnel leading to the central area. 'Ben's' had been there long before the airport. It started life as a place for lorry drivers travelling along the Bath Road. It always seemed to be open at any time of the day or night. It was also one of the few places for miles around where you could buy cakes. Goodness knows how they got around the problem of sugar rationing. They served up a superb breakfast, but the place was so full of smoke you couldn't see across the place – but the grub was excellent and at that time the only place that staff could get anything hot to eat. There was another little place along the Bath Road inside a converted house that sold cooked food and run by a lady from what would have been her front room.

A little later a place called the 'Green Dragon' took over and a company called Airwork undertook the passenger catering. It was located just inside the airport boundary and had once been a freight shed. I'm not sure how it got its name; perhaps the doors had been painted green.

Business consultant Tony Hesketh-Gardener recalls Nissen huts alongside the Bath Road that

provided the best afternoon teas for miles. Tablecloths, monogrammed china, silver-plated cutlery and waitress service. Furthermore, it was a place where many of us congregated for breakfast after hunt balls or the three annual Sandhurst balls. Tails, uniforms, dinner jackets, evening dresses abounded on those early mornings – usually between 3.30-4.30 am. The place never seemed to close and there was a full waitress service, tablecloths, china. My, how times have changed!

* * *

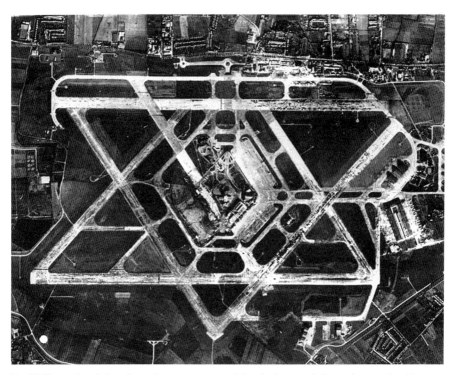

By 1955 much of the airport's passenger activity had moved from the north side to a new diamond-shaped area in the centre of the photograph which included a smart new passenger air terminal known as the Europa Terminal, a world-class control tower, a special building for airport visitors and car parks. (*Author's Collection*)

London Airport became a magnet for people seeking jobs in the exciting world of air transport. In addition to employment as airline ground staff to work on check-in desks and escort passengers to waiting aircraft, there were vacancies for skilled aircraft engineers (and thanks to the RAF they were in good supply), cargo-loaders, and office administration staff. For every job vacancy at London Airport there were at least fifteen applicants and many were snapped up on the same day as advertised.

Between 1950 and 1955, Gwen Humphries from Hounslow, Middlesex worked in the airport's personnel office – a Nissen hut known as 'Hut 29' and located on the Bath Road at Harlington Corner – for a weekly wage of £2 5s. Gwen remembers:

> Our job was to recruit staff for the airlines, including BOAC and Qantas, and scores of people came in every day looking for work. I remember that on one particular day 108 people came through our door wanting jobs at London Airport – and we found employment for them all as

aircraft engineers, aircraft cleaners, clerical and catering staff. They came on their bikes, on the bus and some even walked. They also came for interviews with their parents in chauffeur-driven Rolls-Royce cars, the sons and daughters of lords and ladies.

People used to fill in their job application forms resting on the walls of the Nissen hut as there were only a few tables and chairs and no room to spare. Lots of young men and women wanted jobs as cabin staff because they travelled to places where they could buy ladies' nylons, which were virtually unobtainable in England at that time.

Throughout the 1950s the size of aircraft flying in and out of London began to grow from the small fourteen-seat Douglas DC3 'Dakota' used by Westpoint Aviation to the sleek forty-seat Lockheed Constellation used on services to the United States and Asia. (*Author's Collection*)

Our hut was about one hundred yards from a runway used by York freighter aircraft bringing exotic animals into the country. We liked to watch people's faces when they travelled along the Bath Road in open-top buses and suddenly saw a giraffe appear above the trees, followed by elephants.

A notice was attached to a small gate warning airport staff to make sure they looked both ways before crossing the runway.

In later years our office moved to a more modern building with a spiral glass staircase and we couldn't understand why seats directly beneath the stairs were so popular with men filling in their application forms. We later realised that as we came down the stairs the men could look up our skirts!

There was a wonderful spirit among everyone in those early days. You felt you were really working at the start of something wonderful – and, of course, we were. They were happy days.

In December 1953, passenger traffic at London Airport hit the 1 million passenger mark for the first time. By the end of the year, 1.2 million passengers had flown in and out of London's premier air gateway on more than 62,000 flights. Some 23,000 tons of cargo had also passed through the airport and 527,000 members of the public had paid 6d to pass through the turnstiles at the public enclosure to thrill at the sight of giant silver aeroplanes from all over the world appear in the sky overhead and land at London Airport.

Chapter 11

The New Elizabethan Age and the Russians are Coming

Writer Paul Townend observed in 1951 that air travel

> has made the world shrink like a walnut in its shell. Already airliners like the Stratocruiser and Constellation take 50-70 passengers and already the de Havilland Comet heralds the age of the jet airliners – and before very long we shall probably travel to work by helicopter instead of the 8:47 to Waterloo. Aviation will one day be as safe as a rural bus service and London Airport, the aerodrome of the future, will lead the world.

By the end of 1951 – the year in which the country celebrated the Festival of Britain – 796,092 passengers were travelling through the airport annually and its temporary prefabricated terminals were reaching the limit of their capacity. It was time to call in the builders once again to begin working on the next phase of the London Airport development plan; a plan to create the world's largest and finest airport.

In 1950 the British architect Frederick Gibberd had been appointed by the Ministry of Transport and Civil Aviation to create stunning new futuristic designs for the airport. His work was brought to the attention of the post-war Labour government's Minister for Town and County Planning, Lord Silkin, who commissioned Gibberd to draw up plans for a new town in Harlow, Essex. The project resulted in the creation of the country's first purpose-built peacetime town, an architectural model of its time. In later years Gibberd was also principal architect of Liverpool's Roman Catholic Cathedral and a planning consultant to new towns in Swindon, Nuneaton and Leamington Spa, creating bright new shopping centres in the middle of old, worn-out and bomb-damaged communities. Where possible his schemes were integrated within existing designs and Gibberd's new shopping centres were often found behind original Victorian frontages.

However, London Airport was another matter. There were no Victorian frontages behind which Gibberd could conceal a large and modern public airline terminal, office buildings and a multi-storey control tower. The architect was given a blank canvas on which to create the first permanent buildings for

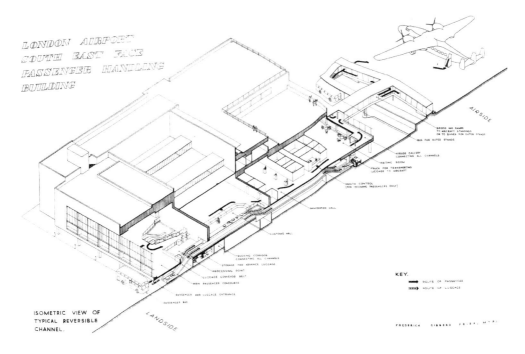

In 1950, British architect Frederick Gibberd was appointed to create stunning new futuristic designs for London Airport costing £21 million. Pictured here is one of Gibberd's original plans for the new passenger terminal – now demolished – located on an island surrounded by runways and reached by a road traffic tunnel. (*Frederick Gibberd and Partners*)

an 'airport city', which would exist within a large 'island' inside the runway triangles. Ground space allocated was generous, covering a 158-acre triangular site.

The airport's central area was designed with a degree of foresight as well as more than £21 million of taxpayers' money. Although the Ministry expected airport buildings to handle passenger traffic for many years to come, additional space was available within the site for at least two additional terminals. Early planners, however, did not think beyond the end of the 1960s. The idea that the airport might eventually require more terminals towards the end of the twentieth century and even more in the twenty-first century had not entered into their 1950s' thinking.

Despite this lack of long-term foresight (and who in the 1950s could ever have imagined what the airport might be like more than seventy years later?), plans taking shape on Frederick Gibberd's drawing board were unlike anything ever seen before at an international airport. They were approved by the Royal Fine Art Commission and prior to building gangs moving in, Gibberd commented:

The airport's design and construction embody the results of many years of study and experiment and no effort has been spared to ensure that the aesthetic appeal of the buildings matches the importance of their function. There is room in the central area to accommodate enough buildings to handle all the passengers and freight that the runways can deliver to them.

The focal point of Gibberd's 'airport city' was a new 122ft-high control tower building that would be at the centre of a highly-complex system of radio and radar navigational aids, airfield lighting and ground movement control. Gibberd proudly stated: 'It is expected that these technical facilities, when installed, will be the most advanced and comprehensive in the world.'

Just across the street from the control tower would be an advanced passenger terminal that would be a world of difference away from the temporary prefabricated buildings travellers were experiencing less than a mile away on the airport's north side. It would be super-modern, spacious and comfortable, containing everything sophisticated air travellers would soon come to accept as normal from a mid-twentieth-century air-conditioned airport passenger terminal including shops, restaurants, cocktail bars, lounges, large panoramic

The focal point of Frederick Gibberd's 'airport city' was a 122ft-high control tower building providing uninterrupted views of the entire airfield. It provided fifty-eight years of unbroken service before being demolished in 2013. (*Taylor Woodrow Construction Limited*)

windows, smart check-in desks and facilities allowing passengers to pass through controls and board aircraft quickly and efficiently.

Adjacent to the terminal would be another building containing space for airport and airline offices, airline briefing rooms, a meteorological office and facilities for the airport's resident press corps. On its roof would be a special place for airport visitors, complete with viewing galleries offering the public grandstand vistas of aircraft arriving and departing to all four corners of the globe.

Gibberd designed his 'airport city' on a grid of 12ft with a steel-framed main structure on which would hang external walls of high-fired red bricks, stone and glass.

It was estimated that the new control tower would be ready for use in July 1955, the terminal in September 1955 and the office building with a public viewing area in January 1956. Some of Britain's leading companies were hired to turn Gibberd's vision into reality. Sir William Halcrow & Partners were the principal consulting engineers, with Taylor Woodrow Construction Ltd in charge of laying the foundations and the main building work and Redpath, Brown & Co. responsible for the steel framework in each building.

To reach the new central area in the middle of the airport, travellers passed through a half-mile-long tunnel running underneath one of the main runways. (*Taylor Woodrow Construction Limited*)

BUILDING A ROAD UNDER AN AIRPORT : AN AERIAL VIEW OF THE 2000-FT.-LONG TUNNEL WHICH IS BEING CONSTRUCTED UNDER
THE NO. 1 RUNWAY AT LONDON AIRPORT—BRITAIN'S BUSIEST AIRFIELD.

This remarkable aerial photograph presents what is otherwise impossible—a comprehensive view of the progress which is being made with the great vehicle tunnel which is being built across London Airport to link the Bath Road with the new main south terminal disembarkation area. As can be seen in the photograph this huge subway—2000 ft. long and 80 ft. wide—is being constructed by the open cut method, and already 600,000 cubic yards of earth have been excavated. The tunnel consists of two carriage-ways, each 25 ft. wide, with two suspended cycle tracks. In the foreground are huge derricks and travelling shutters for the walls. The floor of the tunnel is about 30 ft. below ground-level and there is to be a 10-ft. cover of soil over the roof. It passes under No. 1 Runway, which is normally the busiest, but recently traffic has been diverted to No. 5 Runway. During 1951 London Airport became Britain's busiest, beating Northolt with 796,092 passengers against 749,727. The main work of the tunnel, which is being done by Taylor Woodrow, Ltd., is expected to be completed by the end of the year.

The tunnel was described as a 'cut and fill' job, whereby a huge trench is dug out and
the tunnel is built in the form of an oblong concrete shell before re-covering with earth.
(Illustrated London News)

The airport's new nerve centre, passenger and public buildings would be connected to the old airport area and Bath Road by a 'vehicular subway' running underneath the original main runway and three parallel taxiways. The airport's famous tunnel was constructed from a large and deep trench, known in the building trade as a 'cut and fill' job.

Gibberd designed the trench, half a mile long, 200ft wide and 40ft deep, to house a rectangular reinforced concrete shell that would be sub-divided to provide two dual-lane carriageways each capable of handling 2,000 motor vehicles per hour, including cars, double-decker buses and airport vehicles, plus two separated cycle tracks and pedestrian pathways. Once the concrete shell was in place, the tunnel would measure 2,060ft long, 86ft wide and 23ft high.

A call went out for volunteers to ride through the tunnel in a London Transport double-decker bus. Although the tunnel was tall and wide enough to take a bus with room to spare, concerns were raised that a large public vehicle full of passengers travelling at certain speeds through a restricted space could meet with disaster halfway through. Similar doubts were voiced when a train travelled through a railway tunnel for the first time.

Volunteers were called to ride through the airport's new tunnel in an 81B double-decker bus full of passengers. There were fears that travelling through an enclosed area at speeds of 30mph might have an effect on some passengers, but all the volunteers managed to survive the half-mile-long ride and were rewarded with a cup of tea at the end of their journey. (*Author's Collection*)

London Airport's traffic tunnel was an immediate success and today more than 60,000 cars, taxis, buses and coaches pass through. (*Author's Collection*)

There was no shortage of volunteers wanting to be among the first to travel under the airport's tunnel as bus number 81B made its way towards the entrance from the Bath Road. Large crowds of airport workers stood at either end as the bright red bus slowly made its way towards the inward entrance, followed by an ambulance and fire engine, just in case.

The bus driver gradually increased speed as he travelled along the tunnel and shot out at the other end at a speed of 30 mph; safe, unharmed and all in one piece. Many millions of buses have passed safely through the tunnel since that day.

While construction was taking shape, London Airport's traffic figures were rising steadily. By 1952, 860,760 passengers travelling with 23 airlines on more than 52,000 flights were using the airport, which declared itself 'the busiest in Europe and one of the world's largest international air terminals.'

Elsewhere, more builders were at work, many of whom had been in steady employment at the airport for nearly seven years. Three aircraft maintenance areas had been completed. The largest, covering 240 acres east of the runway system, contained temporary hangars used by BOAC, while a new headquarters complex and hangars rose on the skyline for use in 1954. The headquarters building eventually found its way into the record books when its four 336ft-span pens won it the accolade of being the world's largest reinforced concrete structure. It would be known affectionately to BOAC staff as 'The Kremlin'.

The tunnel beneath the runway pictured in the 1950s and 1970s. (*Author's Collection*)

Eight out of ten new hangars built for BEA were also opened on a site nearby and used to maintain Ambassador and Viscount aircraft. A 91-acre site was set aside for future development on the airport's south side and would eventually become the location for the airport's dedicated cargo terminal.

Airline luggage stickers from BOAC and BEA are much sought after by collectors of airline memorabilia across the world. (*Author's Collection*)

The Europa terminal was very different to the former military marquee used as a terminal on the airport's north side. It was spacious, bright and offered plenty of room for airline passengers and their luggage. It included shops, restaurants, bars, rest rooms, viewing terraces, a children's playroom and a speedy check-in service. (*Brenard Press*)

While foundations were being poured for London Airport's buildings of the future, new British aircraft designed to cross the world's air lanes were ready to enter service. The jet age was about to arrive at London Airport.

* * *

After the air disasters, the Comet never really regained its foothold in the commercial airline market, but modified versions remained in the air until 1997. (*Author's Collection*)

The de Havilland Comet 1 was a revolutionary new form of air transportation and the world's first pure jet passenger aircraft to enter commercial scheduled service. With flying speeds of over 500 mph, it was in 1952 way ahead of its international rivals, designed to give BOAC a competitive advantage over foreign airlines, and it was British.

It looked different to any other aircraft seen in skies over London Airport: sleek, futuristic and with almost invisible engines contained within swept-back wings. It was designed to fly at previously unheard-of altitudes of 40,000ft requiring effective cabin pressurization and at speeds of up to 500 mph. The Comet 1 was a world away in terms of speed and comfort from Avro Lancastrians and Yorks and entered service less than three years after its first test flight, during which it broke a handful of point-to-point speed records along the way.

The man in charge of putting the Comet through its testing paces was John Cunningham DSO, OBE, DFC and bar and known across the country as Johnny 'Cat's Eyes' Cunningham following his RAF career commanding the famous 'Mosquito Squadron'. He had joined de Havilland at the age of 18 and following the war had worked on the Comet project since it was a plywood mock-up. As the airliner's chief test pilot, Cunningham flew hundreds of hours in the aircraft before it entered service with BOAC in 1952.

The late John Balding from Ashford, Middlesex joined BOAC as an apprentice engineer at Whitchurch, south of Bristol, in October 1940. Whitchurch was BOAC's secret wartime headquarters and was requisitioned by the Air Ministry for the duration of the war. After working for the airline in Egypt, he returned home in October 1946 to work on Vikings, DC3s,

The de Havilland Comet was the world's first pure jet passenger aircraft to enter commercial scheduled service in 1952. For the era, it offered a relatively quiet, comfortable passenger cabin and was commercially promising on its debut. However, within a year of entering airline service, problems started to emerge, with three Comets lost within twelve months in highly-publicized accidents after suffering catastrophic in-flight break-ups. (*Author's Collection*)

Lancastrians and Yorks at London Airport. In 1951 he was appointed an airframe inspector on BOAC's new aircraft, the Comet. John remembers:

> I shall never forget my first sight of the Comet. It was amazing, sleek and beautiful with her engines hidden inside the wing. None of us had ever seen anything like it before. Mind you, we engineers all thought that the aluminium used to make the aircraft was too thin. It had been cut down to the absolute minimum in order to make the plane light. In fact, everything appeared to be rather on the thin side.
>
> After the Comet had been in service for a while, we all felt very confident in the aircraft and what it could do. Of course, we had no idea of the problems and tragedy that lay ahead for this wonderful plane.

Captain Cliff 'Alibe' Alabaster, by now flying BOAC Argonaut services to South America following BSAA's absorption into BOAC, became involved with the Comet during its development phase. He remembers his own first sight of the Comet 1 and recalled that 'she looked absolutely smashing' but learning to fly the new aircraft was different to piloting piston-engine equipment. After taking a Comet training course with other pilots at de Havilland's aircraft factory at Hatfield just before Christmas 1951, Alibe was one of the first pilots to fly the aircraft – G-ALYP – when it entered service on the 6,724-mile London-

Johannesburg route on 2 May 1952. Hundreds of spectators and airport staff turned out to witness the departure of the world's first jet service. It was a great day for British civil aviation.

The Comet 1 travelled via Rome, Beirut, Khartoum, Entebbe and Livingstone and Cliff was at the controls for the final section between Beirut and Johannesburg carrying thirty-six passengers. Somewhere along the route, BOAC chairman Sir Miles Thomas demonstrated just how smoothly the Comet performed in flight by pulling down a seat-back table and standing a four-sided foreign coin up on its end. Two hours later the coin was still standing in the same position.

More than 20,000 onlookers turned out to see the world's first jet aircraft passenger service land at Johannesburg after a flight lasting eighteen hours and forty minutes: a new record for the route, which was previously covered by BOAC's piston-engine aircraft in thirty-two hours and twenty-five minutes.

The Comet landed in South Africa in a blaze of publicity, but news reporters covering its arrival were unaware of the drama that had taken place on board 40,000ft above Africa. Cliff Alabaster explains:

> During the sector between Beirut and Khartoum I casually asked how much further we had to travel before landing and was told that there was still about one hour and a half left. It was then that I realised that there was not much fuel left in the tanks to cope with any diversion we might have to perform for one reason or another. There was just enough to get us to Khartoum, flying in over a canal zone operated by the RAF. We sent out a May Day signal and just managed to land in Khartoum. The passengers were none the wiser. It was human error and it never happened again.

A few days later the Comet was on its way back to London Airport at the end of its 13,000-mile round trip and arrived seven minutes early. At the airport BOAC chairman Sir Miles Thomas predicated that from now on world travellers were going to demand jet-propelled aircraft and this would be good for British aircraft manufacturers: 'It is a complete vindication of BOAC's faith in the Comet when we ordered it straight off the drawing board and it makes a wonderful beginning to the Elizabethan age.'

Everyone wanted to fly in the Comet 1. The Queen Mother and Princess Margaret became the airliner's first royal passengers, and stars of stage, screen and sports were happy to be photographed in front of the plane before and after flights. In September 1952 an extended version of the Comet 1, the Comet 3, was announced (the Comet 2 being an experimental test plane not built for commercial service). The new model would take up to seventy-six

The Comet was immediately popular with passengers including Queen Elizabeth, the Queen Mother and Princess Margaret, who were guests on a special flight on 30 June 1953 hosted by Sir Geoffrey and Lady de Havilland, and they became the first members of the British Royal Family to fly by jet. (*Author's Collection*)

passengers and was designed for transatlantic crossings. Orders were received from BOAC and Air-India and Comet pilots, including Cliff Alabaster, were drafted in to help sell the aircraft to American carriers.

'I was detailed to show some Pan American pilots over the Comet at London Airport,' Alibe recalls. 'They were very impressed because there was no equivalent American machine. They went back to their airline stating that they were going to recommend the Comet to their board.'

In October 1952, the president and founder of Pan American Airways, Juan Trippe, announced that his company had placed an order for three Comet 3 airliners for delivery towards the end of 1956, with an option for an additional aircraft. The Comet 3s would be the first jet airliners used by an American carrier and their purchase was the first occasion that a US company had gone outside the United States to buy airliners for regular services. It was explained by Sir Miles Thomas that the delivery date of 1956 had been made possible because BOAC had agreed to release to Pan American Airways early deliveries of Comet 3s earmarked for the corporation.

At around the same time, Captain Eddie Rickenbacker, president of Eastern Airlines and famous American fighter 'ace' of the Great War passed through

Comet crashes became front-page news in 1953 and 1954 and the aircraft were withdrawn from services while an inquiry took place into the cause of the disasters. (Daily Express *Archives*)

London Airport on his way to discussions with de Havilland. He later flew in the Comet 2 prototype and expressed satisfaction with its performance, saying he was prepared to spend about £35.7 million on Comet aircraft and spares. He added that on returning to the US he would investigate whether jet airliners projected by the Douglas, Boeing and Lockheed companies would be ready as late as 1960. If he found this was the case, he would be prepared to take delivery of Comet 3s in 1957. Captain Rickenbacker also said: 'There is nothing available like the Comet in the USA in any stage of conception, let alone the drawing board.'

Then on 26 October 1952, less than six months after the inaugural Comet service had left London Airport, disaster struck. A Comet 1 service flying from Johannesburg to London crashed on take-off with thirty-three passengers on board after a scheduled stop in Rome. It was a wet evening and the plane careered off the runway, hitting a large pile of soil which ripped out the undercarriage. There were no fatalities and pilot error was identified as the cause. The captain was later demoted to flying York freighters. In January 1953 a Comet 1 undershot the runway at Entebbe, killing an airport worker, and in March a Comet crashed at Karachi while being delivered to an airline in Australia. The crew of five plus six technicians were all killed and the new plane was completely destroyed. Pilot error was again blamed, but the airline cancelled their order for a further two aircraft.

On 2 May 1953, on the first anniversary of the Comet's inaugural service, Comet 1 G-ALYV flying from Singapore to London exploded in flight during a tropical storm somewhere close to Calcutta. Forty-three passengers and crew were lost. Weeks later a Comet 1 operated by a French airline overshot the runway at Dakar and was destroyed; the fifth Comet accident in eighteen months. American airlines cancelled their orders, losing de Havilland £40 million. Suddenly the future of Britain's great passenger jet airliner looked bleak.

In January 1954, BOAC Comet G-ALYP flying from Singapore to London disintegrated at 27,000ft near the Mediterranean island of Elba. Twenty-nine passengers including ten children, plus six crew, perished in the disaster. The airline issued an urgent statement to passengers through the media:

> As a measure of prudence, normal Comet passenger services are being temporarily suspended to enable minute and unhurried technical examination of every aircraft in the Comet fleet to be carried out at London Airport. Sir Miles Thomas (BOAC Chairman) has decided to devote himself almost exclusively to probing the Comet mishap, with Sir Geoffrey de Havilland and the highest authorities in Britain. His decision is based on a desire to retain the good name of the Comets.

Close inspection of the grounded aircraft produced no clues as to why there had been so many accidents. Modifications were conducted, including fitting special armour plating around the engines. The Ministry of Transport and Civil Aviation's Accident Investigation Branch continued their inquiries, using pieces of crashed aircraft brought back to the UK from various sites. Detailed investigations also took place following each crash. Meanwhile BOAC was losing £50,000 for every week it kept its Comets on the ground and ten weeks after the Elba tragedy it re-introduced the aircraft into service.

John Balding was part of the team assigned to examine every inch of the Comet for defects. He recalls:

> We spent three months examining the aircraft in great detail and couldn't find anything significantly wrong. By this time the engineers who were sceptical about the Comet's abilities at the start were now totally confident about what it could do. We had changed from having doubts and worries about the aeroplane to being totally confident in its abilities. We thought it was a great machine, even though it was now in trouble.
>
> The aircraft's designers gave us a long list of modifications to undertake. When it was allowed back into service we were sure that the Comet would once again prove itself. But disaster stuck once again.

Despite sabotage theories appearing in the media, plenty of people still wanted to fly in the Comet and by April 1954, the aircraft was back in service.

One of the BOAC aircraft was loaned to South African Airways for services from London to Johannesburg. On 7 April the aircraft arrived in Rome for a scheduled refuelling stop when an Italian engineer discovered thirty wing bolts had become loosened and the fault traced back to BOAC engineering at London Airport. After a long delay while the bolts were tightened, the aircraft continued on its journey with fourteen passengers and a crew of seven. Just minutes out of Rome the aircraft disappeared from the radar screen, killing all on board. Comets were again removed from service.

More than 100 people had lost their lives flying in Comets and the aircraft now had the worst safety record in civil aviation history. The aircraft's Certificate of Air Worthiness was officially removed and Comets were stranded on three continents. BOAC was forced to take some of its older, smaller and slower Hermes, Constellation and Stratocruiser aircraft out of mothballs and reintroduce them on long-haul routes. John Balding says that the older planes kept BOAC in business until the Comet came back into the fleet and the Bristol Britannia was introduced: 'another plane which had more than its fair share of teething problems when it first arrived.'

Investigations continued and BOAC donated one of its Comets for destructive testing at the Royal Aircraft Establishment's investigation centre at Farnborough. Similarities from crash sites began to emerge. Sabotage theories were dismissed. Close internal examination of crash victims revealed similar types of injuries that could only have been caused through explosive decompression and that the Comet's fuselage was unable to withstand the pressure of flying. Minute investigations led accident investigators to believe that metal fatigue had affected the bodywork, causing the aircraft to blow apart while in flight. The fatigue could be specifically narrowed down to the corner of a window in the aircraft's cabin and two positions along the fuselage.

An official court of inquiry opened in October 1954 and sat for twenty-two days over a five-week period under the direction of Lord Cohen. It published its report in February 1955, stating that exhaustive investigations had been conducted with a view to reconstructing the actual disasters. These investigations were described by Sir Lionel Heald, representing the Crown, as 'one of the most remarkable pieces of scientific detective work ever done.' It had included a novel method of testing a whole Comet immersed in a huge water tank and subjected to heavy pressures. In his report Lord Cohen stated that he had 'unhesitatingly' reached the decision that the Elba disaster had been caused by the structural failure of the pressure cabin brought about by metal fatigue. Although it had been impossible to recover any appreciable wreckage from the second disaster and thereby give a positive verdict on its cause, in view of the similarity of the circumstances, it was 'at least possible' that the cause of the Naples disaster had been the same.

In addition to water tank pressure tests, another Comet manned by more than twenty scientists had carried out experimental flights for more than 100 hours under conditions as near as possible to those known to exist at the time of the crash. 'The accidents were not due to the wrongful act or default or to the negligence of any party or any person in the employment of any party,' said Lord Cohen.

John Balding said that a small number of aircraft engineers knew about metal fatigue, which was almost unknown to the wider circle of aviation professionals.

The Comet 1 remained grounded and a new version, known as the Comet 4, was announced containing major structural modifications highlighted by the crash investigations. In March 1955 BOAC announced plans to order twenty of the new aircraft for delivery in 1958, but in the meantime Britain had no commercial jet aircraft in use and lost time as the United States forged ahead with its own jet-age plans.

The Comet made a terrific comeback. More than 100 went into service before the de Havilland production line closed in 1962. Most provided BOAC, BEA and several foreign airlines plus the RAF Transport Command with many years of excellent service. Many were successfully sold on to other airlines including Gatwick-based Dan-Air, which was still using the aircraft well into the 1970s, but Comet air accidents made many foreign airlines nervous of purchasing British aircraft. American carriers who had originally shown interest in the Comet switched their orders to new home-grown jet aircraft taking shape at Boeing's production line near Seattle and the Douglas

The greatly-modified Comet 4 first flew in April 1958 and received its Certificate of Airworthiness in September of that year. It went on to become a highly-successful aircraft. Deliveries to BOAC began on 30 September 1958 with two forty-eight-seat aircraft, which were used to initiate the first scheduled transatlantic services. (*De Havilland Archives*)

Airlines using Comet aircraft had to really go out and re-sell it to sceptical passengers, but the advertising worked and soon Comets were full of passengers flying on both scheduled and charter flights, mostly to European destinations. (*Author's Collection*)

The Boeing 707 jetliner soon took the place of the Comet on many routes. It was faster, offered passengers more space and allowed airlines using it to prepare a wider choice of in-flight meals for passengers. (*Pan American Archives*)

aircraft factory near Long Beach, California. The 130-passenger Boeing 707 'Stratoliner' and 125-passenger Douglas DC-8 were both successfully sold to US-based airlines and scores of others across the world, triggering off another transatlantic race with London Airport as the starting-post for BOAC.

In October 1959, BOAC and Pan American went head-to-head on whose jet airliner would be first across the Atlantic. BOAC's Comet 4 was scheduled to fly from London to New York, while Pan American's shining new Boeing 707 would fly to Paris. Who would be the winner? Did it really matter? Publicity people working for both airlines thought so and BOAC won the day when their Comet 4 touched down in New York minutes ahead of Pan Am's Boeing 707 landing in Paris.

While BOAC won the day, British aircraft manufacturers lost the race to produce the first truly successful passenger jet airliner to remain in continuous service with commercial airlines. For every new British airliner, there would always be an American rival. The Bristol Britannia's rival was the Douglas DC-6, while the Vickers Viscount was forced to square up against the Lockheed Electra. In later years the Vickers VC10 and de Havilland Trident found favour at home with BOAC and BEA plus a few other carriers, but were rejected as unsuitable by American companies. The story would be similar a decade later when Britain and France came together to produce the world's first supersonic passenger jet, the Concorde.

Whatever the aircraft type – British, American, French, Anglo-French, Dutch, Swedish or Russian-made – they all became familiar sights at London's number one airport. In today's dynamic and competitive world of aircraft production, market leaders remain America's Boeing and Britain through its role in the Airbus consortium, shared with France, Italy and Spain.

* * *

The Cold War was at its height in the 1950s, a period when the world's two great superpowers – the United States and the Soviet Union – waged a continuous war of words which occasionally resulted in dirty deeds. Britain was often caught in the middle, and despite fears of sometimes discovering 'a red under the bed', trade agreements between the UK and the Soviet Union continued.

By 1956, Russian airline Aeroflot had been running limited operations between Moscow and London Airport using a noisy Li-2 propliner, which carried a small number of business travellers plus staff working at the Soviet Embassy in London (each of which was suspected of being a spy). No tourists travelled on the flight as entry visas were impossible to obtain and the only people wanting to visit the Russian capital were trade unionists and members of the British Communist Party.

March 1956 and the first Russian jet aircraft, a TU104, touches down at London Airport. It took everyone by surprise. (*Author's Collection*)

In March 1956, Aeroflot announced that it would be bringing a different aircraft to London on the 22nd of the month. The airline said that instead of flying its usual Li-2 from Moscow, it would be bringing a new plane to London: a jet designed by the legendary Russian aircraft designer Alexei Tupolev. On board the plane – a TU104 – would be Colonel Ivan Serov, the Soviet Union's top security chief for military intelligence, arriving to make sure that arrangements were satisfactory for an official visit later in the month of Communist Party First Secretary, Nikita Khrushchev, and Soviet Premier Nikolai Bulganin.

Because the Comet had been grounded and America's Boeing 707 had still to be introduced into service, the arrival of Aeroflot's new aircraft in UK airspace marked the return of a commercial jet aircraft to London Airport, and no one quite knew what to expect. They were in for a shock.

Instead of the ancient and clapped-out Li-2 boneshaker, a slim and sleek silver-painted jetliner with a red flag decorated with a hammer and sickle on the tailplane was approaching the runway. A glass nosecone gave the game away that it had originally been designed as a bomber.

The Russians were eager for their new aircraft to be seen and the press was invited to record its arrival and interview the sinister Colonel Serov. There was just one problem. Once it had landed, the TU104 stood higher off the ground than any other aircraft using London Airport at that time – including the Comet – and there were no passenger steps tall enough to reach the Russian aircraft's doorway. While the Comrade Colonel and his delegation remained in their seats looking down at the hoard of press people on the tarmac below, airport officials were dashing around trying to find something – a ladder, perhaps – that could be used to get the Russian VIPs onto the apron.

Fortunately, a set of flexible steps used by BOAC aircraft engineers was found to be tall enough – just – to reach the aircraft doorway. They were shaky and only one passenger at a time could stand on them, but they served their purpose.

When the door finally opened, Colonel Serov was first in the doorway. Wearing a huge greatcoat and fur hat, he stood at the top of the makeshift steps smiling broadly and proudly showing off a set of stainless steel false teeth. 'This beautiful plane is friendship plane,' he told reporters. 'I come here in friendship. UK, USSR, let's be friends.'

After the colonel's motorcade had whisked him away to Claridge's where Khrushchev and Bulganin would also be staying after arriving in Britain on board a Soviet naval cruiser, the press were allowed to enter the new Russian jet to see if it looked just as good on the inside as it did on the outside.

However, instead of discovering a luxuriously fitted aircraft interior, the press walked into something that one described as 'more like the inside of a second-class Victorian railway carriage.' Draped over the seat backs and armrests were lace antimacassars: ornate covers that would have been more at home in Mr Khrushchev's Kremlin apartment. Ornate brass lamps with heavy shades were fitted to the walls, making the plane look more like the corridor of a dubious hotel or on the Trans-Siberian railway.

The reporters were delighted to discover a pair of double doors at either end of the passenger cabin. On opening them, a small ante-room was discovered containing a two-seater red velvet upholstered settee where passengers could wait before entering yet another small room: the aircraft toilet; just two loos in the entire aircraft for fifty passengers and five crew.

Aeroflot officials who had remained on board the aircraft were delighted with the media response, reading their excitement and popping flashbulbs as British approval of their beautiful new plane, which the Russians were hoping to sell to British airlines in desperate need of a reliable jet aircraft.

The following day's newspapers were full of TU104 pictures and stories asking readers if they could believe that inside this modern jet exterior was a concealed time capsule containing interior design dating back to the days of the tsars.

Yet the Russians had the last laugh. Although none of the aircraft was ever sold to western nations, they served Aeroflot well for the next thirty years. While the antimacassars and ornate lights eventually made way for more modern interiors, the settees remained in the toilet ante-room, usually surrounded by rattling crates of a drink that Aeroflot claimed was lemonade but which passengers said tasted more like gunpowder.

* * *

There was to be one other major aircraft disaster at London Airport before the end of the 1950s. On 1 October 1956 a large group of special guests gathered in the VIP lounge to welcome the arrival back in Britain of the Avro Vulcan bomber, which the RAF had taken on a worldwide sales tour. The giant delta-wing bomber would not normally land at a commercial airport, but facilities for guests and the media at London Airport were deemed superior to those available elsewhere and the airport was chosen for its publicity value.

While VIPs enjoyed hospitality, a severe rainstorm lashed the tarmac. As the Vulcan began its approach to London Airport the crew was told about local weather conditions and reduced visibility. They were invited to divert elsewhere if they were unhappy about conditions at London Airport and it was confirmed that the Vulcan carried sufficient fuel to fly elsewhere.

On board was Air Marshal Sir Harry Broadhurst, air officer commander-in-chief of RAF Bomber Command as

A 1956 Avro Vulcan crash was a military aviation accident that occurred at Heathrow Airport on 1 October 1956 following a round-the-world trip to showcase the aircraft's advanced design. Vulcan B.1 XA897 crashed while attempting to land at the airport in poor weather. The pilot and co-pilot ejected to safety but the remaining four crew were killed. This trade advertisement appeared in *Flight* magazine just a few days before the disaster. (*Author's Collection*)

co-pilot, a crew of three other RAF officers and a representative of the aircraft manufacturer Avro.

Shortly after 10.00 am and at a height of 1,500ft and 5 nautical miles from touch-down, the aircraft began its descent, talked down by an air traffic controller. It was agreed that once the Vulcan's altimeter reached 300ft, it would still be possible to overshoot the runway and begin climbing again if weather conditions remained unsuitable.

While the weather was at its worst the Vulcan violently struck the tarmac, removing both undercarriage units and throwing the bomber's controls into confusion. The plane then rose up sharply to a height of between 200ft and 300ft, totally out of control. An order was given to abandon the Vulcan and the captain triggered his ejector seat. After repeating the order, the co-pilot

Due to heavy rain with visibility reduced to 500ft, Vulcan XA897 was on a ground-controlled approach and had been informed by Heathrow's air traffic control that they were above the glide slope and needed to lose altitude. However, the crew reduced their height too much, with their air speed close to the minimum drag point for a gear-down configuration. As a result, the Vulcan was 1,030 yards short of the runway and the initial contact with the ground tore out the aircraft's undercarriage. (*Author's Collection*)

also ejected. Both pilot and co-pilot must have realized when the order was given that owing to the low altitude both they and the other Vulcan's occupants had little chance of escape and their own chances of survival were negligible. Seconds later the nose and starboard wing dropped and the Vulcan crashed into a field on the airport's edge. The crew that remained on board plus the single passenger all perished. Both the pilot and co-pilot that had ejected survived.

A court of inquiry found nothing to suggest any technical failure in the aircraft, but concluded that the captain made an error of judgement flying below the agreed 300ft altitude and that the air traffic controller should have warned the pilot of his proximity to the ground. There was later speculation that Air Vice Marshal Broadhurst had ignored advice about diverting to another airport so as not to disappoint VIPs waiting to welcome the Vulcan home. It was rumoured that instead of travelling in the co-pilot's seat, Broadhurst was actually at the Vulcan's controls as it approached London Airport. This was never proved.

Chapter 12

The Show that *Must* Go On

The new brick and glass airport city in the centre of the runway triangle was nearing completion in April 1955, and the queen had promised to officially open it once finishing touches had been completed and the site cleared of builders and their construction vehicles.

Taylor Woodrow, the main contractors, produced a special brochure for the occasion. It is worth quoting some of the sections here, if only to share some of the copywriter's enthusiasm for London Airport's new central area, known locally to staff as Skyport City:

The tunnel at London Airport is the smooth, mysterious link between an old world and a new one. Beyond the tunnel, like a diamond set in a paste of emeralds, lies the streamlined capital of Britain's airways – precise, brilliant, compact. Here, inside a pattern of eight miles of runways, the administration, air traffic control and passenger-handling buildings are fitted like a perfect jigsaw. Here, design and planning have been concerned even with the smallest details. This is London – London Airport Central. One of the major visible tokens of the resilience of twentieth-century Elizabethan Britain.

To the non-stop drama of the airport, the tunnel is the curtain-raiser – ingeniously ventilated and subtly lit, the tunnel is itself a monument to British engineering.

But the tunnel is only the beginning. The first thing that opens the motorist's eyes as he cruises up out of the tunnel into a new world, is an arresting two-storey, T-shaped building crowned by a nine-storey tower. This is the air traffic control building; and the control room with the sloping blue glass windows surmounts the tower – the electronic brain of the diamond city. From this tower every movement of every aircraft on the ground or in the London air is charted and controlled. Fascinated visitors might be tempted to think of all this as the most magnificent clockwork toy in the world. But there is more to this than clockwork. And this is no toy.

The air traffic control building was built to last – and also built to please. It was constructed in steel framework encased in concrete, and the finishing touches were put to its outside walls with a pleasing combination of brick, stone and tiles. Like the other new London Airport buildings, it gives an enduring impression of elegance married to strength. And it introduces our visitors to the charm of English brick.

In the lower part of the tower: the management offices. In the left of the T, on the south side: the staff restaurants and kitchens. The design and decoration of the staff restaurants are enough, in themselves, to make appetite easy. A lavishness of height in the rooms, a generosity of space between tables, a superb acreage of window glass, an unashamed gaiety of colour – all of these the stuff of which relaxation is made. And they are the essential condiments of eating. Here, for a change, you eat surrounded by the twentieth century. And, however old-fashioned you may think you are, you like it.

The control tower was something of a marvel. It contained under-floor heating, something unheard-of in Britain during the early 1950s. Its offices were straight out of an American movie: bright, spacious and modern. It was also said that from the top, air traffic controllers could see Windsor Castle in one direction and the chimneys of Battersea Power Station in the other.

If the control tower is the electronic brain of the diamond city, the heart is the passenger-handling building. To the passenger arriving in London by air for the first time in recent years, the elegant glass and stone gallery which runs the whole length of the building looks like a sudden piece of magic. This is London? This *is* London! This symphony of glass-walled footbridges, this gay and debonair pattern of blue and yellow is London's new front door.

Walk into the central entrance hall, then walk up to the first floor. There you find yourself in something which could be the foyer of the grandest and most civilised of Grand Hotels. This is the main concourse, complete with shops, post office, buffet, car hire agencies, children's nursery and two hairdressing salons.

And so, outside again, where passengers in the lounges and waiting rooms look out through the long glass gallery and down upon a world of birds of passage. And where, from the terraced roof-garden 'waving base' friends and relatives wave their 'hellos' and 'goodbyes' to the passengers of the airlines of fourteen nations.

The non-stop drama of London Airport is one of the most magnetic spectacles of the world of 1955. Played on a stage of 2,820 acres, with a cast (in 1954) of some 1,724,000 passengers – it is something which no conceivable Hollywood epic could contrive to emulate, either for scale or for the feeling of actuality. This is the show that *must* go on.

Heathrow's new terminal, control tower and aprons officially opened for business in December 1955. (*Frederick Gibberd and Partners*)

The eastern apex building, which continues the airport's distinctive theme of brick, stone and glass, is designed to meet the needs of two distinct groups of people: those who help to make this spectacular show, and those who come to watch it. That is to say, the aircraft crews and the operational staffs of the international airlines on one hand, and the spectators on the other.

A staircase leads from the entrance hall up to the exhibition hall on the first floor; and this hall opens out into a large roof garden overlooking the airfield and aprons. Wherever the spectator goes within the eastern apex building he has a seat in the stalls.

So, there it is – London Airport Central, one of the wonders of twentieth-century Britain. Not all of it is completed yet. Some if it may not be completed until 1960. In the traditional British manner, London's airport was a quiet starter. Highly-polished new-built airports in Holland and Germany and France and elsewhere were glinting their welcome to air passengers for some years before London Airport was opened for operations. But when it is finally completed this airport may well prove to be the principal monument by which – for fulfilment of purpose, for distinction of design and for excellence of construction – British architecture and constructional engineering would choose to be judged by future generations. In fact, the whole face of London Airport is set fair towards the jet-age future.

Well might the visitor, who had been privileged to see the whole machinery of the airport, remark: 'The new London Airport is the proudest thing that has been built in Britain since the war.'

* * *

The queen inaugurated new buildings in the centre of London Airport. Her Majesty arrived by car with the Duke of Edinburgh and was greeted by a guard of honour made up of air crews from the British and Commonwealth airlines. The daughter of the Minister of Transport, Sarah Boyd-Carpenter, presented Her Majesty with flowers from around the world that had been flown in by four Commonwealth airlines. The name of the principal new building was only revealed at the end of the queen's speech as she unveiled a plaque naming it 'The Queen's Building'. (*Author's Collection*)

Queen Elizabeth II, with the Duke of Edinburgh, inaugurated the buildings in London Airport's shining new diamond city on 16 December 1955 and revealed that the 'Eastern Apex Building' would be re-named 'The Queen's Building'.

Her Majesty told invited guests:

The inauguration of this great terminal today marks an important stage in the story of London Airport. In the ten years which have passed since the earliest development of the site, the airport has grown in size and in international fame. Until today we may say with pride that it ranks among the foremost in the world. Whatever form air travel may take in future, and we may be certain that striking changes lie ahead, London Airport will I am sure continue to grow in importance as one of the world centres of air traffic.

The main passenger terminal was christened 'the Europa building' and designed to handle passengers and aircraft travelling to all parts of Europe. A special section at the western end would be used for domestic traffic and named the 'Britannic' area.

* * *

Thanks to new aircraft and an ever-growing demand for air travel, airlines began to develop interesting new ways of flying to London from different parts of the world during the closing years of the 1950s.

In 1957, a new direct service to London Airport from Los Angeles was introduced by American airline TWA flying over the North Pole in a Lockheed Constellation. This became the world's first non-stop flight from California to London, covering 5,500 miles in eighteen hours and thirty-two minutes and creating a new world endurance record for distance and time in the air for a civil airliner. Previously the journey had taken twenty-four hours, travelling via New York. TWA proudly boasted that the new route followed 'the Great Circle' flying 150 miles south of the magnetic North Pole, crossing northern Canada and the Hudson Bay, passing the southern tip of Greenland, across Ireland and onwards to London. Today's transatlantic airlines flying to and from California still follow the same polar route, covering the journey in ten to eleven hours.

The first American jet aircraft to enter commercial service made its passenger debut in August 1958. Originally named the 'Stratoliner' and later re-named the Boeing 707, the aircraft soon became an American icon. Pan American, the first carrier to operate the plane, planned to use it on its prestigious New York-London routes and in September 1958, just one month after it had entered commercial flying service, the Boeing 707 touched down at London Airport on a training mission for the company's air crews, and without passengers. The aircraft would also be measured for noise as it arrived and departed from the airport following serious concerns about the din the new jet might create once it entered regular service.

Boeing also hoped that the 707's London visit would help to persuade BOAC that the American-built jet would fit perfectly into the airline's fleet. It had the opposite effect. Days before the 707 touched down in London,

Pan American's first Boeing 707 arrives at Heathrow on 8 September 1958. (*Brenard Press*)

BOAC announced that its own newly-delivered British-built Comet 4 aircraft would be used on transatlantic routes from October – three weeks before Pan American received certification to fly passengers over the Atlantic in 707s – on routes from New York to Paris. BOAC claimed the distinction of operating the first transatlantic jet service by flying two Comet 4s simultaneously from London to New York and New York to London days ahead of their American rivals.

BOAC's ability to quickly exploit this opportunity stole some of Pan American's thunder by using a jet aircraft on the route. It would be another five weeks before Pan American had sufficient 707s in its fleet to offer a daily New York-London service, by which time BOAC had established itself as the premier transatlantic jet operator. However, once passengers had the choice of flying with either jet operator, Pan American won the day. The 707 flew faster than the Comet 4, it carried more passengers and the service was sold through an aggressive advertising campaign that emphasized speed, comfort, and low air fares.

The campaign worked. By 1958, the British public were in love with everything American thanks to the glamour created by its movies, television shows, rock 'n' roll music, people, casual clothing, wide open spaces, thrilling cities, laid-back lifestyle, and fabulously designed jet planes. More than 19,000 passengers flew across the Atlantic to London or Paris with Pan American during the Boeing 707's first six weeks of operation, compared with nearly 4,000 on BOAC's Comet services.

It was another eighteen months before BOAC took delivery of its first Boeing 707 to use on routes between London and New York. (*Brenard Press*)

BOAC realized that while its Comet 4 and Bristol Britannia aircraft were excellent pieces of equipment, they were no match for the Boeing 707. Dozens of airlines had placed orders for the aircraft and the media began to declare that unless BOAC also signed up with Boeing, the state airline would be left behind. In response the airline declared that it was 'satisfied that our fleet requirements for well into the 1960s are already met by the (British-built) aircraft on order.'

A year later, BOAC changed its mind and obtained permission from the government to place an order for fifteen Boeing 707s costing £2.9 million each. There was some consolation for Britain's aviation industry: the engines would be provided by Rolls-Royce. BOAC's first Boeing 707 entered service on London-New York routes on 28 April 1960.

The arrival of American aircraft was similar to the cavalry riding over the hill to rescue the wagon train. BOAC desperately needed a new prestige route service and in April 1959 inaugurated a round-the-world service. Introduction of the 707s and new Comet 4s freed up some of its gas turbine-powered Bristol Britannia turboprops to perform the task. The global operation was, in fact, the joining up of two different services travelling around the world in different directions and meeting up in Tokyo, where passengers swapped aircraft for the rest of their chosen route. Eastbound services travelled from London Airport via Frankfurt, Beirut, Karachi, Delhi, Calcutta, Bangkok and Hong Kong before landing in Tokyo, while the westbound service travelled via New York, San Francisco and Honolulu to Tokyo.

The round-the-world service was offered twice-weekly in both directions and was truly a long haul, taking three and a half days to fly eastbound routes and four and a half days to fly the 25,000-mile route westbound. Not only were there stops every few hours in either direction, there was also a twelve-hour layover in San Francisco and a twenty-four-hour stopover in Hong Kong.

Only certain parts of the route were a success for BOAC and as the airline moved towards the 1960s financial problems experienced by both the airline and London Airport began to rear their heads in a very public way.

Chapter 13

The Swinging Sixties and Plane-Spotting on the Queen's Building

The smart new terminal at the airport's centre relieved the old temporary prefabs on the north side of 60 per cent of its passengers. Now that the old terminal was less congested, airlines were able to build their own private lounges for increasing numbers of travellers prepared to pay higher fares to fly first-class to long-haul destinations in North America, Africa and Asia. It would be another six years before passengers using the terminal would be given a shining new glass and chrome terminal of their own within the diamond city.

BOAC engineer Don Parry recalls the relaxed style of working at the old terminal:

In the mid-1950s I was posted to BOAC's Britannia fleet. At that time crews reported for duty an hour and a half before departure. Most of us arrived early in order to grab a pre-flight meal at the adjacent aircrew mess, where Brown Windsor soup was a staple. It was a gentle start to a trip that allowed everyone to meet and get to know each other. There was no designated crew car park and those fortunate enough to have a vehicle parked it on the side of the road or on a patch of spare ground. There was never any difficulty in securing a spot.

As the flight engineer, I would then walk over to the engineering office (a hut, actually) to check on the state of the aircraft and then stroll over to our plane, which nestled neatly among the Stratocruisers, Constellations and DC6s bearing the great names of aviation like Pan American, TWA and the exotically-named Panair do Brasil.

In retrospect it all seemed so relaxed. The refuelling bowser was always available and not in a rush to go somewhere else. No problems with air traffic control take-off slots. We just called the control tower when we were ready to start. Departure was simple; we just taxied out and took off. There was rarely more than one aircraft ahead of us and we had all the convenience of a swift, rolling start out on the runway.

Sometimes my wife would accompany me to see me off. I never recall her not having a seat in the north side terminal coffee shop. I would then leave to go to the engineering office and she would pass through the restaurant to the small enclosed viewing areas at the rear. As the Britannia taxied out, we could offer mutual waves. Innocent days, gone forever. No wonder I have a degree of sympathy for today's crews. Commercial aviation's romantic phase is long past.

By the spring of 1956, visitors watching the non-stop procession of the world's airliners had turned the roof garden above the Queen's Building into London's most visited attraction. The admission price of one shilling for adults and sixpence for children generated thousands of pounds in revenue for the airport and roof garden admission soon outrivalled Windsor Castle, Madame Tussauds and the Tower of London.

Everybody wanted to watch aircraft take off and land from the rooftop viewing area of the Queen's Building, which in its first year of opening attracted 1 million visitors.

It offered all the ingredients of a great family day out in the second half of the 1950s and throughout the 1960s. First there was the experience of travelling through the famous tunnel (well worth the 2d bus fare alone) and

The Queen's Building provided the best place in England to go 'plane-spotting'. During weekends and school holidays its terraces were packed with spotters – 99 per cent of them boys – armed with their Ian Allen *Book of Civil Aircraft Markings*, a cheap biro and ruler to underline the aircraft spotted and a battered duffel bag containing their picnic lunch. A splendid time was guaranteed for all. (*Brenard Press*)

Visitors to London Airport appear to be wearing their best clothes in this photograph taken from one of the balconies overlooking the apron in the main terminal. The building in the background with a BOAC advertisement on the side had been Richard Fairey's old aircraft assembly building, but in the 1950s was used as the airport fire station. The old public viewing area on the airport's north side closed for business on Saturday, 16 April 1955. The airport officially opened its doors to passengers and visitors the following day and thousands passed through the tunnel to reach the central area by car, bus, coach, taxi and bicycle. There was even a half-mile-long public walkway through the tunnel for those without any form of transport. With picnic baskets on their arms, families swarmed onto the terraces of the Queen's Building and terminal balconies to get a grandstand view of arriving and departing aircraft. (*Author's Collection*)

getting off at the entrance to the Queen's Building. Then came the pleasure of climbing the staircase, passing fantastic ultra-modern aircraft pictures and Festival of Britain-inspired drawings on the walls. Then out into the spacious roof gardens, built to handle 10,000 people at any one time and often attracting that many spectators in the space of a single day. From here, visitors enjoyed a vast panorama of the airport with wonderful views of aircraft movements and watching passengers walking to and from Viscounts and Vanguards, Caravelles, Elizabethans, Dakotas and Comets and all kinds of strange-looking aircraft flying to London from the Soviet Union, Hungary, Czechoslovakia and Poland.

The friendly invasion of the Queen's Building represented a special day out for visitors happy to dress up for the occasion. Men put on suits and ties, wives dressed in their best frocks and matching hats while children wore school uniforms. It was as if each and every visitor wanted to be mistaken for a passenger instead of a day-tripper, despite packed lunches and picnic hampers and thermos flasks of tea brought along in case the Queen's Building cafés and restaurants proved too expensive.

Day-trippers came to London Airport from across the country, prepared to sit in a stuffy charabanc for four or five hours in order to spend just a short time on the Queen's Building or climb onto another coach for a guided airport tour before driving home again to Wales, Yorkshire or Devon. They also came from towns and villages surrounding the airport. Vincent Vere from Richmond upon Thames, Surrey spent two years as a BOAC visitor guide. He remembers:

> I was escorting a coach full of visitors around the airport's perimeter road and proudly announced to passengers that if they looked to their right they could see a runway which was made in the late 1940s and a lady at the back of the bus said 'Yes I know, it used to be part of my back yard.'

Staff working for BOAC were encouraged to bring their families and friends to the airport on Sundays for free guided tours of the airline's hangars and engineering base. Former employee Don Parry remembers:

> The visits allowed us to show our nearest and dearest the airport in action. They always ended with an excellent afternoon tea back in the airline's headquarters known as 'The Kremlin' – a utilitarian-designed building which a newspaper once claimed had been named because it reflected the number of communist trade unionists who worked inside.

The Ministry of Transport and Civil Aviation claimed that the Queen's Building expresses the recognition by London Airport of the new role international airports must accept. For today, in addition to organising the dispatch and reception of passengers and freight by air to and from the most distant parts of the earth, a great airport must be prepared to be treated as, in itself, a place of interest.

Former Flying Officer Flo Kingdon, who had served with the WRAF in the 1950s, including a spell as a broadcaster with the British Forces Network in Egypt and Cyprus, was one of two commentators on the roof of the Queen's Building. Like hundreds of others returning to Civvy Street after serving in the forces, Flo needed a job:

Former Flying Officer Flo Kingdon became one of the first public commentators on the Queen's Building roof gardens. (*Author's Collection*)

The airport's new terminal offered restaurant diners a chance to watch aircraft movements over-looking the apron as they ate their food from a table with a grandstand view. Note the tomato ketchup bottles on the tables, an important item that no family dining table was without in the 1950s. (*Author's Collection*)

Just after coming out of the WRAF, I attended a course designed to help officers re-settle into civilian life. I was there alongside Group Captains, Wing Commanders, Flight Officers and other ranks. One morning during a tea break, we took it in turns to look through a copy of *The Times* lying on a table.

We were searching through the appointments section for our first jobs in 'Civvy Street'. Someone saw a position advertised at London Airport for a public enclosure commentator on the Queen's Building and said: 'You can do that, that's just the job for you,' so I applied. I'd been turned down for other jobs and was surprised to be invited to an interview with the Ministry of Civil Aviation in Berkeley Square. They asked me how familiar I was with civil aircraft. I'd been used to RAF military aircraft for the past few years, so told them I didn't see any problem recognising civil aircraft. But they turned me down. And then a couple of days later they contacted me to say that the successful applicant had backed out and was I still interested? A week later I was in the glass-walled commentary box on the roof garden viewing area on top of the Queen's Building telling crowds of visitors about aircraft arriving and departing to and from all parts of the world.

My colleague was a man called Stan Little, a natural entertainer who always appeared in pantomimes at Christmas-time. He was the airport's

It might have been a new airport terminal, but flight arrivals and departures still had to be chalked onto a blackboard informing passengers, 'meeters and greeters' about aircraft movements. Electronic information boards came along in the 1960s, saving the airport authorities a fortune in chalk…

... and by August 1960 arrivals and departures boards were all operated electronically. (*Brenard Press*)

first public enclosure commentator and we took it in turns to do the job, often doubling up on busy weekends. It wasn't unusual to work 10-hour-long shifts.

Those were great days. We used to get information about aircraft movements from a daily schedule which told us what flights would be passing through the airport, times they would be moving in and out and the type of aircraft used. We also spoke regularly on the 'phone with the control tower who would alert us when aircraft were approaching ready to land or preparing for take-off. A typical commentary might go like this: 'And if you look over to your left, you will see a BOAC Bristol Britannia arriving on runway number five from Montreal. This British-built airliner has four turbo-prop engines and can carry up to 149 passengers, depending on its series. It can fly for up to 5,000 miles at a cruising speed of 325 mph.'

The public lapped it up and our commentaries probably created a desire to travel by air with more people than many advertising campaigns. People looked down from the Queen's Building and saw the first members of the jet set boarding aircraft. Naturally, they wanted to be down there on the tarmac with them, too – and a few years later many were doing exactly that.

We were also responsible for telling the public about any celebrities who might be on board aircraft. I'd tell the public that on the BEA Viscount directly in front is the film star Diana Dors, and hundreds of people would drop their telescopes and sandwiches and rush to the railings to wave and try to get a glimpse of her. Most celebrities were very good and would usually look up and give the spectators a nice big wave. Some might even blow them a kiss.

I recall an occasion when an Air-India Boeing 707 jet was unable to lower its nose wheel and attempted to land on runway 28-right. I was aware of the problem but didn't immediately tell the spectators in case it managed to land normally. I held my breath as it got closer and sure enough, sparks and smoke flew in all directions as it scraped along the runway and out of my field of vision. I then told the public: 'Probably some of you might have noticed that the aircraft just landed has experienced a few nose wheel problems and our airport emergency services now have the problem under control. Now the next plane arriving in front of you will be …'

I worked as a commentator for nine years and had a wonderful time. People were very polite and well-behaved, although plane-spotters often used to come and knock on the window and ask dozens of questions about what planes might be landing in the next six hours.

If anyone became bored watching aircraft and listening to commentaries, there was a small children's playground, a paddling pool, a souvenir shop, a sunken garden, easy chairs and coin-in-the-slot telescopes. If it rained, there was plenty of cover. If it was hot, it was a safe place for schoolchildren to be on a warm school summer holiday day out, armed with a duffel bag containing a sandwich box, bottle of pop, pair of binoculars and a copy of Ian Allen's Civil Aircraft Markings book which no true plane-spotter could be without. They were mostly boys aged between 11 and 16 who would pour out of double-decker buses and invade the Queen's Building for eight hours at a time before going home for tea. They would be back again the following day, out of their mothers' way, out of trouble, out of harm and hungry to see aircraft dropping in from all over the globe, dreaming of the day when they, too, would become passengers or – better still – behind the controls of a Comet, Britannia, Super Constellation or a Boeing 707. The Queen's Building is probably responsible for inspiring more young people to apply for jobs with airlines or aspire to travel to far-flung places. The roof gardens and spectator balconies were a place where dreams were made, careers planned and excitement about aircraft and travel generated.

By 1959, 1 million annual visitors were paying visits to the roof gardens. By the late 1980s this had dwindled to just a few thousand plane-spotters. When it finally closed its doors to visitors in the 1980s after the airport authorities (quite correctly) considered it to be the perfect place from which to launch a terrorist attack on aircraft, the Queen's Building roof gardens had become a tatty version of its former self. Watching aeroplanes was no longer a novelty. In an age when the public uses planes in much the same way as the London Underground, the airport was no longer a fabulous place for a great day out. New passenger piers and building extensions had also begun to obscure the perfect views once enjoyed by visitors. Now die-hard aircraft-spotters preferred to watch planes from positions beneath the flight path.

Yet for millions of visitors during the heady days of the late fifties and sixties, the Queen's Building was a magical and wonderful place, remembered with affectionate nostalgia for great days gone by at London Airport ...

Chapter 14

Britain's New Front Door and BOAC in Debt

I n August 1961, Peter Thorneycroft, the latest politician to stand in shoes owned by the Ministry of Aviation, told Parliament that the Conservative government 'is determined that British airports should pay their way.' He added: 'We have been seeking to put our airports on a commercial basis; we don't regard them as part of the welfare state.' For years the airports had been running at a loss trying to keep up with the level of money

The chairman of the British Airports Authority (BAA) Sir Peter Masefield recalled: 'The history of British airports had been an appalling catalogue of costly and time-consuming public inquiries, decisions deferred, decisions overturned, decisions that were obviously mistaken – and seen to be so at the time – and golden opportunities missed. We British have a history of dragging our decisions for as long as possible, as if time and money were unimportant.' It was Sir Peter who decided to change the airport's name from London Airport back to Heathrow. (*Wikipedia*)

In August 1961, Peter Thorneycroft, the latest politician to stand in shoes owned by the Ministry of Aviation, told Parliament that the Conservative government 'is determined that British airports should pay their way.' He added: 'We have been seeking to put our airports on a commercial basis; we don't regard them as part of the welfare state.' (*Wikipedia*)

invested in them. The worst offender was London Airport. The cost of creating the airport in the first place followed by massive investments building the new central area meant that it would be years before it would ever recover its costs and go into profit.

Former chairman of the British Airports Authority (BAA), Sir Peter Masefield – who began his professional career working for Richard Fairey's aircraft-building company – recalls:

> The (history of) British airports had been an appalling catalogue of costly and time-consuming public inquiries, decisions deferred, decisions overturned, decisions that were obviously mistaken – and seen to be so at the time – and golden opportunities missed. We British have a history of dragging our decisions for as long as possible, as if time and money were unimportant.

In 1959 the government considered handing airports serving the capital over to an independent body and published a white paper two years later in June 1961. The Airports Authority Bill was presented to Parliament on 6 November 1964, resulting in the creation of the British Airports Authority (BAA) which controlled the running of Heathrow, Gatwick, Stansted, Prestwick and other

An aerial view of London's splendid new showpiece airport showing the control tower, passenger terminal, public viewing area and a variety of piston-driven aircraft on the tarmac. (*Author's Collection*)

smaller airports. The organization actually commenced control of the airports on 1 April 1966, 'on April Fool's Day, of course,' remembers Sir Peter. At that time 12.2 million travellers were passing through London Airport.

BAA inherited a bureaucratic and loss-making airport system and Sir Peter later claimed the airports had suffered under poor management for years 'and the only directive handed down by the government was that we should run the airport properly, consulting with local residents but not interfering with navigation services.' In reality, Masefield's team had to become familiar with the airports and their problems from day one, introduce new operating procedures 'appropriate to a harsh new commercial environment', find and equip offices, recruit staff and decide endless details of future policy.

An army of opponents tried to block every move and Sir Peter remembers the outrage when it was announced that he would be BAA's first chairman and perceived as 'pro-aviation' which was considered a bad thing. 'Back in the 1830s a vociferous minority tried to stop the railways,' he notes in his memoirs, *Flight Path*.

It was not only airports that were in serious financial trouble. In 1963 a government white paper called 'The Financial Problems of BOAC' set out plans for turning the airline's fortunes around and extend government powers to make further loans to finance deficits on revenue accounts.

BOAC defended its poor performance by stating that 'the corporation could not be purely commercial.' It said that, where possible, it had tried to buy British aircraft and help the industry build new airliners. The corporation claimed 'it was completely wrong that it should be expected to do something which was not commercial and yet get nothing for it and crazy that when the airline had lost money it should be expected to go on paying interest on that money until kingdom come.'

The truth was that while BOAC was a prestige international airline, it was in debt up to its tail fins. Between 1946 and 1951 the airline enjoyed a monopoly on routes from London Airport to 'the colonies' and had created favourable partnerships on routes linking Commonwealth nations. However, the corporation's costs were abnormally high – mainly the result of flying wartime aircraft adapted for civil use during the late 1940s – and receiving £32 million in grants from the Exchequer during these years.

Despite the Comet disasters in 1952/53 and subsequent purchase of Boeing 707s, the corporation showed a profit between 1952 and 1956 but made a loss of more than £80 million in subsequent years. The airline attributed this to the independence of many colonies who had started their own national carriers, the cost of introducing new aircraft into the fleet, investments in associate companies and internal organization and management costs.

There was talk of a merger between BOAC and BEA. The two airlines could combine common functions in engineering, catering and some short-haul routes. One airline could also act as a 'feeder' for the other. BOAC admitted that this would not solve its immediate problems and BEA 'felt that any merger would destroy our singleness of purpose and *esprit de corps*.' Talks of the merger ground to a halt for the time being and staff from both airlines breathed a huge collective sigh of relief for the next decade.

In 1959/60 BOAC employed 191,131 staff. The following year this had risen to 20,787 and by 1962/63 21,686 staff were employed by the airline. In order to claw money back, BOAC sold its 15 per cent equity in the Hong Kong-based airline Cathay Pacific, 40 per cent holding in Ghana Airways, 16 per cent share in Nigeria Airways and 48 per cent share in Lebanese carrier MEA. It released its 90 per cent shareholding in the Caribbean airline BWIA for just £520,000, while at the same time losing a managerial contract to run Kuwait Airways.

It would take BOAC more than a decade before it returned to profit, by which time it had finally merged with BEA, axed hundreds of jobs and non-profit-making routes and launched itself onto the London Stock Exchange.

* * *

The old and 'temporary' prefabricated terminal buildings on the north side of London Airport was an embarrassment to the thirteen airlines still using them at the end of 1961, but it didn't matter. In November of that year they would finally start to close down the old buildings for good, although they would remain standing for several more years, used as a base for the airport's cargo operations. Most of the terminal's furniture, fixtures and fittings were also thrown into the skips. They had been installed at the end of the 1940s and now looked shabby, faded and as out-of-date as Avro Lancastrians as Britain entered an exciting new decade of promise dubbed 'the Swinging Sixties'.

On 13 November 1961, BOAC and some of its associated airlines set up shop in their gleaming new home: a building again designed by Frederick Gibberd, but instead of using red brick for his terminal, the architect used steel, glass and marble. Dubbed 'Britain's new front door', it was known to the rest of the world as the 'Oceanic' terminal. Other long-haul carriers would follow BOAC through the tunnel over the next few months at the rate of one new airline every six weeks until the move was complete in March 1962.

Like the control tower, 'Europa' and 'Britannic' terminals, the new building was located inside the runway triangle at its south-west corner and on the exact spot where a small settlement called Heath Row had once stood just fifteen years earlier. The 'Oceanic' terminal was built for international jet-

Terminal 3 was originally called the 'Oceanic' building and is still used by long-distance carriers. (*Author's Collection*)

setters: passengers who turned up at the airport in their best clothes, carrying expensive luggage and handing over large tips to airport porters. It was rectangular in shape, 430ft by 55ft and designed to handle several thousand passengers each hour of the day.

Built at a cost of £3 million, the terminal was a modern, fashionable and brightly-lit building with marble floors, open-plan staircases, buffet-style restaurants, cocktail bars – including a famous one known as 'The Tavern in the Sky' – shops selling duty-free goods, newspapers and London souvenirs.

Before opening its doors to passengers, its exterior was used in a film called *The V.I.P.s* starring Richard Burton, Elizabeth Taylor, Orson Welles and Margaret Rutherford plus a host of other international performers. The plot involved a mixed bag of travellers passing through the new terminal but stranded by fog. The interior of the new building was accurately recreated on a sound stage at MGM-British Studios, Borehamwood, Herts, where the sound of jets taking off and landing would not get in the way of filming. Playing the part of a young Brenard's airport reporter attempting to interview the Orson Welles character was a young man who would later become one of television's best-known faces. His name was David Frost.

The new terminal was uncomfortably hot in summer and freezing cold in winter and no amount of maintenance could solve the problem. Then in

Before opening its doors to passengers, the Oceanic terminal's exterior was used in a film called *The V.I.P.s* starring Richard Burton, Elizabeth Taylor, Orson Welles and Margaret Rutherford plus a host of other international performers. The plot involved a mixed bag of travellers passing through the new terminal and stranded by fog. (*Author's Collection*)

the 1980s, when the terminal had been open for more than twenty years, a refurbishment programme began which revealed that a 1960s' tile-cutting machine had been left deep inside the building's labyrinth of utility ducts, blocking the heating and air-conditioning vent. Suddenly temperatures inside the building began to improve for the first time since 1961.

A set of twelve chandeliers graced the ceiling above the check-in area. Each light fitting hung from a steel cable attached to a large winding mechanism located within the ceiling cavity. Engineers could unwind and gently lower chandeliers to the ground for cleaning and maintenance. On one occasion, maintenance men were attempting to lower one of the chandeliers and could not understand why it refused to descend. On further investigation it was discovered that a wheel mechanism controlling the light fitting had become jammed. Engineers, however, failed to notice the steel cable gently unwinding in great coils. Suddenly the chandelier dropped at great speed towards engineers on the ground below. They scattered in all directions, being chased by forty bouncing 100-watt lamp bulbs. Fortunately, the chandelier reached the end of its travels about 2ft above the terminal floor. The engineers spent the rest of their shift sweeping up thousands of tiny fragments of glass from the terminal floor. They all lived to tell the tale.

The floor of the terminal's dedicated car park was originally laid with an unusual coating: peanut shells. Partly as a low-cost experiment and partly as a political gesture towards an East African country, someone in a high place had the bright idea that the shells would make an ideal surface if held in place with ex-railway sleepers. The idea was a disaster and motorists using the car park hated the idea, especially ladies wearing high-heeled or open-toed shoes. The English weather eventually made the porous surface wet and soggy and before long the entire surface was ruined and substituted with concrete.

The 'Oceanic' terminal was always busy, and the number of passengers passing through was swelled by 'meeters and greeters' plus hundreds of local people to whom the airport was a prime source of evening entertainment. As night fell, entire families would pile into their cars and drive through the tunnel from nearby towns, park for free and enter the terminal to 'people-watch'. Here was a rare chance to see real Arabs wearing traditional dishdasha robes, dainty Japanese ladies in kimonos, Africans and Asians wearing a variety of strange-looking hats and colourful robes and tall Texans who appeared even taller in their 'good old boy' cowboy boots and Stetsons.

Visitors also came to the terminal to enjoy 'frothy coffee', American-style muffins and Danish pastries at the snack bar. They, too, wanted to be mistaken for international jet-setters and by mingling with different nationalities in the terminal, that is exactly what they became for an hour or two every evening. Besides, you never knew who you might also catch sight of in the 'Oceanic' terminal: a famous film star, a millionaire, Miss World ... or your next-door neighbour.

* * *

After all the airlines had moved from the north side shanty town, all that was left of the original airport complex were the offices and warehouses forming the airport's cargo terminal, a maintenance department and a scattering of two-storey offices used by airlines and other commercial companies.

Years before, Bill Brenard had moved his newsroom and photographic darkroom from one of the primitive ex-military caravans to one of the former residential houses along the Bath Road – known as Fern Villas – and turned it into editorial offices. A former fish and chip shop next door was converted into a darkroom, and its manager Geoff Matthews swore that he could still smell cod frying well into the 1960s.

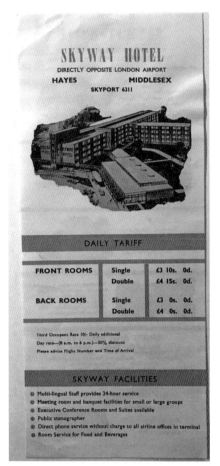

Two large American-style airport hotels opened along the Bath Road in the 1960s. Largest was the 160-room Skyways Hotel which was so popular that within a year of its opening a further 100 rooms were added. The second hotel was a circular building close to the airport's telephone exchange called The Aeriel. A joke circulating around the airport was that when everyone was asleep in the hotel's bedrooms, their feet all met in the middle. (*Author's Collection*)

A new airport telephone centre called the Skyport Exchange was also opened along the Bath Road and every airport company was assigned a number with the prefix SKY. Brenard's news agency somehow acquired the unique number of SKY 1234, while the airport switchboard ended up with SKY 4321. There was further confusion when Harrods, the famous Knightsbridge store, was assigned the telephone number of SLO (as in SLOane) 1234. Every day scores of elderly and short-sighted ladies would mistakenly misdial the number and instead of talking to Harrods, ended up speaking to Brenard's newsdesk staff. On slow news days, young news staff would take advantage of this by answering the phone and pretending to be the store's ladies' foundation underwear department or a non-English-speaking person in the food hall. Neither Brenard's nor Harrods refused to give up their prestige telephone numbers, creating hours of endless fun for the young reporters and endless confusion for lady telephone users in Middle England.

Two large and designer-built American-style airport hotels had also been opened along the Bath Road and opposite the airport's perimeter track. Largest was the 160-room Skyways Hotel which was so popular that within a year of opening a further 100 rooms were added.

The hotel boasted that it offered a swimming pool, was soundproof and that every room was equipped with a television and a telephone; something almost unheard-of in a British hotel in the early 1960s. The Skyways Hotel also offered guests 'the longest upholstered bar in the country'. This, however, was not its main claim to fame. One of the first VIP guests to stay at the hotel was Italian film star Sophia Loren whose jewellery was stolen from her room while she took dinner in the restaurant. None of Sophia's jewels, necklaces, tiaras and earrings was ever recovered. 'I shall never stay at this hotel again,' Sophia told a Brenard's reporter. 'Miss Loren should have placed her valuables in the hotel safe,' said the manager.

The second hotel was a circular building close to the telephone exchange called the Aeriel. A joke circulating around the airport was that when everyone was asleep in the hotel's bedrooms, their feet all met in the middle.

* * *

By the end of 1962, London Airport was handling 6.1 million passengers. Since its opening sixteen years earlier, 41.6 million passengers had flown in and out of the airport. By the end of 1963, 1 million passengers would be passing through the airport every month. In 1966 Heathrow was named fourth largest in the world in terms of passenger throughput. It was identified as seventh largest in terms of aircraft movements and fifty-first in terms of

Members of the British Olympic team board a BEA Viscount aircraft to fly to Rome in August 1960 to participate in the XVII Olympic Games where Great Britain won twenty medals and finished in twelfth place. (*Brenard Press*)

aircraft movements. This was a boom time for mass passenger travel as more people around the world travelled further afield for holidays and to conduct business.

Unless they were scared of flying, anyone who was anyone in the world of show business, sport or current affairs eventually found themselves passing through London Airport. The same applies today, but in the 1960s the passengers everyone wanted to see were four young Liverpudlians who had taken the music world by storm: The Beatles. John, Paul, George and Ringo had already passed through the airport following a sensational visit to America in February 1964.

In the US the group had appeared on Ed Sullivan's television show. A few months earlier, Sullivan and his wife were checking in at Terminal 3 for a flight home to New York and heard the sound of screaming coming from the other end of the building. They saw dozens of hysterical teenage girls running through the building, chased by police. When the poker-faced American TV presenter asked an airline check-in girl what the problem might be, he was told that The Beatles were travelling from the airport that day. 'Who are The

The Beatles – Paul McCartney, George Harrison, John Lennon and Ringo Starr – regularly travelled through the airport and were greeted by thousands of adoring fans, no matter what day of the week it was. Other pop groups arriving at Heathrow, including The Osmonds and the Beach Boys, also brought thousands of fans to the airport to greet their heroes. However, like Donny Osmond and his four singing brothers, pop stars of the day enjoyed being met whenever they arrived or departed from Heathrow. (*Brenard Press*)

Beatles?' asked Sullivan. Four months later, The Beatles flew from the same terminal to appear on his Sunday night American TV show.

The pop group's triumphant return to London has become part of the airport's history. It was deemed so important that it was transmitted live on television. Nearly 4,000 fans – mostly teenage girls – descended on the airport to catch a glimpse of their idols. Queen's Building commentator Flo Kingdon, who later went on to be an airport public relations officer and part of the Queen's Building management team, remembers the day:

Fans began to arrive at the airport early in the morning and immediately caused problems when they began to gather inside the terminal building. The police decided to divert them all towards the Queen's Building where they could be better contained. Many of them didn't want to leave the terminal, where they thought they would have a chance to reach out and touch one of The Beatles and several became rather hysterical and had to be taken to the airport's medical room to recover.

Once the kids arrived on the roof gardens, I began to assure them over the loudspeakers that this was by far the best place to see the

'Fab Four'. Pan American planned to taxi the aircraft – a Boeing 707 – around to the tarmac directly in front of the Queen's Building instead of at Terminal 3.

The pandemonium began all over again as soon as the aircraft approached the runway. Girls were fainting, weeping, climbing on top of walls and seats and I began to be concerned that there might be an accident. But once the aircraft taxied around the corner and came to a standstill in front of the Queen's Building, the kids were given a fantastic grandstand view of all four Beatles as they appeared in the aircraft doorway. The trouble was that as soon as the aircraft door opened and The Beatles appeared, everyone surged forward to get a better look and part of a wall collapsed. It could have been a disaster, but fortunately, apart from a few cuts and grazes, no one was seriously hurt. The Beatles waved to everyone from the aircraft steps and never stopped waving, even when they reached the tarmac. This was at the height of what was known as 'Beatlemania' and the screaming was deafening. I don't think anybody could hear my commentary that day. Today, whenever you see TV documentary programmes about The Beatles, they always show this famous airport arrival.

Nine cars were damaged by hysterical Beatles fans at London Airport that day and the pop group's management generously settled all insurance claims. Such was the power of publicity for the group – and also for Pan American – that television and newspaper stories about the London Airport arrival reached all four corners of the world.

When The Beatles flew out of the airport with TWA the following year, each member of the group was presented with a special red airline bag containing their name and the airline's logo. One of these bags was recently sold at auction in the United States for $25,000.

There would be many other welcomes to pop performers at London Airport throughout the 1960s and '70s – for the Beach Boys, The Osmonds, David Cassidy – when the Queen's Building would again be pressed into service as the best possible viewing point for fans to see their idols. Teenage fan worship still exists, but nothing like it did in the Swinging Sixties when all you needed was love, love, love and anyone could fly with Lucy in the sky … with diamonds ….

* * *

The 1960s was a boom time for mass passenger air travel. Heathrow entered the 1960s by handling more than 5 million travellers. By the end of the decade this had risen to around 15 million. British airlines using Heathrow Airport

In November 1963 BOAC introduced the British-made VC10 into its fleet and began phasing out Comets and Britannias on its Eastern and African routes. The aircraft turned out to be one of the noisiest commercial aircraft ever built. (*Author's Collection*)

used the biggest, fastest – and often the noisiest – aircraft to transport record numbers of passengers in and out of 'swinging London'.

In November 1963 BOAC introduced the British-made VC10 into its fleet and began phasing out Comets and Britannias on its Eastern and African routes. The aircraft, as much a child of the sixties as Carnaby Street and The Cavern, was built at Vickers' manufacturing base in Weybridge. It was designed to compete with American jets which, by now, had set the standards for international air travel.

The VC10 was described by BOAC as

an exciting new shape in the sky and the most advanced airliner BOAC has ever brought into service … it is a quiet, smooth and comfortable plane. With its clean swept-back wings and smooth engine nacelles snuggling close to the fuselage beneath a high tailplane, the sleek lines of the VC10 convey an impression of purposeful energy …. The engines are positioned at the rear so that the broad sweep of the wings may be kept free for high-lift devices, which give the aircraft its modest appetite for concrete compared to the vociferous demands of earlier jetliners of similar weight and size.

BOAC ordered 12 standard VC10s and 30 larger, long-range 150-passenger 'Super VC10s' together costing over £150 million. They gave the airline years of excellent service, but they were noisy. As the VC10 came thundering down the runway and almost stood on its tail as soon as the front nose wheel left the ground, it emitted a deafening roar from its Rolls-Royce Conway turbojets, breaking all previous aircraft noise levels. Complaints about aircraft noise from local residents and people living under the flight path reached all-time records once the VC10 came into regular passenger service.

BOAC's VC10s became as familiar a sight at Heathrow as BEA's Tridents, a short to medium-range aircraft powered by rear-mounted turbojets and built to accommodate 100 passengers. By March 1965, fifteen Tridents had been delivered to BEA and were flying all over Europe and a further eight joined the fleet the following year. The Trident became the backbone of BEA's fleet and a very popular plane with passengers and the airline's Heathrow-based engineering staff. Larger versions of the Trident followed in later years and, unlike the VC10, were also bought by a variety of other commercial airlines including Cyprus Airways and thirty-three were sold to the Central Aviation Administration of China.

Another popular British aircraft from this time was the BAC One-Eleven, a jet designed to carry around eighty passengers on short-haul routes. Unlike the VC10 and Tridents, the One-Eleven was successfully exported to a number of other countries in Europe, Africa and the Far East, and to at least one American operator.

The international aircraft manufacturing market remained competitive, but few airlines on the European side of the Atlantic truly appreciated that a new type of aircraft was taking shape on designer drawing boards at Boeing's

On 3 July 1968 an Airspeed Ambassador operated by BKS Air Transport crashed at Heathrow damaging two parked Trident airliners as it cartwheeled into an incomplete Terminal 1 still under construction. Six of the eight people on board were killed, along with eight racehorses being transported on it. The crash was blamed on the failure of a flap-operating rod due to metal fatigue, resulting in asymmetrical lift.

Seattle plant. The prototype design was known as the 'Jumbo Jet' simply because it was designed to carry up to four times more passengers than anything else available in commercial aviation. To handle the new big jets, airports receiving them would need to invest in enlarged passenger piers to cope with expanded numbers of people using the new aircraft and extend the length of runways from which they would land and take off.

The Burtons – actor Richard and his wife Elizabeth Taylor – both wearing their best summer clothes at Heathrow in 1971.

However, in the mid-sixties, few European airlines were paying attention to what was soon to take shape in an American aircraft manufacturing plant. Britain and France were too busy concentrating on another project. In December 1962 it was announced that a joint UK–French agreement had been signed to develop the world's first supersonic jet. Nobody was sure what it might look like and some newspapers even attempted to create their own designs, which looked like a cross between something out of a Dan Dare story in the boy's comic *The Eagle* and a low-budget Hollywood science-fiction 'B' movie. Nevertheless, the joint project did have a name: 'Concorde'.

Chapter 15

The Sad Tale of British Eagle

O ne of BAA's first tasks when it took over management of London Airport in 1966 was to change the airport's name back to Heathrow, or to be correct Heathrow Airport (London). For the last twenty years the airport's name had been abbreviated to LAP; now it would be known as LHR: London-Heathrow. It would take years for the name to catch on and many former airport staff now retired still refer to it by its old name.

In 1968, BAA opened its latest terminal, known as 'Terminal 1' and home to all BEA's pan-European services. The original 'Europa' terminal was re-named 'Terminal 2' and used by continental European airlines, while the 'Oceanic' building was re-named 'Terminal 3' and used by all long-distance carriers.

When Terminal 1 was opened by the queen in April 1969, it became Europe's biggest airline terminal in terms of space, passenger capacity and the number of aircraft boarding gates available. It was also the third terminal designed by Gibberd, who now had three different architectural styles on view at Heathrow. Each was efficient and functional, yet each looked different, reflecting the architect's own vision at the time of design. Many agreed that three terminals designed by the same man looked odd. Gibberd countered that each was built with different requirements in mind and that air transport had grown so rapidly since his first terminal opened thirteen years previously that new buildings based on old designs would not solve the airport's problem of how to deal with rising demand for usage.

Whereas BEA and BOAC were the airport's principal UK airlines, there was also a small squadron of other British carriers that provided airline passengers with alternatives on many domestic and short-haul European routes from Terminals 1 and 2. Many of the airlines had been created following the formation of the Air Transport Licensing Board in 1960, which led to the formation of long-forgotten airlines such as BKS Air Transport, North-East Airlines, Cambrian Airways and Derby Airways (which eventually became British Midland).

Prior to 1960 several other airlines had also arrived and departed, merged or gone bankrupt: Hunting Clan, Skyways, Olley Air Services, Euravia Limited (which later become part of Britannia Airways) and Westpoint Aviation. Then there was British Eagle, a successful and popular airline prepared to take on the big boys but allowed to die a swift and very public death.

* * *

British Eagle began life as Eagle Aviation in 1948 during the Berlin Airlift. It was founded by a pilot called Harold Bamberg who had plenty of enthusiasm, technical ability and a pair of aeroplanes: former RAF Halifax bombers used to fly 7,300 tons of food and coal to the beleaguered German city on more than 1,000 flights over a ten-month period.

Following the end of the airlift in 1949, Bamberg set himself up as a charter carrier and purchased an Avro York. His reputation plus the flair that was to characterize him in later years resulted in the introduction of scheduled services between Blackbushe Airport in Surrey and Belgrade; the first post-war British air link to the Yugoslav capital. Services to Denmark and Sweden followed. By 1955 Eagle Aviation was operating ten Vickers Vikings and two DC3s and Bamberg was directing his considerable energy into building a truly British independent airline.

Bamberg moved into a plush office at Marble Arch, ordered a fleet of Douglas DC-6s and began campaigning to become Britain's first low-cost carrier. He called his plan the 'VLF' (Very Low Fares) challenge: an idea to offer fares much lower than those available through BEA and other domestic airlines. The scheme met with resistance from the government who finally decided what airlines could charge.

In 1959, Eagle flew more than 170,000 passengers and had acquired a valuable contract to transport British troops from and to Blackbushe on behalf of the government. The airline's fleet continued to grow and Bamberg now offered competitive services to Italy, Austria, France, Luxembourg, Belgium, Majorca and the Channel Islands.

Until this time, under the Air Corporations Act of 1946, private airlines were excluded from scheduled routes except – under exceptional circumstances – as 'associates' of the major corporations. Government liberalization at last removed the monopoly held by BOAC and BEA, allowing British Eagle to expand both its fleet and routes. Bamberg responded quickly by introducing scheduled services to Bermuda and the Bahamas and entered into an equity partnership agreement with the Cunard Steam-Ship Company to operate competitive fares across the North Atlantic.

Bamberg dreamed of becoming the second British long-haul airline alongside BOAC transatlantic routes and Cunard provided British Eagle with the capital support it needed to purchase modern jets 'plus the prestige of Britain's great history of trading on the North Atlantic and the experience

British Eagle began life as Eagle Aviation in 1948 during the Berlin Airlift. It was founded by a pilot called Harold Bamberg who had plenty of enthusiasm, technical ability and a pair of ex-RAF aircraft. The airline collapsed twenty years later when British Eagle was faced with heavy bills for fuel, landing charges and wages that rendered the company insolvent. (*Author's Collection*)

of our 17 sales offices on the North American continent.' Cunard was the operation's majority shareholder.

In 1960 British Eagle transferred operations from Blackbushe to London Airport in readiness to become a major player on the European and transatlantic airline scene. In December 1960 the newly re-named Cunard Eagle Airways ordered a pair of Boeing 707s at a cost of £2.6 million each for delivery in 1962. In May 1961 the airline was granted a licence to operate daily services between London and New York in direct competition with BOAC, Pan American and TWA, but with just three months to go before the new American-built jets were due for delivery, BOAC appealed against the decision and Cunard Eagle's licence was revoked by the Minister of Aviation who cited 'excess capacity' on the route.

With his customary energy, Bamberg set about renegotiating his North Atlantic licences by applying for routes over the 'mid-Atlantic' between London and Miami and new transatlantic jet services were launched in May 1962. A second route between London and Jamaica followed and the airline's engineering base tooled up in readiness to begin working on Boeing 707 equipment.

However, dirty work was going on behind the scenes. BOAC wanted Bamberg's airline crushed and entered into secret negotiations with Cunard to form a new airline to be called BOAC Cunard. This new £30 million company then snatched Bamberg's Atlantic licences, its two Boeing 707s and some crew. Cunard Eagle was left with only a few scheduled services and a top-heavy engineering organization geared to the operation of big jets.

Bamberg had been 'sold down the river' by Cunard. He had two options available: close down his airline or sell his interest to another company. He chose the latter route and arranged for a management buy-out of Cunard's 60 per cent holding in the Eagle group.

Eagle was re-born on 1 March 1963 as British Eagle International Airlines and the name Cunard was unceremoniously dropped. Once again Bamberg was in charge of the airline he had founded fifteen years earlier; a company he stated was 'a forward-thinking and industrious British independent airline.' In 1963 the airline carried 153,436 passengers, employed 850 staff and made a loss of £80,000. By 1966 Bamberg's airline carried more than 1 million passengers, had created jobs for 2,500 staff, made a profit of £600,000 and operated a fleet of seventeen Bristol Britannias, six Vickers Viscounts, five BAC One-Elevens and a pair of Boeing 707s. A rosy future lay ahead …

Then in November 1968, Bamberg's airline came crashing down around him. None of the 2,500 staff were expecting it, although regular articles by Bamberg in the airline's staff newspaper warned them that Harold Wilson's Labour-controlled government was not giving independent airlines an easy time. The airline's Heathrow passengers were confronted with notices on check-in desks telling them that flights were cancelled and British Eagle had ceased trading. The last British Eagle flight to operate was a BAC One-Eleven service from Liverpool to Heathrow. When it had taken off, the airline had been a going concern. When it landed in London less than an hour later, the crew were told that they no longer had jobs.

So what went wrong?

The government of the day had done its best to slap down the country's independent airlines, taking away their scheduled services and preventing them from growing, thereby depriving them of the power to generate income and the opportunity to obtain long-term, low-cost financing. BOAC was still claiming that Eagle's weekly service to the Bahamas was hurting its own operations to the destination and pleaded with the government for help. The government saw fit to revoke Eagle's licence just as the airline was about to sign new financial agreements for the next stage of its expansion. In the eyes of BOAC, British Eagle had the effrontery to offer opposition to a state-owned carrier that screamed blue murder every time a new route was given to an independent airline, with the result that it was usually revoked. According to BOAC, every new route awarded to an independent airline threatened to put it out of business. As a result, backers, bankers and investors got cold feet, saw that the government was not prepared to help independent airlines, and pulled the plug on their support.

The government was also winding down the number of military bases it operated overseas and had drastically reduced the number of troop flights British Eagle operated on its behalf.

The final straw came at the end of October 1968 when British Eagle was faced with heavy bills for fuel, landing charges and wages that rendered the company insolvent. Hambros, the airline's bankers, had been prepared to assist other ailing companies but regarded British Eagle as a lost cause. The *Sunday Telegraph* accused Bamberg of 'being brim full of bright ideas but he lacks the capacity for detailed administration and Hambros was unconvinced that the airline was sufficiently well run to be worth bailing out. Even so, Mr Bamberg emerges with credit. He offered to throw in his entire personal fortune.'

Why didn't the government step in?

The government's attitude towards privately-run airlines was equivocal, regarding them as something to be suffered rather than nourished. The Board of Trade thought that if commercial bankers were not prepared to support a private airline, it did not see why public funds should be used. There were also serious doubts about the quality of British Eagle's management. The government knew that the public at large would not suffer because BEA and BOAC would mop up British Eagle's passenger and cargo traffic.

A dramatic advertisement in *The Times* on 13 November 1968, written and paid for by Lawrence W. Levine, a Wall Street banker representing several American airlines and addressed to 'the political leaders in England – especially the Prime Minister', stated that

> if the government wants to help the country move forward, if it wants England to have a major role in civil aviation without hurting BOAC, if it wants those 2,500 Eagle jobs back with a possibility of making that 5,000 jobs later on – then I suggest that it cuts the 'double talk' and stops sitting around trying to figure out how to liquidate the empire that took thousands of years to build – and give Eagle's liquidators a couple of routes and give them quickly – instead of waiting around for a report by a distinguished commission whose conclusions anyone in the industry, in my opinion, could have given two years ago.

Former British Eagle staff member Dennis Martin from Woking, Surrey, remembers:

> It is ironic that the same day that Terminal 1 opened for business coincided with the announcement that British Eagle was to go into liquidation. Our first flights to Edinburgh, Glasgow and Belfast all left on schedule, and then at about 2.00 pm the news came through that our backers (Hambros Bank) had withdrawn their support on the basis of future plans (or lack of them) in the aviation industry by the government. Everyone was stunned. The airline had been part of our lives – and suddenly it was no longer there. We were powerless to do anything.

Jim Russell from Staines, Surrey, remembers that British Eagle staff were summoned to the airline's main hangar at Heathrow 'to be told the airline had run out of money and that operations would cease.'

He adds:

> The wind-down of British bases overseas and the withdrawal of Cunard's interest all seemed to come too near together. We worked damned hard to keep our airline going, but it was not to be.
>
> I remember well that evening, walking around Heathrow wondering how I was going to support my family: my wife Liz (who didn't yet know the situation), my two boys, Iain and Colin whose birthday party was that evening, a mortgage and two dogs.

Shortly after leaving British Eagle Jim opened a DIY shop in Staines and was later joined by Dennis Martin who introduced a gardening, plumbing and electrical department at the shop, known as 'The Handyman'.

So British Eagle was allowed to die, quickly and in pain; Heathrow lost one of its major airlines; and hundreds of airport-based staff were thrown out of work. Harold Bamberg later re-emerged as a private businessman in charge of Bamberg Enterprises, which specialized in commercial building schemes, including the creation of polo-playing arenas. He also became the UK representative for the American executive jet manufacturing company Beechcraft.

Bamberg's name is now almost forgotten by the UK's airline industry, but his legacy has resulted in the creation of a new breed of airline entrepreneurs prepared to take on the government and competing airlines in order to break their monopoly and offer lower fares to popular destinations. Others who followed in Bamberg's wake included buccaneering Sir Freddie Laker, Virgin Atlantic's Sir Richard Branson and founders of the late-twentieth-century's low-cost 'no frills' airlines, EasyJet and Ryanair. It is to Harold Bamberg that they owe a debt of gratitude, although most will not admit it.

Chapter 16

Heathrow Scoop!

This author spent twelve years (1966–78) reporting the news from Heathrow for the national print and broadcast media and it was great fun. I met film and sports stars, glamorous models, prime ministers, presidents, potentates and assorted other politicians from home and abroad, business tycoons and ordinary everyday people who for one reason or another found themselves in the news. Here are a few photographs of a few well-known 'faces' who travelled through Heathrow.

For over seven decades, Heathrow has been one of the country's single most productive news-gathering centres. The press was there on its first day

Photographers and reporters working for Brenard Press at Heathrow met with at least one showbiz star – sometimes more – every day. All the pictures that follow were taken by 'button-pushers' (an affectionate name given to photographers) who were always ready to snap photos of the great and the good from the business of show, including Hugh Hefner, founder and publisher of the *Playboy* empire, who flew to London in 1970 with an armful of Bunny Girls in his own jet-black DC9 jet, known as 'The Big Bunny'. It cost $5.9 million and is said to have included a large round waterbed for Mr Hefner's personal use in a special compartment … (*Brenard Press*)

and more than seventy years later, the airport still provides a steady flow of news copy and picture stories for the international media.

Bill Brenard's airport news-gathering operation finally closed its doors in the 1980s. In that time many of the company's photographers had been called 'paparazzi', but most of the celebrities they photographed were delighted to see them waiting as they emerged from their first-class cabins and headed off down airport corridors. For many, their picture would be in an evening newspaper that same night or in a daily newspaper on the following morning's breakfast table. Agents, PR people and promoters would go out of their way to let the airport press corps know that their clients were passing through Heathrow and the great and the

Comedian Tony Hancock and his wife Cicely laugh for the cameras before flying off to Italy on holiday.

good, the bad and the ugly always took care to disappear into aircraft toilets to wash, brush up and put on fresh make-up as their aircraft approached London air space.

There is no such thing as a permanent Heathrow press team any more. Airports are no longer glamorous or exciting places because millions of everyday people now travel through airports every year. They are no longer exciting places to visit. Airports are confusing, crowded and confounded, especially if flights are delayed or cancelled for one reason or another. Today's airports are expensive shopping malls that passengers have to walk through before passing along endless corridors in order to reach their aircraft. Airport toilets are far apart, seating is uncomfortable, food and drink expensive to buy and so-called 'duty-free' shops are a rip-off. So if Heathrow appears in the news today it usually concerns the controversial construction of a new runway, a strike or foul weather causing flight delays, cancellations and inconvenience for thousands of travellers. A film star, pop singer or a footballer travelling through Heathrow is no longer news, meaning that reporters and photographers have no need to be based at the airport from sun-up to sun-down to get a story unless it is about something very special.

There was a time up to around fifteen years ago when a band of airport pressmen were classed as 'trust-worthies' and carried passes allowing them to

French superstar actress Brigitte Bardot flies into London in 1967 to make a Western film with Sean Connery called *Shalako*.

Charlie Chaplin flies into London with his wife Oona to receive a knighthood from the queen in 1975. He is surrounded by police and other hangers-on, including this author who can be seen at the back surrounded by policemen and wearing glasses.

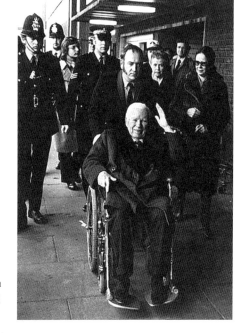

Opera star Maria Callas was always fashionably dressed whenever she passed through the airport. Here she is in 1958 wearing garments – including a hat – designed and made for her by Christian Dior. (*Brenard Press*)

An airport Nissen hut once used as a staff canteen became a press conference room when Laurence Olivier and Vivien Leigh travelled to London Airport to say goodbye to Marilyn Monroe and her playwright husband Arthur Miller after filming *The Prince and the Showgirl* at Shepperton. (*Author's Collection*)

Come fly with us! Rat-packers Dean Martin and Frank Sinatra leave a BOAC jet ready to travel into London to give charity concerts at the Royal Albert Hall.

move – more or less – freely throughout the terminals and walk right up to the doors of arriving and departing aircraft. The airlines loved them, especially when showbiz superstars chose a particular airline to fly with. Heathrow's management loved them because they kept the airport in the news day after day. Airline staff loved them too, because they enjoyed watching photographers rushing around taking pictures that helped fill the pages of their favourite newspapers the following day.

Chapter 17

The Supersonic Seventies:
Jumbo Jets, Concordes, Terrorists
and Time to Call in the Army

The 1970s was the decade when the world became a smaller place and far-flung cities could be reached faster and cheaper than ever before. It was the decade of mass transit air travel and Heathrow was at the epicentre of this activity. As the decade began it was handling 15.4 million passengers. At its end it was handling 27 million.

The airport's runways had to be extended from 9,000ft to 12,000ft during the autumn and winter of 1969 in readiness for the arrival of the first Boeing 747 'Jumbo Jet' in January 1970. Many of the world's leading airlines had placed orders for the massive aircraft, built to carry 385 passengers in comfort on routes that crossed the globe.

Heathrow invested £11 million in a major refurbishment programme to accommodate the giant aeroplane and the large influx of passengers it would carry to and from London. The age of the wide-body Jumbo Jet began at the airport shortly after 2.00 pm on 22 January 1970 when Pan American ferried the first 324 fare-paying Boeing 747 passengers across the Atlantic seven hours late thanks to technical problems in New York.

Dennis Stone Esq
Airport Photo Services Ltd
Resident Press Room
Queens Building
HEATHROW

In 1971 the airport celebrated its twenty-fifth anniversary with a first-day cover postage stamp and envelope. (*Author's Collection*)

The age of the wide-body Boeing 747 'Jumbo Jet' aircraft began at Heathrow after 2.00 pm on 22 January 1970 when Pan American ferried the first 324 fare-paying passengers across the Atlantic, seven hours late thanks to technical problems in New York. The 747 was also built in an all-cargo version and used by airlines including Flying Tigers in transatlantic routes from Heathrow. It could carry up to 100 tons of freight. (*Brenard Press*)

Airport staff and hundreds of sightseers who turned out to see the new aircraft land could scarcely believe their eyes when the first of Pan Am's twenty-five Boeing 747s roared its way into Heathrow. They had read about it in newspapers and seen television bulletins about the aircraft's trials, but now they were seeing it for themselves and wondered how anything so gigantic could ever get off the ground, let alone carry more than 300 passengers plus crew and a belly full of freight over the Atlantic.

The monster plane was due to return to New York later that evening but problems with one of the 747's doors caused take-off to be delayed for four hours. The 350-ton aircraft had encountered a multitude of problems during its development stage. There was concern over the kind of engines to be used to power the massive aeroplane, followed by others concerning the speed it might take to evacuate passengers if the plane experienced an emergency. The Heathrow delays were simply the latest problems to be overcome.

By the time the first aircraft had landed in London, BOAC had ordered eleven Boeing 747s but a pay dispute by pilots threatened to delay its introduction.

Within six months of its first New York–London service, Pan Am had carried more than 1 million passengers on the Boeing 747. A year later, nearly 100 Jumbo Jets were in operation with 17 airlines and the number of passengers travelling on the plane increased to 7 million. Since then, the aircraft's safety record has been good and although it has been involved in several incidents and accidents, none has been directly attributable to a fault with the aircraft, making it one of the most successful ever built. The Boeing 747 has dominated the airline passenger and cargo world for more than three decades, although that changed when the Airbus A380, seating between 555 and 840 passengers, came into commercial operation at Heathrow in 2006.

* * *

Concorde was designed to fly at twice the speed of sound, the result of equal partnership in design and technology between England and France. The supersonic aircraft made its unofficial Heathrow debut dramatically and unexpectedly on a wet Sunday afternoon on 13 September 1970; five years and four months before it was due to enter full commercial service. By this time, Heathrow's former commentator on the Queen's Building, Flo Kingdon, had moved on to become a member of the airport public relations team and remembered:

I was busy working with reporters and photographers who had come to the airport to report the arrival of British hostages who had been unfortunate enough to be on an aircraft hijacked by Palestinian terrorists. The passengers had been brought across the airport to hold a press conference in a building on the airport's northside and we were just finishing when suddenly there was a loud roar outside. I looked out of the window through the mist – and suddenly Concorde zoomed past out on the runway.

Concorde was designed to fly at twice the speed of sound; the result of equal partnership in design and technology between England and France. The supersonic aircraft made its unofficial Heathrow debut dramatically and unexpectedly on a wet Sunday afternoon on 13 September 1970; five years and four months before it was due to enter full commercial service. (*Brenard Press*)

All the press crowded around me immediately wanting to know what was going on. Concorde was towed to a stand close to where the press conference had been held and I rushed over and climbed the aircraft stairs and knocked on the door (which was open). I asked to speak to whoever was in charge. It was Brian Trubshaw, Concorde's chief test pilot. I could see that seats had been taken out of the cabin and replaced with all kinds of monitoring equipment and I edged my way to the front, where I told Mr Trubshaw that I had a large press group with me who were interested in Concorde's mysterious arrival. I asked him if he was prepared to give an impromptu press conference. He laughed and then agreed to meet everyone in the Queen's Building. He told me that Concorde had flown out of Farnborough to conduct some test flights and was heading for Filton, near Bristol. But Filton was fogged out and he needed somewhere else to land – and he was bursting for a chance to try out Heathrow's runways, which would eventually become its main UK operating base.

That was typical of Heathrow. You never knew what was going to happen next. The press was delighted. They had come to the airport for one story and went away with two.

Concorde's next Heathrow visit was on 21 January 1976 when the supersonic aircraft made its maiden flight from London to Bahrain in the colours of British Airways, the airline created by merging BOAC and BEA in 1974. An Air France Concorde was scheduled to depart from Paris to Rio de Janeiro at the same time and a massive party was held in an airport restaurant for the media and VIPs, including government ministers, members of the Opposition party, British and French plane-makers. Large TV split-screens showed the two airliners waiting to take off on their respective tarmacs in London and Paris at exactly 11.30 am. As the supersonic jets roared down their runways, the room was hushed and all eyes fixed on the front nose wheel of both aircraft. Never mind '*entente cordiale*', everyone wanted to know which Concorde would be first into the skies. Would it be the one outside the window at Heathrow, or the Air France version in Paris? Everyone held their breath, and then the nose wheel of the British Airways service lifted a full two seconds before the French plane.

It was a small victory for Britain, but politicians in the room were triumphant and a great cheer went up. The press corps were happy, too, as some serious betting had taken place as to which aircraft would be first off the ground. One pressman was so delighted with the result that he stepped backwards and onto the foot of an up-and-coming Conservative politician who had been a great champion of Concorde. Her name was Mrs Margaret Thatcher and more than forty years later the reporter still remembers her icy glare in his direction as Britain's future first female PM hobbled away, muttering under her breath something about clumsy reporters who had obviously consumed too much free food and drink on offer that day.*

* * *

Concorde was designed to fly at cruising speeds of 2,158 km/h, allowing it to cover the 1,350 miles to Bahrain two hours faster than subsonic jets. In 1976 British Airways boasted that the one-way fare was 'only £45 above the normal first-class fare.' While flying at supersonic speeds at an altitude that allowed passengers to see the curvature of the earth, those same passengers dined on gourmet meals: canapés, smoked salmon, breast of duck bigarade or fillet steak with Café de Paris butter, fresh strawberries with double cream, English cheeses, a choice of three wines, champagne, cognac… the list just went on. British Airways spent £33 on food and wine for every Concorde passenger. Travellers flying in the economy-class section of the airline's other aircraft were served food and drink costing just £3.50 per head.

Concorde's sleek and modern aircraft galley was built from new lightweight material, controlled by sophisticated electronics to ensure that all meals were simply perfect. It was a million miles away from what Mary Guthrie had to put up with in her primitive Avro Lancastrian 'Starlight' galley thirty years earlier.

---

* The author can testify to the accuracy of this incident: he was that 'clumsy reporter'!

Most of Britain's population took Concorde to their hearts, seeing the aircraft as a strong symbol of European technical co-operation and a great achievement for aviation. Concorde was wonderful to look at but she was a noisy beast. Whenever she roared into the air, hundreds of businesses in the Heathrow area had to excuse themselves while talking on the telephone until she had passed overhead. Every day Concorde triggered off hundreds of car alarms sensitive to the vibration it caused on the ground. The noise was murder for anyone living under her flight path. Everything stopped until Concorde had flown overhead, which was mercifully quick. Yet everyone loved to watch her shoot up into the sky like a beautiful dart, even those at Heathrow who saw her come and go every day. Anyone who ever saw Concorde felt a certain pride in their hearts for this unique aeroplane. Although only a small percentage of the British population ever flew in her, the majority felt ownership of her in some way. She is badly missed.

* * *

British Airways made its first appearance in 1935 as the country's second major airline after Imperial Airways. The brand name disappeared four years later when Britain's airline industry was nationalized and the name of Imperial Airways dominated the world's air lanes. It would be another forty-four years before the name returned after the state-controlled airline sector was

A collection of Boeing 747s, 707s and DC10s on a typical day at Heathrow in the summer of 1970. (*Barry Dix Collection*)

restructured and a single national carrier was created by merging BOAC and BEA into a single 'super' airline called British Airways.

Staff working for the two airlines hated the idea of a merger and attempts to bring the two companies together in previous decades had fallen at the first fence. BOAC, whose intercontinental routes flew the British flag in North and South America, Africa, Asia and Australasia, considered itself vastly superior to BEA, which carried the Union Jack on shorter European routes closer to home.

Prior to the merger, both airlines were hidebound by their respective cultural legacies, lack of focus, rising debt and ineffective management. Many passengers actually hated flying with BOAC. The company's aircraft were safe, reliable and comfortable, but they complained that staff were often snooty and superior in their attitude (as opposed to Pan Am, whose in-flight staff were famous for being rude and uncaring). The media said that once the merger had taken place, British Airways would be abbreviated to BA, standing for 'bloody awful'.

Thomas Marks from High Wycombe joined BOAC's engineering staff at London Airport in the mid-1950s and recalls:

There is no doubt about it, everyone working for BOAC prior to the merger considered themselves superior to just about everyone else working at the airport. Looking back, I now feel ashamed of this attitude. I put it down to the fact that everyone working for BOAC felt they were ambassadors for Britain. We thought we were better in everything we did. BOAC had the best planes and flew to the world's smartest destinations, carrying our great tradition with us wherever we went.

What we didn't know, of course, was that the airline was haemorrhaging money and was deep in debt. We occasionally read newspaper stories about the company's financial performance but didn't believe them because management made no public comment about the company's financial affairs. Every month staff members were given a magazine called *BOAC Review* which was full of articles about how fantastic BOAC was and how staff made this possible. And we believed it. We genuinely thought that everything we did turned to gold, so it came as a massive shock in later years to learn that BOAC had been trading almost insolvent for a long time. People who had worked at the airport for years were forced into early retirement and others made redundant. Even the public turned against us. We used to think that we were 'the world's favourite airline' and came to realise that we were far from being a favourite. We soon stopped feeling superior, I can tell you. At one stage I even avoided telling people who I worked for, such was the public's attitude towards BOAC.

The merger with BEA was a difficult one, but it made perfect sense. It was a chance for the airline to re-invent itself; something it tended to do over again every few years.

In addition to fleets of modern aircraft and route licences to prime destinations, BOAC and BEA also had other major assets: valuable take-off and landing slots at Heathrow Airport, the world's most profitable airport for airlines and real estate where each had its own headquarters and engineering bases.

The purpose of the merger was to combine the strengths offered by the two carriers, eliminate their combined weaknesses and create a profitable and customer-focused carrier, which would eventually become privatized via a stock exchange flotation. Everyone was happy; or so it seemed, apart from staff working for the two airlines. There was talk of industrial unrest. The prospect of redundancies loomed large as there were bound to be job duplications when the two airlines became one. There were many questions, and few answers seemed to be coming from respective managements. As a result, there was wild speculation and inaccurate predications about the outcome.

The merger went ahead, a new joint management was appointed, aircraft were repainted in a new livery and financial losses continued. One member of the airline's accounts team joked that when the time came to produce an annual report and accounts, Tipp-Ex (a white-coloured fluid used to correct typing errors) was delivered to the airline in 100-gallon containers.

At the time of the merger, John Balding had risen to become BOAC's chief investigator of accidents and air safety (a position that later won him an MBE). He recalls that one of the first things the newly-merged airline did was to take air safety into their control, appointing John in charge of air safety on long-distance routes and another staff member on short-haul and regional routes. In 1977 John was named chief air safety investigator for the entire airline. 'And all the time the merger was going through, I thought

British Airways chairman, Lord King, desperately wanted his airline to occupy all of Terminal 4 on an exclusive basis, but following a heated exchange with airport authority chairman Sir Norman Payne, King was told that it was not possible for a single airline to monopolize the building. (*BBC*)

that I would be out of a job and so did hundreds, thousands of others,' he recalled.

In 1991 Margaret Thatcher appointed Sir John King to be the airline's new chairman. British Airways was carrying an overdraft of £1 billion. The corporation was top-heavy with staff and operated many unprofitable routes. Thatcher charged King with the task of turning the loss-making airline around and preparing it for privatization but refused to pour any further state aid into its future. She kept telling King: 'Remember John, there is no money.'

King was forced to cut one-third of all jobs at British Airways, withdraw aircraft from unprofitable routes and reduce capacity. He appointed a new board including several directors from outside the airline industry, who – like himself – could offer plenty of experience and success in other commercial business activities. One such new board member was Colin Marshall, a man with plenty of senior management experience and who became the airline's new chief executive. The challenge facing King, Marshall and the airline's board was to turn British Airways from an appalling to an appealing airline.

A priority task was to make the airline's staff begin to believe in their company once again. An ambitious training programme called 'Putting People First' was introduced across the organization and Marshall himself spent time mingling with staff and passengers. A new advertising campaign was created by Saatchi & Saatchi while Landor Associates, a US-based design company, produced new visual identification for the airline's fleet incorporating elements from the British flag on aircraft tailplanes and fuselages.

In 1997 British Airways was successfully floated on the London Stock Exchange. Staff were given a stake in this success and offered shares in their company. After many years of dissatisfaction, they slowly began to believe in their airline again. The flotation united the company, which went on to become a profitable enterprise. However, it did not put an end to all the airline's woes and over the next few years, British Airways faced many new challenges. More staff and unprofitable routes would be axed and the airline forced to re-think its role in the face of challenges from low-cost carriers such as EasyJet, Ryanair, Norwegian and Whizz Air. Yet, unlike many other national flag-carriers unable to survive problems confronting carriers in the early years of the twenty-first century (such as Sabena, Swissair, Iberia, Alitalia plus other European and American carriers teetering on the edge of bankruptcy), British Airways is a great survivor with an even greater future ahead.

* * *

Industrial relations in Britain reached a low ebb in the 1970s. It was the decade in which the country was plunged into economic chaos and in which a three-day working week and the 'winter of discontent' became potent symbols. A wave of strikes paralysed the country and Britain's European neighbours dubbed industrial unrest 'the British disease'. Disputes involved refuse collectors, deep-sea fishermen, car workers, coal miners, postmen, lorry drivers, ship-builders, hospital workers, civil servants, social workers, printing trade unions, even Yeoman Wardens (better known as Beefeaters) at the Tower of London. They were unhappy with pay, working conditions, or both; they all tried to negotiate with their respective managements and talks had failed. There was only one avenue left open to them: to withdraw their labour and go on strike.

Heathrow had its own share of industrial unrest in the 1970s. In March 1970 the airport was shut down for the first time in twenty-four years when its firemen – employed by the airport authority – walked out over a dispute about shift allowances and working conditions.

It is illegal for an airport to operate without a full complement of fire officers on hand to deal with an emergency, and aircraft sat on the tarmac unable to move for two days. No incoming planes could land either, costing airlines thousands of pounds in lost revenue. Collectively the airlines put Heathrow's management under pressure to resolve the dispute and the airport's owners were forced into reaching a compromise with firemen and allowing the airport to re-open. It took days to clear the backlog of delayed flights and passengers.

The late Fred Gore from Stanwell, Middlesex was at the centre of much of the airport's trade union activity at this time. Born in London's East End, Fred

In March 1970 the airport was shut down for the first time in twenty-four years when its firemen – employed by the airport authority – walked out over a dispute about shift allowances and working conditions. It is illegal for an airport to operate without a full complement of fire officers on hand to deal with an emergency, and aircraft sat on the tarmac unable to move for two days. No incoming planes could land either, costing airlines thousands of pounds in lost revenue. Collectively the airlines put Heathrow's management under pressure to resolve the dispute, and following a mass meeting of firemen (see above) the airport's owners were forced into reaching a compromise with firemen and allowing the airport to re-open. It took days to clear the backlog of delayed flights and passengers. (*Brenard Press*)

Fred Gore was at the centre of much of the airport's trade union activity in the 1960s and 1970s. He remembered Heathrow being 'a wonderful place to work at that time, but industrial relations left a lot to be desired. Although a constitution had been set up by the Labour government of the day – which in many ways was ahead of its time – they did not address day-to-day problems at Heathrow and there were a number of short stoppages and disputes.' (*The Author*)

moved to Hanworth shortly before the Second World War and volunteered for the Royal Navy in 1943 working as a torpedo man. He learned basic electrics in the navy and when the war ended became a member of the electricians' trade union, ETU (Electricians Trade Union). He joined BEA as an aircraft electrician in the early 1950s and recalls:

> Heathrow was a wonderful place to work at that time, but industrial relations left a lot to be desired. Although a constitution had been set up by the Labour government of the day – which in many ways was ahead of its time – they did not address day-to-day problems at Heathrow and there were a number of short stoppages and disputes.
>
> A big electricians' strike in 1961 disrupted the airline for about five weeks. Within a week we had the airline grounded. To get around the problem and to keep flying, BEA airlifted equipment and instruments for maintenance to other airports, which resulted in my getting in touch with these airports. Working closely with the World Federation of Trade

Unions (an international trade union organization which supports and encourages action by trade unions in every country) I flew to these countries asking for their support. For example, I would fly out to Prague, meet with unions there, make lots of contacts and ask them to support our cause by refusing to co-operate with the airline. I did the same in the Soviet Union and countries all around the Iron Curtain states. They were all marvellous and most co-operative. It made the airline's management realise that you couldn't just fly an airliner out to another airport for maintenance work. Lord Douglas, the Chairman of BEA at the time, said that if the strike went on any longer we would all be out of a job – including himself.

Strangely enough, once the dust had settled the airline started to expand its operations and one of the political decisions was to set up a service to Moscow. There were problems about which route the airline would fly. So, I contacted my friends in Russia to see if they could help BEA establish a scheduled route between Moscow and London. Lord Douglas was most helpful in supplying me with all kinds of gifts for me to take there. So, it wasn't all antagonism. The unions were in a position to help management. There was co-operation.

When the airlines merged to create British Airways, there were fears which always exist in a merger that there would be redundancies. If you merge two instrument shops together, you're going to have what management believes will be job duplication and surpluses. So, the new BA Board decided to call a conference for all senior staff and we were asked to submit questions we might have about the future. Management asked for questions beforehand so they could consider their answers. So, we submitted questions asking for guarantees that there would be no redundancies and asked if that question could be addressed as number one.

The question was asked and Roy Watts, BEA's Chairman, read it out and told us that no employer in the country would give workers such a guarantee. I and all the other union representatives – there must have been 200 of us – walked out of the conference and went back to the base to report what had been said. A week later I was sent for by Roy Watts' office and told that the airline was prepared to guarantee there would be no redundancies, on the understanding that trade unions would co-operate with the merger.

We set up various working parties to look at different aspects of the merger and I was elected Chairman. Our job was to look at ways of bringing all sections together. This was an opportunity for workers themselves to try and resolve issues brought about by the merger. As a result, not one dispute arose. There were disagreements about wages, but nothing arising from the merger.

From that day onwards, it was agreed that if unions didn't reach agreement, you went back to the drawing board. It was important to keep on talking and negotiating. Eventually all sections were merged including outstations. My job was to go to all these outstations and talk about the merger. As a result, we reached an agreement in which no one was forcefully made redundant at British Airways. Nobody. As union representatives, our job was to negotiate for good pensions, wages and working conditions. And we achieved that.

A major Heathrow dispute that hit the headlines late in 1969 followed news that a Canadian company called General Aviation Services (GAS) had been contracted to provide a range of ground services and maintenance for Heathrow airlines. After correspondence was passed to the unions indicating that GAS intended to grab contracts for anything from cabin services to engineering, ground staff opposed the arrival of a competitive company and took industrial action. Other unions representing staff working for 200 firms came to their support.

The dispute that followed has gone down in the annals of Heathrow trade union history. Many union veterans now compare the GAS dispute with the 1971 Upper Clyde ship-builders strike in protest about shipyard redundancies and mass action in July 1972 when the state was forced to release five shop stewards – known as the 'Pentonville Five' – imprisoned under Edward Heath's anti-union laws. Fred takes up the story:

GAS generated terrific opposition from the unions, because the company threatened their jobs. GAS opened premises on the airport's northside and bought new equipment – but failed to sign up any airlines. The unions were ready to campaign in opposition to them because our members' jobs were sacrosanct. There was a gradual build-up to opposing this company, which finally secured a contract from Iberia. It claimed to have three others, but I think they were just paper contracts. A mass meeting was called at Brentford Football Ground where I had the job of moving the resolution that unless they withdrew from Heathrow we would 'black' any airline or company using the services of GAS.

It was a terrific mass meeting, probably one of the biggest ever seen in the Heathrow area. About 15,000 people walked out of the airport to attend and the football stadium was full – perhaps the biggest gate ever. It was a terrific effort. The vote was unanimous in favour of a strike. There was also a demonstration in the airport's Central Area where the police used dogs to try and control the men. This resulted in questions later being asked in parliament.

The airports authority, Heathrow's custodians, decided they would have to take action against us and injunctions were served on individuals. Strangely enough, I didn't get one. My colleagues all received one, but I didn't and I don't know why. But it made no difference. We were adamant that we would 'black' any airlines using GAS.

It was just before Christmas and court cases were about to be heard when a statement was released stating that as a gesture of Christmas goodwill, the injunctions would be withdrawn. The National Joint Council (NJC) was meeting on this subject in London and were, perhaps, not on the same wavelength as us who worked at the airport. These were full-time paid officials who didn't see things in the same way as we did. They wanted us to compromise and let GAS have a little bit of business. But we didn't want a foreign company coming into Heathrow, taking revenue from our own country and jobs away from union members.

I had a hell of a job trying to persuade them to see our point of view. Edward Heath (prime minister 1970–74) sent one of his special envoys to see me. He was an elderly man, a farmer, and he said he didn't know why he'd been picked for the job. He said he knew nothing about aeroplanes. His job was to try and build a bridge between the unions and the government of the day and go back to Number 10 with some kind of solution.

At the end of the day the NJC came down in favour of us and GAS went back from whence they came. What we did, we did for the benefit of the country as a whole. We needed to protect the job security of our members. We believed we were doing the right thing.

There were other disputes at Heathrow and according to Fred 'people used to claim that we came out on strike when the daffodils came out', but once the unions had obtained procedural agreement to resolve differences, strikes became a thing of the past and unions and management were in a position to work towards settlements.

A 1971 newspaper described Fred as follows: 'He's left-wing, there's no doubt about that. But he would probably prefer the term progressive to militant.' 'He's not a member of the lunatic left,' said a colleague. 'I knew I could always count on him. I would much sooner see a positive man like Fred. He's ruthless, but a very astute politician.'

On retirement, Fred managed an unemployment centre in Hounslow and became a Labour councillor in Spelthorne Borough. Fred was still actively involved in trade union activities right up to his early death in 2009.

Throughout his life he believed that Heathrow was a great place for a career and actively campaigned for more young apprentices to come to the airport and undergo training schemes:

'I can remember a time when 600 engineering apprentices were going through the system at one time,' he recalled. 'Once they had received their final City & Guilds certification, they could get a job on the shop floor. You would see ordinary working-class lads get an apprenticeship, go to a technical college and be recommended to go on to university. Many of today's airport and airline managers are people who went through that system. Sadly, far fewer apprentices go through it today.'

* * *

Security was another great Heathrow issue in the 1970s. Increasing numbers of aircraft were being hijacked by terrorists and attacked both on the ground and in the air. Many passengers were taken hostage and some were murdered.

Although aircraft hijacking was nothing new, it reached new heights on 6 September 1970 – later dubbed 'Skyjack Sunday' – when five passenger planes were hijacked by militant members of the People's Front for the Liberation of Palestine demanding release of Arab dissidents held in a Swiss jail. The incident involved a BOAC VC10 jet bound for Heathrow from Bombay, a TWA 707 from Frankfurt, a Swissair DC8 from Zurich, an El Al Boeing 707 and a Pan Am Boeing 747, both from Amsterdam.

The BOAC, TWA and Swissair planes were flown to a former RAF airfield in Jordan – known as Dawson's Field – while the Pan Am aircraft was ordered to fly to Cairo. On the El Al flight over Europe a passenger managed to pin down a female Arab hijacker called Leila Khalid who was holding a hand grenade, while an airline steward managed to tackle another terrorist. Shots were fired, killing an Arab militant and wounding a crew member, but the pilot was able to make a daring emergency landing at Heathrow. Leila Khalid was arrested by armed police at Heathrow and taken away to Ealing police station. After 28 days she was released in exchange for more than 400 hostages.

In Cairo, hostage passengers were taken to safety while the giant Boeing 747 was blown up out on the airfield. Captive passengers travelling on planes sitting in the desert heat in Jordan were released and the three jets wired with dynamite and detonated.

Security at Heathrow was stepped up following 'Skyjack Sunday'. Passenger searches and devices for scanning baggage and cargo were introduced. Occasionally there would be breaches of security and someone – usually a newspaper reporter (but not one of the airport's resident press corps) – would

Although aircraft hijacking was nothing new, it reached new heights in September 1970 – later dubbed 'Skyjack Sunday' – when five passenger planes were hijacked by members of the People's Front for the Liberation of Palestine demanding release of Arab dissidents held in a Swiss jail. The incident involved a BOAC VC10 jet bound for Heathrow. On an El Al flight over Europe a passenger managed to pin down a female Arab hijacker called Leila Khalid who was holding a hand grenade, while an airline steward managed to tackle another terrorist. Shots were fired, killing an Arab militant and wounding a crew member, but the pilot was able to make a daring emergency landing at Heathrow. Leila Khalid was arrested by armed police at Heathrow and taken to Ealing police station. After twenty-eight days she was released in exchange for more than 400 hostages. (*Both images courtesy of United Press International*)

claim to have carried a potentially dangerous item on board an aircraft without detection.

Threats to Heathrow security also came from sources closer to home. Following the 'Bloody Sunday' killings in Belfast in 1972 when thirteen men were shot dead by British paratroopers in Londonderry, the IRA stepped up its nationalist terror campaign. BEA flights from Heathrow to Belfast were boarded and disembarked in a special security-monitored area and searches of passengers and airport staff going about their work increased dramatically.

Then one Saturday in 1974, the British army 'invaded' Heathrow Airport. Few people expected to see troops driving around the airport's perimeter roads in armoured vehicles and wandering through passenger terminals carrying guns, including the soldiers themselves.

Following a strong tip-off to government officials that the airport could expect a terrorist attack at any time, Prime Minister Edward Heath ordered soldiers from the Blues and Royals Regiment based in nearby Windsor barracks to descend on Heathrow Airport. The first anyone – including

In 1974, the British army 'invaded' Heathrow Airport. Few people expected to see troops driving around the airport's perimeter roads in armoured vehicles and wandering through passenger terminals carrying guns, including the soldiers themselves. (*Brenard Press*)

airport officials and the police – knew about the troop invasion was when four armoured vehicles rolled through the airport tunnel and proceeded to drive around roads in the central area causing traffic chaos. Military vehicles were also seen on the airport's southern perimeter road.

When an airport reporter (this author) contacted Heathrow's management asking for an explanation, officials were forced to admit that they had no idea what was going on. It soon became clear that the Ministry of Defence had experienced a 'communications breakdown' in attempts to inform the British Airports Authority that the army was on its way to defend Heathrow. The resident media jumped into cars and made their way around airport roads to try to speak to soldiers. They soon encountered an armed vehicle, from the top of which a soldier stood waving his hands at the pressmen indicating that he wanted them to stop. The media men thought they were about to be arrested when the soldier asked: 'Excuse me gents, have you any idea what's going on? Do you know why we're here, because nobody has told us the reason?'

Airport police were furious that the army had descended onto their 'patch' and confirmed that they, too, had not been informed about the army's arrival. Security staff became confused when several armed soldiers demanded to be allowed to pass through passenger controls into departure lounges only accessible to authorized travellers and airport staff holding the correct passes. The soldiers were eventually allowed to pass through airport controls, providing they were accompanied by reluctant police officers. It appears that they only wanted to enter the lounge in order to get a cup of tea from the departure lounge cafeteria.

Hours after the troops had descended on the airport and film of their confused activities had appeared on lunchtime television news bulletins, the Ministry of Defence issued a statement confirming that a terrorist threat had been received and the army had been ordered to place 'a ring of steel' around the airport. The 'ring of steel' was lifted at 5.00 pm when the troops went home to Windsor. They failed to appear the following morning (Sunday) but came back at 9.00 am on the following Monday, pulling out again at 5.00 pm. By the end of the week Prime Minister Heath must have felt that he had made his point to whatever terrorist group had made the threat (it was never made clear who they were), because Britain's '9 to 5' army failed to return the following week and only returned to the airport on the odd occasion. It would be another thirty years before the army returned to Heathrow following a terrorist alert, this time on the orders of Tony Blair.

On Sunday, 19 May 1974 – the same date that Merlyn Rees, then Secretary of State for Northern Ireland, announced a State of Emergency in Ulster – the IRA planted a series of bombs which exploded in Heathrow's Terminal 1 car park. The explosion could be heard across the airport. Two people were injured and rushed to hospital. More than fifty vehicles were damaged in the bomb-blackened car park, some of them totally written off.

Jokes surrounding the comings and goings of the army at Heathrow suddenly stopped. The IRA had been allowed to get as close to Heathrow, its passengers and staff as it was possible to get. Although the damage could have been worse, the terrorists from Ulster had made their presence felt. They had issued their warning signal and nobody complained any more about being searched as they passed through Heathrow's security system.

It was not the last Heathrow was to hear from the IRA. They would return with a series of bombing attacks two decades later.

* * *

Following events in New York on 11 September 2001 when aircraft were hijacked and flown into the World Trade Center and Pentagon buildings, security at the world's airports has never been tighter. Security procedures are a necessary pain. They have cost airports and airlines huge amounts of money and resulted in a 'security tax' built into the cost of airline tickets.

Because of security procedures, passengers now have to arrive at airport check-in desks hours before departure in order to pass through screening devices. Long queues form as passengers remove jackets, coats, belts, watches, mobile phones, loose change and keys into special containers which pass through X-ray machines, while the travellers walk through devices designed to register other suspect objects concealed in passenger luggage. Sometimes passengers are also body-searched and required to remove shoes for closer examination.

A nuisance? Yes. A necessity? Definitely. Heathrow today is one of the safest and most secure airports in the world, although there will always be someone prepared to put this to the test and challenge the limits of security staff and equipment, resulting in even longer queues and delays.

* * *

Back in 1943 when Professor Abercrombie laid out plans for London's new airport he had envisaged a rail connection to central London via an 'electric railway to Waterloo and Victoria by means of a short branch to Feltham. A two-mile extension of the tube railway from Hounslow West would also give direct connection with the Underground system.' The underground railway finally arrived at Heathrow thirty-four years later.

It took the form of a £71 million extension to the Piccadilly Line to Hatton Cross, on the airport's edge and later diving down underneath the airport's runways and curving around to a new Underground station in the heart of the airport's terminal complex called Heathrow Central.

The queen formally unveiled the underground link between Hatton Cross and Heathrow Central on 16 December 1977 when Heathrow became the first airport in the world to offer a rapid rail link to a capital city centre. Heathrow to Piccadilly could be achieved in around thirty-five minutes. Her Majesty travelled to the new station by Tube from Hatton Cross – designated a 'Royal Train' for the three-minute journey – which broke a ceremonial tape as it came to a standstill on the westbound platform. It arrived four minutes late. (*Author's Collection*)

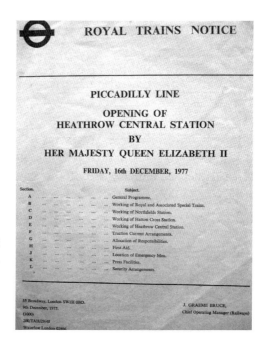

The queen formally unveiled the underground link on 16 December 1977 when Heathrow became the first airport in the world to offer a rapid rail link to a capital city centre. Heathrow to Piccadilly could be achieved in around thirty-five minutes. Her Majesty travelled to the new station by Tube from Hatton Cross – designated a 'Royal Train' for the three-minute journey – which broke a ceremonial tape as it came to a standstill on the westbound platform. It arrived four minutes late.

The queen, whose grandfather George V had pioneered the 'twopenny tube' in 1890, was taken on a tour of the station and actually purchased a ticket from one of the new machines. A reporter covering the occasion noted that she did not reach into her royal purse for coins but was handed 80p by the station's chief booking clerk. The queen paid tribute to airport staff as she unveiled a commemorative plaque marking the opening of the new service, designed to carry 11 million passengers in its first year. The single-fare cost of 80p compared favourably with the £1.00 bus fare into Central London and £5.50 taxi charge. Today (2019) it costs £6.00 for a single fare from Heathrow to Central London; £6.00 travelling by bus; from £35.00 by taxi; and £25.00 by the Heathrow Express train.

Since 1977, the Piccadilly Line to Heathrow has been expanded to include branch lines to Terminals 4 and 5.

In 1999, Tony Blair officially opened the Heathrow Express which provides fast, efficient travel between Heathrow and London-Paddington in fifteen minutes. The rapid rail link was introduced after Heathrow's management announced that its vision was to see half of all passengers using the airport arriving and departing by public transport.

Heathrow Express cost £450m to construct. Trains run at fifteen-minute intervals and services start at 5.00 am, finishing just before midnight. At Paddington visitors can connect to the rest of the London Underground network, allowing them to continue their journey further into London if required. Passengers with return air tickets can check in and complete boarding formalities at Paddington, leaving them free to head straight for the departure gate on arrival at Heathrow.

The Piccadilly Line and Heathrow Express are both examples of late-twentieth-century transport technology for the capital's premier airport, originally conceived in the dark days of the Second World War and finally taking between thirty-three and fifty-four years to realize. Time certainly flies, but the wheels that make airport-city transport links turn take a little longer.

* * *

At a few minutes past 5 o'clock on a quiet Sunday afternoon in June 1972, 112 passengers boarded BEA Trident G-ARPI – known as 'Papa India' – at Heathrow bound for Brussels. Six regular crew members were also rostered to fly on the aircraft that day. Less than two minutes after taking off from runway 28R, the plane dropped out of the sky and 6,000ft later crashed into a field on the edge of Staines, Middlesex; a populous town 3 miles south-west of the airport. 'Papa India' missed the town centre, several residential roads and a large gas storage unit by a few hundred yards.

Eyewitness Adrian Bailey, aged 15, said: 'I heard the plane circling overhead and there was a spluttering sound as though the engines were cutting out – then there was a thud like a clap of thunder.' The fuselage ploughed into trees and the tail section landed 50 yards away from the rest of the wreckage.

Father Peter Knott, Roman Catholic chaplain at Heathrow's St George's chapel, was driving along the A30 when he saw the aircraft plummet into the field. He was one of the first on the scene. He climbed a low fence and rushed to the wreckage, which lay in three large pieces with the tailplane sitting at an angle of 45 degrees into the air. He later recalled total silence apart from the sound of birdsong. Inside the main fuselage he found a scene of total devastation, dead passengers still strapped into their seats. As he moved down the aisle he noticed movement coming from one passenger. Clearly the passenger was close to death and Father Knott administered the last rites.

Moments later the police, fire service and other rescuers were on the scene just as a fire broke out in the crashed plane. Flames were quickly extinguished

At a few minutes past 5.00 pm on a quiet Sunday afternoon in June 1972, 112 passengers boarded BEA Trident G-ARPI – known as 'Papa India' – at Heathrow bound for Brussels. Six regular crew members were also rostered to fly on the aircraft that day. Less than two minutes after taking off, the plane dropped out of the sky and 6,000ft later crashed into a field on the edge of Staines, Middlesex. 'Papa India' missed the town centre, several residential roads and a large gas storage unit by just a few hundred yards. (*Author's Collection*)

and the passenger still alive and discovered by Father Knott – a businessman from Dublin – was removed and taken to a local hospital, where he died shortly afterwards. A young girl was also found alive but died moments after being removed from the wreckage. There were no other survivors and the crash of 'Papa India' marked the first time that more than 100 people had been killed in a British air accident.

Days later, BEA Chairman Sir Henry Marking said that there was 'no reason to suspect sabotage'. A later inquiry by the Air Accidents Investigation Branch concluded that a 'speed error had caused the plane to stall.' An autopsy on Captain Stanley Keys, who was in charge of the flight that day, revealed that he was suffering from a heart condition that may have been causing him pain during the fatal take-off. It was later learned that prior to boarding the flight, Captain Keys had been involved in a disagreement with another pilot in BEA's Heathrow Crew Room regarding a labour issue, which may have raised his blood pressure, in turn impairing his judgement while at the controls.

Other issues arose from the crash, most notably a lack of training among BEA crew about what action to take when a fellow crew member became incapacitated at the controls. It was generally accepted that the plane could have been saved if flying crew had been more aware of danger signals.

The 'Papa India' disaster plunged Heathrow into a state of deep gloom for many weeks following the crash. People living in and around the crash site were in shock. After twenty-six years, the town had grown used to Heathrow. Hundreds of its residents worked there. The Trident's wreckage remained in the field for days while accident investigators carried out their inquiries. Local people passed the crash site every day on their way to and from their airport jobs. They reflected on how close part of their town and scores of its residents had come to being wiped out or injured by an aircraft flying from the place on which many depended for their livelihoods.

Thirty-four years after 'Papa India' fell from the sky, the field where its wreckage came to a halt and 118 passengers and crew died, remained an empty space. In June 2004, the people of Staines remembered the disaster by opening a memorial garden at the scene of the crash and unveiled a specially-commissioned stained-glass window in nearby St Mary's church.

At a service of dedication, local Councillor John O'Hara said: 'All of us associated with that dreadful event have our own memories, but Staines has always lacked a memorial to the tragedy, so that those who wish to reflect may do so in dignity.' The window and garden were the result of moves within the Staines community to remedy the situation. Financial support came from the airport authority, British Airways and the local council.

'The "Papa India" disaster was the worst aircraft accident in British history, and with the exception of the Lockerbie outrage, that remains so today,' said Councillor O'Hara. 'Time heals wounds, but we will never forget.'

Chapter 18

The 1980s: 'We lived at the right time'

A s the 1970s drew to a close, 27 million passengers were using Heathrow each year. Terminals were congested and there was an urgent need for an additional one, although two would have been better. Space in the central area was a problem and there was no room for additional buildings of any size to sit alongside Terminals 1, 2 and 3, but there was space alongside Heathrow's south-east perimeter.

By 1978 when an empty plot of land for Terminal 4 had been allocated, Frederick Gibberd – the man responsible for designing most of Heathrow's key buildings – had retired and the job of drawing up plans for the new building went to the architectural practice of Scott Brownrigg & Turner. Their design was influenced by the post-modernist styles of Richard Rogers' Pompidou Centre in Paris and the London headquarters of the Stock Exchange, although the new terminal's exterior could not have been more different.

The site lay within the airport's boundaries close to the A30 Great South-West Road and £200 million was allocated for its construction once a public inquiry had taken place. Following pressure from local councils surrounding Heathrow, up to half of the inquiry was held within local communities, allowing residents, businesses and elected representatives to state their case on their own doorsteps. To give everyone with something to say a chance, local inquiries were held in town halls and civic centres during afternoons and evenings. The rest of the inquiry took place at London's County Hall starting in May 1978.

In a report designed to promote its case for the new building, the airport authority said that the terminal would create between 3,000 and 6,000 new jobs by 1987. The report promised that impact on local housing would be 'slight' and that road traffic would increase by 'no more than 17 per cent' once the terminal opened. The report also stated that Terminal 4 would allow Heathrow to handle 38 million passengers and that 'the building is needed as soon as possible to ensure the UK remains at the forefront of the world civil air transport industry.'

The public inquiry resulted in the airport authority receiving the green light to go ahead and build Terminal 4. Objections were widespread, mostly on the grounds of noise, use of green belt land in construction of access roads and disruption to community services. Some groups stated that the multi-million-pound investment could be better spent elsewhere in the country.

The spacious new terminal was designed to accommodate twenty of the world's largest aircraft at any one time. Its design would allow arriving and departing passengers to be totally segregated from each other. The departures area was massive, but so was the distance that some passengers had to travel in order to board aircraft parked at the furthest aircraft stands from the passenger lounge.

The terminal's large departure area was deliberately built in the style of a great bare hall in order to discourage what BAA called 'weepers' – friends of relatives travelling to the airport to say goodbye to passengers – from staying too long.

Areas around the building and on the opposite side of the road were carefully landscaped with a small series of undulating hills designed to reduce noise levels created by aircraft and motor traffic using the terminal. The hills separated the terminal and its roadways from part of the small community of Bedfont which almost ran up to the side of the new building.

British Airways Chairman, Lord King, desperately wanted his airline to occupy the entire new terminal on an exclusive basis, but following a heated exchange with airport authority Chairman Sir Norman Payne, King was told that it was not possible for a single airline to monopolize the building.

British Airways, however, did become the terminal's main user when it was finally opened by the Prince and Princess of Wales on 1 April 1986, sharing it with other smaller carriers.

* * *

During the 1970s and 1980s, Heathrow acquired the unfortunate nickname of 'thiefrow' following a number of robberies from airport cargo buildings and passenger baggage. Airport staff were often placed under suspicion. The majority of Heathrow's employees were – and remain – honest, hardworking folk, but occasionally one bad apple would spoil it for the rest of the barrel and be accused of theft.

In November 1983 an armed gang wearing balaclavas and wearing security uniforms carried out Britain's largest ever robbery at Heathrow Airport. More than £25 million-worth of gold bullion destined for the Far East was stolen from a warehouse owned by the Brink's–Mat Company early one morning.

Police estimated that around six people were involved. The men overcame warehouse guards, terrorized them into revealing secret alarm codes, handcuffed them and then disabled electronic security devices. They hit one of the security guards over the head with a pistol and poured petrol over two others.

Once inside the security vault, the robbers used the warehouse's own forklift truck to transport 76 boxes containing nearly 7,000 gold ingots to a waiting van. Some £100,000-worth of cut and uncut diamonds were also seized. Fifteen minutes after the thieves had left, one of the security guards managed to raise the alarm.

Only three members of the gang were ever convicted. Two were jailed for twenty-five years and a third served fourteen years for handling some of the stolen gold. Despite a huge police investigation, most of the gold has still to be recovered, having 'vanished' into the criminal underworld. It is also said that anyone wearing gold jewellery purchased in the UK after 1983 is probably wearing Brink's-Mat gold …

* * *

In January 1986 three people arrived at British Airways' Heathrow headquarters with invitations to a luncheon party in their pockets. All three were no strangers to the airport, although it had been some years since the trio had been there in their capacity as flying crew or airline passengers.

At the door they gave their names to a girl checking invitations. First to arrive was a smartly-dressed 75-year-old gentleman who declined the glass of wine offered on arrival. He gave his name in a booming voice: 'Air Vice Marshal Donald Bennett, CB, CBE, DSO.' The man who had flown the first international flight from Heathrow had returned to the place where the airport's history had begun four decades earlier.

Bennett was guest of honour at a special celebration for 200 guests marking both the airport's fortieth anniversary and the founding of British South American Airways, the airline that had made civil aviation history on 1 January 1946. Since being forced out of BSAA in 1948, Bennett had unsuccessfully dabbled in politics, flown numerous sorties during the Berlin Airlift, started a charter passenger and cargo airline using the same ill-fated Tudor aircraft he had championed at BSAA, attempted to revive interest in flying boats and purchased most of a small airfield in Surrey where the local council refused him development permission, fearing he would turn it into a major airport.

Some claimed that Bennett had become a bitter old man, in the habit of telephoning Heathrow's switchboard demanding to speak to the airport director to protest about their claim that the first Heathrow flight was one that took off on 25 March 1946 and not his Lancastrian 'Star Light' which had departed under the full glare of publicity on 1 January. The airport director ungraciously refused to return Bennett's calls and he was usually diverted

By Patricia Clough

The 40th anniversary of the first passenger-carrying flight from Heathrow Airport, London, was celebrated at the weekend by three members of the original crew.

Air Vice-Marshal Don Bennett, the pilot, Captain Robert Alabaster, the navigator, and Marie Guthrie, the "stargirl" or stewardess, attended the unveiling of a plaque in the Terminal One VIP lounge, commemorating their 36-hour flight to Buenos Aires. Their route went via Lisbon, Bathurst (now Banjul in The Gambia), Natal, Rio de Janeiro and Montevideo, and the crew remained on duty throughout.

The aircraft, a four-engined Lancastrian Starlight, a derivation of the wartime Lancaster bomber, carried 11 passengers and six crew on the first of a series of proving flights to South America by British South American Airways.

Heathrow Airport was not officially opened until five months later, on May 31, 1946.

The three recalled that Heathrow, now the busiest airport in the world, was simply a collection of tents and caravans. The control tower, a single-storey brick building, functioned for the first time for their flight.

"The airport looked like a runway under construction, which was almost what it was", Air Vice-Marshal Bennett said. "We had to ask the contractors three days beforehand if they could clear the runway so we could take off."

Heathrow now handles around 30 million passengers a year travelling to 200 destinations on 70 airlines. It has three main runways and a fourth terminal, which will increase traffic by another eight million passengers, is to be opened in April.

A toast by Captain Robert Alabaster (left), Marie Guthrie and Air Vice-Marshal Don Bennett in front of a photograph of the official inauguration.

In January 1986 three people arrived at British Airways' Heathrow headquarters with invitations to a luncheon party in their pockets. All three were no strangers to the airport, although it had been some years since the trio had been there in their capacity as flying crew or airline passengers. They were Cliff 'Alibe' Alabaster, Mary Cunningham (née Guthrie) and Air Vice Marshal Don Bennett. (*Skyport*)

to the airport's public relations department. Former airport reporter Ray Berry fielded one of Bennett's calls in his later role as an airport PR man and remembers how angry and insulted the old air vice marshal appeared to be as he insisted that his flight be recognized as the airport's first departure.

It would have done the airport authority no harm to have backed down and let Bennett retain the glory that was rightfully his. The airport could, in fact, have championed Bennett and used him as a valuable promotional tool for Heathrow in its fortieth anniversary year. Instead, they ungraciously ignored the old RAF Pathfinder and his early achievements for the airport.

Next to arrive was a smartly-dressed lady, aged 65. Former BSAA colleagues recognized her as 'Star Girl' Mary Guthrie – for the last thirty-five years Mary Cunningham – who had been the country's first post-war air hostess back in 1946. Now living in retirement with her family in Somerset, Mary now rarely visited the airport but was delighted to be back at Heathrow in the company of colleagues she had not seen in years.

As the room began to fill with people, another familiar face from forty years ago arrived at the door: Captain Cliff 'Alibe' Alabaster, navigator on the first flight, a pioneer of in-flight refuelling, one of the first to pilot a Comet in commercial service and last to fly the famous jet when it was withdrawn from BOAC operations in 1965. Pride of place in Alibe's home in Surrey is a scale model of the famous jet with an inscription on a plinth (borrowed from St Matthew's Gospel) reading: 'So the last shall be first, and the first last.' Alibe was now retired, aged 68 and enjoying his free time sailing boats around the Mediterranean.

Meanwhile, over at Terminal 1, another event had been planned for the veterans. Waiting to greet the pioneering Heathrow trio was another airport and BSAA veteran, Keith Hayward, who as a 16-year-old school-leaver had travelled to the airport from London with Bennett and Alibe to witness the departure of the first flight. Now just three years away from retirement and working as senior passenger officer with British Airways in Terminal 1, Keith was the prime mover of today's reunion party and further recognition of the airport's first international departure.

Once the guests had all arrived, they were taken to the airline's VIP lounge in Terminal 1 where Bennett, Mary and Alibe unveiled a framed photograph commemorating their thirty-six-hour flight to Buenos Aires four decades earlier. The air vice marshal must have been delighted that his achievement had at last been recognized, even if it was by British Airways instead of the airport authority itself.

When later asked by a television reporter what Heathrow was like in those days, Bennett reflected:

We didn't have any buildings then. The airport looked like a runway under construction, and that's exactly what it was. We used a hut as headquarters for British South American Airways and there was one other building for flying control. The whole atmosphere wasn't exactly make-do, but we had to get on with it despite the lack of posh buildings and expensive places for passengers to be held up in. We had to ask the contractors if they would clear the runway so we could take off. In those days it was almost exciting, certainly very interesting. Today it's mundane in the extreme. We lived at the right time.

The air vice marshal also used the occasion to take a pot-shot at the way British airports were run in the 1980s. 'Back in 1946 I was one of those who believed that we should have eight airports, not one – and I still think I'm right. If you look around Heathrow on a busy day, you'll see exactly what I mean.'

Seven months later Bennett was dead. He passed away on 14 September 1985, his 76th birthday. Mary Cunningham died in July 2012 and Cliff Alabaster in May 2014. Keith Hayward is still going strong, enjoying retirement, keeping in touch with his children and grandchildren and reflecting on a fine career at Heathrow. At the age of 90, Keith has never left the airport where today he freely gives his time as honorary consultant archivist at British Airways' marvellous treasure trove of an archive. Long may he thrive!

* * *

In December 1988 an anonymous telephone message was received at the US Embassy in Helsinki warning that a sabotage attempt would shortly be made against a Pan Am aircraft flying between Frankfurt and the United States. Details of the call were passed on by the American Federal Aviation Administration to embassies around Europe and to the airline's headquarters, but the information was never made available to the public because it might harm the now ailing airline and cause unnecessary panic among the travelling public. In many areas, the threat was dismissed as yet another hoax.

On 21 December, a Pan Am Boeing 747 'Maid of the Seas' carrying 259 passengers and crew took off from Heathrow to New York. Around forty minutes into the journey, the flight disappeared from radar screens at Prestwick Air Traffic Control Centre. There were reports that an explosion had taken place on the ground 15 miles north of the Scottish border. The plane had crashed from a height of 31,000ft onto the town of Lockerbie, between Carlisle and Dumfries. Everyone on board was killed. A further eleven people on the ground also lost their lives that day as the wreckage plunged

On 21 December 1988 a Pan American Boeing 747 'Maid of the Seas' carrying 259 passengers and crew took off from Heathrow to New York. Around forty minutes into the journey, the flight disappeared from radar screens at Prestwick Air Traffic Control Centre. There were reports that an explosion had taken place on the ground 15 miles north of the Scottish border. The plane had crashed from a height of 31,000ft onto the town of Lockerbie, between Carlisle and Dumfries. Everyone on board was killed. (*Daily Mail*)

through twenty houses and numerous cars, ploughing a deep crater into a residential street. The plane then exploded into a ball of fire, propelling debris across a wide area. The impact registered 1.6 on the Richter scale. 'It was virtually raining fire, liquid fire,' said an eye witness.

The crash had been caused by a massive explosion in a baggage container positioned on the left-hand side of the forward cargo hold, scattering passengers, baggage, cargo and wreckage over a wide area of Lockerbie.

The subsequent police investigation was the biggest ever mounted in Scotland and was turned into a full-scale murder inquiry once evidence of a bomb was found by Britain's Air Accidents Investigation Branch. The organization later confirmed that the Pan Am jet had been sabotaged and traces of Semtex high explosives discovered in the wreckage. The bomb had been hidden away inside a portable radio cassette player concealed in a suitcase.

Two men accused of being Libyan intelligence agents were later charged with planting the bomb in a piece of baggage checked in at Frankfurt Airport and due to be transferred to the ill-fated Pan Am jet at Heathrow. One of them was jailed following an eighty-four-day trial under Scottish law and held in Holland, while his alleged accomplice was found not guilty.

Once again Heathrow was placed on alert and security screening increased. Passenger baggage and cargo containers were placed in special 'decompression chambers', which scanned units for suspect devices. Passenger searches were intensified and travellers advised to arrive at airport check-in desks extra early in order to undergo additional security checks.

Today more than one-third of Heathrow's employees work in security-related jobs. BAA was the world's first to introduce 100 per cent total baggage screening and new security techniques are constantly being pioneered at the airport.

* * *

At the same time as plans were still being drawn up for Terminal 4 in the 1970s, secret talks were taking place at the airport authority's London offices for a fifth terminal, a building much larger than the others and built on the only site still available on what was now an extremely congested airport, considered one of the finest and most successful in the world.

One of the last tasks facing Sir Peter Masefield before he retired as the airport's chairman in 1972 was to oversee plans for Heathrow's fifth terminal, which the organization expected to be fully built and ready for use in 1990 on the redeveloped site of the Perry Oaks sludge works on the airport's western side. Knowing that a large-scale public inquiry would have to take place before builders moved in, BAA quietly put the Terminal 5 plans to one side, for the time being. The organization had one other major plan to oversee before it could do anything else.

The plan was to float its shares on the stock market in 1987. Market analysts were sceptical about the success of the flotation, but investors brave enough to buy shares saw excellent returns within a short time. Now Heathrow – and other airports run by the newly-renamed BAA plc – had to operate on a commercial basis. The world watched and quickly saw that privatizing airports was an extremely good idea.

Chapter 19

The 1990s: Dirty Tricks, the IRA and the Longest Public Inquiry

More than 40 million passengers were using Heathrow at the start of the 1990s and behind the scenes plans were being finalized for the largest and most controversial construction project in Europe: Terminal 5.

It was no secret that BAA wanted another terminal to be sited on land covering 251 hectares on the airport's western edge on land once occupied by the small country settlement of Perry Oaks, now site of a sewage works owned and operated by Thames Water Utilities. It was the only place large enough to accommodate a massive new terminal and the surrounding infrastructure needed to successfully feed cars, coaches, lorries and underground trains plus the world's largest airliners – including the giant A380 – to and from the building.

Naturally, a public inquiry would be mounted to examine evidence for and against construction of the new terminal and a secretariat was set up well in advance of BAA's application being received in order to have everything ready for the time when organizations and individuals would come forward to raise their objections and give their points of view.

By February 1993, BAA was ready to submit forty separate formal applications, orders and appeals under the Planning, Highways, Civil Aviation and Transport and Works Act. By the following month, the organization had submitted a further twenty applications relating to Terminal 5, including schemes to relocate the sewage works, divert two rivers running around the site, building a new road connecting the terminal to the M25 motorway (which would be widened to cope with massive amounts of extra traffic), improvements to the M4 and extensions to the Heathrow Express railway and Piccadilly Underground lines.

BAA put forward a strong argument in favour of a terminal designed to handle 17 million annual passengers and boost the airport's annual throughput to 80 million annual travellers by 2017. Estimated cost was in the region of £3.7 billion. It stated that as the world's busiest airport, Heathrow's success was 'vital to the local economy and the country as a whole.' It predicted that the number of people wanting to fly is forecast to double in the next fifteen years. Heathrow's existing four terminals cannot cope with this demand and the airport needs to expand. Both Gatwick and Stansted airports are growing fast but London needs Terminal 5 as well if it is to meet the needs of the twenty-first century.

According to BAA, 'without Terminal 5, Heathrow's position as Europe's leading gateway could be lost to other airports. Airlines seeking to grow their business could take their investment and jobs to Paris, Frankfurt and Amsterdam instead of London.' The organization promised that 'thanks to expected advances in aircraft technology, there will be no overall increase in noise levels … and BAA will accept a legally binding guarantee that this is so.'

The terminal would also generate employment for thousands of people 'and provide around 6,000 construction jobs.' BAA claimed the project 'has the support of the travel industry, trade unions, business groups and many community representatives, and local polls show residents are strongly in favour.'

BAA's early Terminal 5 publicity failed to mention that the terminal also had a large number of objectors, including thirteen local authorities. Out of fifty major parties participating in the inquiry – including environmental groups and residents living around Heathrow – over 95 per cent were opposed to the terminal. Around 5,000 individuals and organizations formally registered to speak for or against the construction project: 3,000 giving oral evidence and 2,000 submitting written representations. So large was the demand to give evidence that a special library had to be created containing all applications, statements and representations.

* * *

While arrangements for the Terminal 5 public inquiry rolled on, Heathrow and British Airways were both under attack from different quarters.

In 1993, British Airways ended one of the most bitter and protracted libel actions in aviation history following a humiliating courtroom climb-down. In the High Court, Christopher Clarke QC publicly apologized 'unreservedly' for an alleged 'dirty tricks' campaign against rival airline Virgin Atlantic.

The airlines had competed with each other head-to-head on transatlantic routes ever since Virgin had transferred operations from Gatwick to Heathrow in July 1991. Virgin's boss, Sir Richard Branson, claimed that he had evidence that British Airways' staff were in the habit of 'poaching' Virgin's customers and tampering with confidential company files. Branson also claimed that British Airways' PR consultants had been undermining him and his company in the City and through the media.

In an open letter to British Airways' executive directors, Branson accused the airline of 'sharp business practices'. They responded by accusing Branson of publicity-seeking and the accusation was repeated by British Airways Chairman, Lord King, in a staff newspaper. The statements formed the basis of Branson's libel case and both British Airways and Lord King counter-sued over Virgin's original allegations.

The High Court heard that British Airways agreed to pay damages of £500,000 to Branson and £110,000 to his airline, as well as picking up legal costs of around £3 million.

In June 1993 Lord King retired from British Airways six months earlier than expected, to be replaced by Colin Marshall (now Lord Marshall). That year the airline made a pre-tax profit of £301 million while Virgin Atlantic declared an operating loss of £9.3 million. Virgin moved back into profit, however, in later years and went on to rival British Airways on major airline routes to Africa, Asia, Australia and the United States.

*　*　*

No one working at Heathrow Airport in March 1994 will ever forget three terrifying days when the IRA launched a series of mortar attacks on the airport, partially paralysing the capital's main air route. Their plan was to blow up runways, cause death and injury to airport staff and passengers – including the queen – and damage to aircraft, including Concorde.

Attack number one happened on the evening of 9 March when IRA terrorists carried out a mortar attack from a car park next to the airport's Hatton Cross Underground station. The attack followed a coded telephone warning to the airport switchboard. Although five mortars fell inside the airport estate, none of them exploded. Concorde had touched down at Heathrow from New York just a few moments earlier. Police and security services searched the area looking for other vehicles containing mortars but none were found.

The second attack came thirty hours later when another coded warning alerted the airport to expect further assaults on Terminal 4. Passengers and staff were evacuated from the building and runways closed, causing congestion and confusion in other terminals. This time the IRA had positioned themselves in a wooded area on the western side of the airport from where they launched four mortars over the perimeter fence. Once again, none exploded. An RAF plane with the queen on board landed at Heathrow while security forces were conducting a search of the terminal. Police carried out minute searches but discovered no further mortars.

Attack number three came on 13 March when four IRA bombs were fired from a heavily-camouflaged launcher buried in scrubland along the airport's

In March 1994 the IRA launched a series of mortar attacks on Heathrow, partially paralysing the capital's main air route. Their plan was to blow up runways, cause death and injury to airport staff and passengers – including the queen – and damage aircraft, including Concorde. Although the IRA attacks failed to kill, maim or damage Heathrow's passengers and staff, they brought business to a standstill on three consecutive occasions and demonstrated just how vulnerable Heathrow was to a terrorist strike. (*Author's Collection*)

southern perimeter. The airport was closed for two hours following the mortar attack and none of the devices exploded.

Although the IRA attacks had failed to kill, maim or damage Heathrow's passengers and staff, they had brought business to a standstill on three consecutive occasions and demonstrated just how vulnerable it was to such strikes.

* * *

Early in 1995, Roy Vandermeer QC was appointed chief inspector of the Terminal 5 inquiry. In April and May he called a series of pre-inquiry meetings to identify thirty different parties who would go on to play an active part in the proceedings, examine the main issues, how they would be handled, agreeing day-to-day ground rules and how formal evidence would be exchanged. It was stated that once the inquiry was under way, it would operate on totally transparent lines with daily verbatim transcripts of proceedings made available in printed form via a special website.

A major problem facing Vandermeer and his team was where the inquiry itself should be held. There were few venues in the Heathrow area large enough to accommodate both an inquiry hall and the large amount of office space needed to support the proceedings. The venue also needed to be close enough to Heathrow and the surrounding community and it was agreed that an airport hotel could offer neutral ground for what was expected to be a long and controversial inquiry. Three hotels along Heathrow's famous 'strip' – the nickname given to the section of the Bath Road running alongside the airport, which for the past thirty years had come to resemble the famous Las Vegas thoroughfare housing hotels, casinos and nightclubs – were suggested. However, none of the hotels were keen to hire out their ballrooms or conference centres for a long and indefinite period because they risked losing regular clientele.

Then the manager of the Ramada (now Renaissance) Hotel – adjacent to the site where the airport's first flight had taken off in 1946 – suggested that the hotel's under-used swimming pool be converted into a meeting hall. It would mean that he could keep his function rooms open and for a capital outlay, rent out the former swimming pool for what was expected to be a long period plus a further fifty ground-floor bedrooms to be used as offices by the major parties and secretariat; a nice piece of business!

The government had previously agreed that in view of the exceptional nature of the inquiry, the Department of the Environment, rather than a local planning authority, would cover the cost of the main inquiry accommodation.

After two years of preparation, the Terminal 5 inquiry finally opened on 16 May 1995. More than 400 people turned up on the first day. The major players were identified as BAA plc (the applicant), British Airways (the terminal's major supporter), the Highways Agency (promoting Highways Orders), the London Borough of Hillingdon (the local planning authority opposing Terminal 5), Spelthorne Borough Council (also opposing), plus LHRT5 (a consortium of ten local authorities also against the terminal development). The Environment Agency and Royal Parks Agency were also involved for part of the time. More than thirty barristers, solicitors and advocates, including twelve QCs, appeared for these and other parties during the course of the inquiry.

Around twenty small third parties and individuals played a regular part in the proceedings, including the environmental and noise action groups Friends of the Earth and HACAN Clearskies. The groups represented themselves as the secretariat had no resources to assist with anyone's legal costs, although some bedrooms were made available for office use by smaller groups.

Despite deep feelings aroused by many people, the inquiry was conducted in a co-operative and orderly atmosphere throughout. More than half the inquiry time was taken up by three topics: the economic/aviation case for the proposals, surface access to the new terminal, and noise. These covered the main issues of concern to objectors, although the effects of the terminal on land use/ecology, air quality and construction impact were also important to local people.

Thirty-five parties made closing submissions at the end of the inquiry, taking forty 'sitting days'. BAA's closing speech alone took fourteen 'sitting days'.

The inquiry finally closed on 17 March 1999 when recommendations were submitted to the Department of Trade and Industry. It had sat for 525 days spanning 3 years and 10 months and entered the *Guinness Book of Records* as Britain's longest-running planning inquiry (overtaking the Sizewell B Nuclear Power Station inquiry which had run for 340 days). The inquiry had cost more than £80 million, of which £64 million was borne by BAA and British Airways and £17 million by central and local government. Local authorities opposing Terminal 5 spent more than £7 million on opposing the terminal plan. Evidence was given by 734 witnesses representing more than 50 major parties. More than 600 pieces of evidence were submitted, along with 22,500 written representations; most of them expressing opposition to Terminal 5. The inquiry had generated 5,000 documents covering 80,000 pages and 30 million words. Under the inquiry rules, everyone had a statutory right to be heard and challenge the views of others and time allocated to hear their views.

They then held their collective breath as they awaited a decision...

* * *

The final outcome of the inquiry came on 20 November 2001 when the government gave its blessing to allow the terminal to go ahead with the next stage of planning. It would be ready for business in 2008. Thousands who had spent time gathering and giving evidence to the inquiry were disappointed. Others said that the outcome had been a foregone conclusion and that the inquiry itself a cosmetic (yet highly expensive) exercise for what was an inevitable outcome.

As the twentieth century drew to a close at Heathrow, BAA announced that 61.9 million passengers had passed through the airport in 1999.

Chapter 20

2000 and Beyond:
Heathrow and the Third Runway

While the Terminal 5 inquiry trundled on, eighty of Britain's top archaeologists were making plans to excavate the 250-acre site, which they were confident would reveal some fantastic objects from history buried underneath the airport for thousands of years. Excavation plans were formulated as soon as BAA announced its intention to build a terminal at Perry Oaks.

Before the army of builders moved onto the airport, archaeologists from Wessex Archaeology and the Oxford Archaeological Unit brought their teams together for the largest excavation in British history. They were given just over a year to complete their 'dig'.

Before long, archaeologists were unearthing evidence of communally-farmed land divided into individual and family-owned plots dating from around 2,000 BC. They discovered evidence of wells and boreholes and 80,000 individual objects including a 3,500-year-old wooden bowl and one of only two wooden buckets ever found from the same period. Two 1,000-year-old pottery cups were also uncovered along with 18,000 other pieces of pottery and 40,000 pieces of worked flint.

One archaeologist described the Terminal 5 site as one giving 'unprecedented insight into the way mankind had used the landscape over the past 8,000 years,' with pieces found from the Mesolithic or Middle Stone Age period and earliest farmers of the Neolithic period or the New Stone Age. Items from the Bronze and Iron ages, Roman, Saxon and Medieval periods were all brought to light.

John Lewis, one of several archaeologists in charge of the 'dig' said: 'It was fascinating to discover that within the boundaries of the world's biggest international airport lies a record of how people used the landscape for 8,000 years, from the time when people were hunter-gatherers to the earliest farmers and later.'

The archaeological finds are now on permanent show at the Museum of London and display cabinets in Terminals 4 and 5.

* * *

Eighty of Britain's top archaeologists came to Heathrow to excavate the 250-acre site for Terminal 5, which they were confident would reveal some fantastic objects from history buried beneath the airport for thousands of years. Before the army of builders moved onto the airport, archaeologists from Wessex Archaeology and the Oxford Archaeological Unit brought their teams together for the largest excavation in British history. They were given just over a year to complete their 'dig'. Before long, archaeologists were unearthing evidence of how communally-farmed land was divided into individual and family-owned plots dating from around 2,000 BC. (*Author's Collection*)

Around 450 armed troops were back at Heathrow at dawn on 12 February 2003 after a suspected Islamic plot to fire a missile at an airliner prompted Tony Blair to send in the army once again.

Troops used armoured Scimitar and Spartan reconnaissance vehicles to patrol the airport's 17-mile perimeter road, tunnel entrance and multi-storey car parks. Soldiers carrying semi-automatic weapons patrolled terminals just as the first of the airport's 150,000 daily passengers began checking in. A back-up force of 1,300 police officers stood ready to be called if needed. The soldiers came from the 1st Battalion Grenadier Guards and Household Cavalry.

There was a heavy police presence around the airport too, and also in areas where aircraft taking off and landing might be low enough in the sky to be hit by a rocket missile. Scotland Yard said the security was 'precautionary' and related in part to the possibility that 'the end of the Muslim festival of Eid may be used by Al-Qaeda and associated networks to mount attacks. The strengthened security, which is most likely to be visible to the public at Heathrow, relates to a potential threat to the capital.'

Some politicians accused the government of calling out the army simply to send signals to potential terrorists that the airport could swiftly be protected in the event of any threat. However, following the 11 September attacks on

Around 450 armed troops were back at Heathrow at dawn on 12 February 2003 after a suspected Islamic plot to fire a missile at an airliner prompted Prime Minister Tony Blair to send in the army once again. Troops used armoured Scimitar and Spartan reconnaissance vehicles to patrol the airport's 17-mile perimeter road, tunnel entrance and multi-storey car parks. Soldiers carrying semi-automatic weapons patrolled terminals just as the first of the airport's 150,000 daily passengers began checking in. (*Brenard Press*)

New York, no one was taking any chances. It was later learned that Home Secretary David Blunkett had seriously considered shutting the airport down, but he later admitted this would have signified a victory for terrorists and been 'catastrophic' for Britain's trade and economy. 'We decided we needed to act and put in place preventative measures to pre-empt any action that was threatening us,' said Blunkett.

Passengers departing from Heathrow seemed reassured by the increase in security measures, but it came as a shock to arriving travellers who saw armoured vehicles sitting on the tarmac next to refuelling, baggage and catering vehicles waiting for their aircraft.

Today, terrorism is never far from the minds of Heathrow's security forces. They are frequently reminded that the airport is a prime target, and sometimes the reminders come from the strangest sources. In July 2004 a motorist who had stopped to buy petrol at a Heathrow fuel station spotted a large bound document blowing along in the wind. The motorist recovered it and discovered that it appeared to contain confidential information detailing how terrorist threats were planned on potential sites, including Heathrow.

Instead of turning the dossier over to the police, the motorist thought it better to hand it over to the *Sun* newspaper, which made a big splash of the story before surrendering the file to the authorities. The newspaper said the document had been written in the previous month and set out ways in which an airport could be protected from terrorist attack.

The newspaper claimed that the dossier had said that Heathrow 'affords an excellent site to attack departing aircraft. The firing point is just over the fence into the field. This is a very large site with little cover. The only way to patrol this area is on foot. Consider dogs and the air support unit.'

David Blunkett later commented: 'The plans were obviously very good. Someone disposing of them in a way that allowed that to happen is very bad.'

* * *

Friday, 24 October 2003 was a sad day in Heathrow's long history. Nobody had died; nobody was ill. Nobody had lost their job and no airport companies had gone into liquidation that day, but millions of people were about to lose a friend and they turned out in their thousands to say goodbye ... to Concorde.

On that day, the legendary Anglo-French sky goddess in British Airways' colours drooped her long nose for the final time after twenty-seven years of supersonic history. Twenty Concordes had been manufactured and fourteen went into service in 1976, split equally between Air France and British Airways.

The supersonic jets had completed 50,000 flights and flown for more than 140,000 flying hours, 100,000 of them at supersonic speeds. During that time 2.5 million passengers had flown for 140 million miles, drinking 1 million

On 24 October 2003, thousands turned out to say goodbye to Concorde. (*Brenard Press*)

bottles of champagne along the way. Now Concorde was making its final arrival before being consigned to aviation museums and aviation history.

Thousands of Concorde fans ignored BAA's pleas to stay away from the airport and took a day off work to say an emotional farewell to their favourite aeroplane. They lined airport access roads, stood on top floors of multi-storey car parks and buildings to pay their last respects to the aircraft they all loved but in which only a few had flown. As the last three passenger flights approached Heathrow, many had tears in their eyes.

The final trio of Concordes landed at Heathrow within minutes of each other, carrying a mixture of show-business celebrities, business tycoons and ordinary people who had won a competition in which a ride in the world's best-known plane was first prize. One arrived from New York, another from Edinburgh and a third after completing a trip for invited guests around the Bay of Biscay. All three taxied to British Airways' engineering base, their crews hanging out of cockpit windows waving Union Jacks to the crowds.

Concordes have now found homes in aviation museums in Barbados, Seattle, Manchester, Edinburgh, Brooklands Aviation Museum in Surrey, a museum of flight in East Lothian and at Filton Airport near Bristol, where much of the plane's early development work was undertaken. Pieces of the famous plane along with its distinctive crockery and glassware have also been sold at auction for sky-high prices. The nosecone of a French Concorde was sold for $500,000 in 2003.

Former British Airways Chief Executive Rod Eddington said that there was 'a mixture of sadness and celebration' about the final flights. 'Concorde is a wonderful plane, an icon, but its time has come. It's an old plane – it doesn't look it – but it was designed in the 1950s and built in the 1960s.'

Although Heathrow will always be one of the first airports in the world to welcome new-age aircraft, it will never see the likes of Concorde again. The day will come when people will say 'I remember Concorde flying in and out of Heathrow. She was beautiful.' Those people of all ages who came to bid farewell to her in October 2003 will turn to Concorde pictures in books and proudly show them to children, grandchildren, nieces and nephews, who will ask why the world's first supersonic plane is no longer flying. If they can get an answer, they will hear that Concorde outlived its usefulness, that airlines could no longer get the spare parts needed to keep her in the air, that she was expensive, no longer profitable, and noisy. They might hear how Richard Branson made a last-minute bid to buy all of British Airways' remaining Concordes for his Virgin Atlantic fleet and how BA had rejected the offer.

Concorde was the beautiful bird in which British skill and technology played a major part in its creation. It will be a long time before we see its like once more.

* * *

News that Heathrow was to get a new control tower was a surprise to everyone, except air traffic control staff working in the old tower, opened in 1955. Back in those days, the brick-built tower had allowed controllers visual contact

Heathrow's elegant new control tower – which went into service in 2006 – is located at the western end of the airport's existing central terminal area and stands 87 metres tall, taking on the appearance of a giant lighthouse. Dwarfing Nelson's Column, it gives controllers unrivalled views across the entire airport and west London. The glass cab at the top is more than five storeys tall, weighing over 860 tonnes. The tower was built in pieces before being towed to its site on three massive flatbed transporter lorries. A 25m-tall section was jacked up to a height of 12m to allow a prefabricated mast section to be slotted in underneath until the building was completed and settled into its foundations. (*The Author*)

with all of the airport's runways. However, by the end of the 1990s, terminal extensions and new car parks had interrupted their field of vision and it was time to design a taller, more modern structure able to cope with the demands of an airport expected to be handling nearly 90 million passengers by 2030.

The new and elegant tower – which went into service in 2006 – bears no resemblance to the old one. Located at the western end of the airport's existing central terminal area and standing 87 metres tall, the tower takes on the appearance of a giant lighthouse. Dwarfing Nelson's Column, it gives controllers unrivalled views across the entire airport and west London. The glass cab at the top is more than five storeys tall itself and weighs more than 860 tonnes.

The tower was built in pieces before being towed to its site on three massive flatbed transporter lorries, similar to ones once used by NASA to carry the space shuttle.

A 25m-tall section was jacked up to a height of 12m to allow a prefabricated mast section to be slotted in underneath and so on until the building was completed and settled into its foundations. The tower was designed by the Richard Rogers Partnership and it quickly became a new Heathrow symbol in much the same way as the old tower had become an icon half a century earlier.

There was another major change at the airport on 15 October 2012 when the name British Airports Authority – or BAA – was dropped to be replaced by … wait for it … Heathrow Airport Limited. Chief Executive Colin Matthews said:

> We are a different company today from when BAA was formed. Over the last few years we have sold our stakes in Gatwick, Edinburgh, Budapest and Naples airports and the BAA name no longer fits. We do not represent all British airports; we are not a public authority and practically speaking the company is no longer a group as Heathrow now accounts for nearly 95 per cent of our business.

* * *

One of the last iconic remnants of the 'old' Heathrow was demolished in 2013. The distinctive nine-floor red-brick old control tower was pulled down as part of Heathrow's ongoing transformation and was removed to make way for roads to serve a new £2.5 billion terminal in the Central Area: Terminal 2.

The iconic old control tower, with its instantly recognizable glazed Air Traffic Control Room and white radar dome, had stood over the ever-evolving airport since 1955. It replaced the old RAF Control Tower shortly after the first modern runway and terminal building were opened by Queen Elizabeth.

Designed by architect Sir Frederick Gibberd, who was responsible for the Liverpool Metropolitan Cathedral and Didcot Power Station, the old control tower closed in 2012 after almost sixty years of service. It was home to offices for the last five years of its life after Air Traffic Control moved to the new control tower in 2007.

Once the tower had been flattened, the only original building still standing in the Central Terminal Area was a boiler house. The tower was built in the same era as the Queen's Building and Europa terminal, both of which had also been demolished.

The new Terminal 2, which is the latest phase of an £11 billion refurbishment programme at Heathrow, became home to Virgin Atlantic domestic routes and STAR Alliance and Aer Lingus flights when it opened in 2014. At a cost of £2.5 billion, the terminal building, satellite stands and aircraft parking stands became the largest privately-funded construction project in the UK. Heathrow said it expects 20 million passengers a year to use the new terminal.

* * *

By March 2005 and two and a half years into construction, work on Terminal 5 was more than 50 per cent complete and ahead of schedule. More than 4,000 workers were employed on the site, many engaged on raising the terminal's massive 'wave-style' roof structure into place. When put into use in 2008, this spectacular single-span structure provided passengers and staff with a bright and airy environment plus stunning views.

Work on raising the roof began in April 2004 when the first of six 2,500-tonne steel sections was lifted 39m into the air. Each 117m arch section was assembled at ground level and roofing components fitted before being jacked up 40m to its final position. One year and five subsequent lifting operations later, the dramatic roof was fully in place. The internal superstructure is made up of 26,000 tonnes of steel, which was installed at the rate of 700 tonnes each week.

At the same time, the historic twin rivers, an essential landmark on the Heathrow site since the seventeenth century, were successfully diverted along a new course around the edge of the Terminal 5 site. The Longford River and Duke of Northumberland's River had originally run through the middle of the construction site. It was necessary to alter their course and a two-year project began in which engineers created 6 km of new concrete channels to carry the twin rivers along the airport's western boundary to meet with their original courses at the southern edge of the terminal site.

A major part of the river work had been making sure that as well as being ecologically sound, the watercourses continue to provide an enhanced habitat for native fish, plants and other river life in which to thrive. More than 80,000 pre-grown plants of 37 species were brought from Norfolk to live in the new river channels. More than 4,500 fish were caught, including bream, chub, sticklebacks and eels, and were released into the nearby River Colne, while 550 freshwater mussels were transferred by hand into the new channel.

* * *

When Terminal 5 finally opened its check-in counters to passengers in 2008, Heathrow Airport was sixty-two years old and the world's largest commercial aircraft, the Airbus A380 'super jumbo' – capable of carrying more than 800 passengers – had been in operation for two years.

According to a report published by British Airways in 2005, more passengers will travel by air in the future as air fares fall in price; the result of innovative fares offered by low-cost airlines and the introduction of bigger aircraft. The report says that in 1991, the cost of a return flight to Australia was equivalent to five weeks' average salary in the UK and in 2005 it accounted for just over two weeks' average earnings. By 2015 the return air fare from London to Sydney amounted to the equivalent of just one week's average weekly earnings, and by 2025 half of that again.

Does Heathrow have room for millions of extra passengers and aircraft movements? Do Terminal 5 and the new Terminal 2 solve all of the airport's problems for the distant future? The answer to both questions is no. BAA stated (in its 'Heathrow Airport Interim Master Plan', June 2005) that with Terminal 5, Heathrow will be equipped to handle around 80 million annual passengers by 2010/11. This rose to 78 million passengers in 2017 and could rise to between 90 and 95 million passengers in its eighty-fourth anniversary year of 2030.

Where will these extra passengers be processed and dispatched to and from airliners of the future? Is there sufficient runway capacity at Heathrow to handle this additional traffic?

A government White Paper titled 'The Future of Air Transport' published in 2003 made it clear that the government supports 'a short (2,000m as opposed to 4,000m) third runway at Heathrow'. The document claimed (as such documents often do) that there is a good case for further airport development:

> The airport is of vital importance to the UK economy, attracting business to London and the south-east and supporting 100,000 jobs (direct and indirect). A short third runway would yield net economic benefits of some £6 billion (net present value) – the largest of all the new runway options examined in the run-up to the White Paper.

The airport's current runway system involves using one runway for take-offs and the second for landings. The new runway could be 'mixed mode', catering

The London Borough of Hillingdon claims that 'the villages of Sipson and Harmondsworth will essentially be demolished to make way for Heathrow's new runway', stating that two historic sites would be lost or forced to relocate: Harmondsworth's Great Barn built in 1426 and the twelfth-century parish church of St Mary plus its churchyard. (*Airport Expansion Consultation Document, January 2018*)

Three years after it had closed, the entire contents of Heathrow Terminal 1 were auctioned. Over a hundred bidders of all ages competed to buy items of aviation history, from check-in desks to toilet signs.

for both take-offs *and* landings, which are currently alternated to provide relief for local residents.

The paper recognized that further expansion would have a degree of environmental consequences and stated that any further development would be conditional on air quality standards, creation of no additional noise and improvements to public transport (especially rail) access to the airport in order to relieve pressure on the surrounding road network.

Where might this new short runway be located? In an interview with Heathrow's weekly newspaper, *Skyport*, BAA's former Chief Executive Designate Mike Clasper said: 'A third runway would require passenger-handling facilities north of the Bath Road if it's going to make sense. If you want to call that Terminal 6, fine.'

Ironically, the site Clasper suggested is similar – yet smaller in area – to one originally identified as a possible site for future airport expansion back in 1946; an area approximately 3.3 miles long and around half a mile wide north of the Bath Road and the airport's existing runways and immediately south of Junction 4 of the M4 motorway. The new runway would be linked to Heathrow's existing runway system by a half-mile-long narrow taxiway running parallel with the M4 spur road linking the motorway with a road heading towards the airport tunnel. Plans show that at the end of the new taxiway, the area will open out to accommodate the new runway which will partially devastate the ancient communities of Harmondsworth and Sipson, 700 homes, schools, playing fields, public parks, shops, an industrial estate and a large hotel within those communities. Compensation plans have been made available to 'homes blighted by these plans'.

BAA's 'Heathrow Airport Interim Master Plan' cleverly reproduced the airport's original plans for 1946 in the document, widely circulated to the general public, local authorities and other interested parties. Other maps show various options the airport operating company might follow if the new runway is given the green light, including another terminal, arrivals and departure gates and aircraft parking stands. It also revealed plans to spend a further £3 billion over the next decade to 'rejuvenate and develop the rest of the airport.'

The London Borough of Hillingdon – one of the councils most vocally opposed to Terminal 5 – says that 'the villages of Sipson and Harmondsworth would essentially be demolished to make way for the new runway and terminal buildings.' The council claimed that two historic sites would be lost or forced to relocate – Harmondsworth's Great Barn built in 1426 and the twelfth-century parish church of St Mary and its churchyard – located next to the village green.

Other councils have made it clear that they will fight vigorously to defeat the proposal for the third runway. Some have set aside a fighting fund of £100,000 to argue the case and have joined forces with various anti-noise and environmental groups to make their voice heard even louder.

BAA said 'We've found a way to retain both the Harmondsworth Tithe Barn and St Mary's Church and graveyard. We do not underestimate, however, the scale of other impacts.' Such impacts may include noise that might be magnified for those living directly under new flight paths. Local roads would be under considerable strain from extra traffic generated by a busier airport, causing congestion and bringing roads to frequent gridlock. The price of building a third runway would be the demolition of nearly 800 homes at Longford and Harmondsworth, plus an increase in flights from 480,000 to 740,000 a year.

Extra activity from planes, cars and buses may also bring serious consequences regarding the air we breathe. It is claimed that in 2015, even without a third runway, 14,000 people were exposed to levels of nitrogen dioxide exceeding EU limits. This figure could rise to 35,000 people if a third runway is built.

Mick Temple, a former managing director of BAA Heathrow, said:

> Heathrow is one of the world's great airports, but we recognise that it needs modernising. Terminal 5 gave us an opportunity to transform Heathrow and this interim master plan is an important step towards achieving that.
>
> The aviation industry is constantly changing to reflect the evolving needs of air passengers and as an airport operator we also have to respond to meet these needs. What is certain is that Heathrow cannot afford to stand still. We need to plan for the future and ensure we provide excellent customer service and facilities to both our passengers and airlines.

* * *

In June 2015, after forty-seven years of service, Heathrow's Terminal 1 closed its doors to passengers for the last time. BEA was the first operator to fly from Terminal 1 to Edinburgh when it was opened by the queen in May 1968 and the final departure was a British Airways flight to Hanover.

At its peak, more than 9 million annual passengers passed through Terminal 1, which was once the largest short-haul terminal in Western Europe. It was also the last of the central area heritage buildings built in the 1950s to be demolished by the wrecking ball. The new Terminal 2 has now taken the place of Terminal 1.

Three years after it had closed, the entire contents of Heathrow Terminal 1 were auctioned off. More than 100 bidders of all ages turned out to the auction at an airport hotel in an attempt to buy items of aviation history ranging from seats to check-in desks and even toilet signs.

Larger items, including baggage carousels and escalators, were sold at a later date. Thousands of other bidders from across the world made their bids online.

Potential buyers included seasoned travellers wanting a bit of something to remind them of where they had once travelled from, serious collectors of airport-related memorabilia, staff who had once worked in Terminal 1 and former plane-spotters now turned into adults looking for nostalgic reminders of their visits to Heathrow. Commercial ventures bidding for items included nightclubs, pubs and restaurants seeking something unique to hang on their walls.

Operators from other airports in the UK and Europe came to the auction to bid for security cameras and scanners, while others came for toilet signs to use at amusement parks and zoos.

Before the auction had reached a dozen lots, it was clear that Heathrow Terminal 1 was more loved than weary passengers and staff might have imagined. Britain's biggest airport was literally making money for old rope! A short length of red velvet rope used for cordoning off a VIP area, together with two posts, sold for £900. Moments earlier, a small sign reading 'Gate 7' raised £1,050.

Because no one was sure how much demand there would be for the entrails of an obsolete 1960s airport terminal, there were no reserve prices. However, as soon as bidding began for Lot 1, a sign reading 'Welcome to Terminal 1', it was clear that the auction would raise hundreds of thousands of pounds.

A piece of airport signage that would normally have ended up in a skip rose swiftly to £1,200. Soon afterwards, an online bidder paid £4,750 for a large utilitarian clock that had hung in the main departures area. A row of four black leather seats from which travellers watched delays tick from minutes into hours sold for £800.

A check-in desk, complete with scales and conveyor belt, sold for £3,000, while a pair of information desks went for £450 each. Even a baggage trolley, with a slogan attached stating 'Making every journey better', was an object of desire, selling for £250.

Almost three hours into the auction, a series of ten original enamel-on-steel art works by Polish artist Stefan Knapp came up for sale and were sold for £57,000, while in keeping with the hierarchy of air travel, signs for 'Economy', 'Business' and 'First Class' went for £325, £375 and £600 respectively.

Chapter 21

Alternative Airports and
(possibly) the End of Heathrow!

L ondon has six commercial airports in its metropolitan area, making it the world's busiest airports system. However, the question of how to expand the system's capacity to cope with growing demand for air travel is an issue that successive governments have failed to properly and responsibly address since the 1960s.

By 1960, it was clear that further air capacity near to London was needed. Stansted, a former military airfield in Essex, was proposed as a third airport in 1963. A government White Paper endorsed Stansted in 1967 but in 1968, after an inconclusive public inquiry, the government appointed the Hon. Mr Justice Roskill to head the commission on the Third London Airport (the 'Roskill Commission') to review sites for a brand-new airport. Cublington in the Vale of Aylesbury was its chosen site, offering the best access as it was situated on the key London-Birmingham axis, away from built-up areas and would cost less than the alternatives. The proposal met with strong opposition from local people and more broadly from politicians and voters, making Cublington politically untenable.

Proposals for alternative airport sites also included the following:

Maplin (Foulness)

The Roskill Commission proposed an alternative site at Maplin Sands, Foulness, in the Thames Estuary, opening the door to strong political opposition against Cublington. In April 1971 the government announced that the Maplin site was selected for the third London airport, even though it was the most remote and expensive option. In due course the Maplin Development Act received Royal Assent in October 1973 and a Special Development Order was made under the Town and Country Planning Acts granting planning permission for the project. The project would have included not just a major airport, but also a deep-water harbour suitable for new container ships then coming into use; a high-speed rail link together with the M12 and M13 motorways to London; and a new town for the accommodation of thousands of workers who would be required. The new town would eventually cover 82 square miles for its predicted population of 600,000 people. The cost was estimated at

£825 million, which many – particularly in the Labour Party, which was in opposition at the time – regarded as unacceptable.

The Maplin project was scrapped in July 1974 when Labour came to power. A reappraisal of passenger projections indicated that there would be capacity until 1990 at Heathrow, Gatwick, Stansted and Luton, aided by regional airports. The scheme was abandoned in favour of a cheaper plan to enlarge Stansted rather than build an entirely new airport.

Cliffe (North Kent)

In 2002 a Department for Transport study identified a site at Cliffe on the Hoo Peninsula in north Kent as the leading contender among potential sites for a new airport for London. The proposal was for up to four runways arranged in two east–west close parallel pairs, with a possible fifth runway on a different alignment, for use at night and in particular weather conditions. In December 2003 the government decided against Cliffe on the grounds that the costs of a coastal site were too high and there was a significant risk that the airport might not be sufficiently well used.

Isle of Sheppey (Thames Estuary)

A proposal was put forward in the 1990s for an airport to be built on an offshore artificial island in the Thames estuary, north-east of the Isle of Sheppey, but the idea was once again scrapped. When the proposal was put forward again in a government 2002 consultation, it was rejected on the grounds of insufficient information and prohibitive expense.

Shivering Sands (Whitstable, Kent)

The proposal was revived in 2008 by then Mayor of London, Boris Johnson, with the site relocated to the east towards the Shivering Sands area, north-east of Whitstable. In November 2008 the mayor appointed Doug Oakervee (executive chair of Crossrail) to lead the Greater London Authority's preliminary feasibility study which determined in October 2009 that there was 'no logical constraint' to the plan.

London Britannia Airport ('Boris Island')

A Thames hub airport to be called London Britannia Airport (but popularly known as 'Boris Island' after Boris Johnson, the Mayor of London) proposed the construction of a four-runway hub airport located on the Isle of Grain in Kent. The plan was to combine rail, freight logistics, aviation, energy, flood protection and regional development in the Thames Estuary connecting the infrastructure to a trade and utilities spine running the length of the country. It would eventually totally replace Heathrow Airport which would close down to be replaced by 'the London Borough of Heathrow – a technopolis centre for regional high-technology enterprises, new homes and parkland for 300,000 people and provide direct/indirect employment for over 200,000 people.' The plan was to open London Britannia Airport in 2029 with an initial handling capacity of 110 million annual passengers.

The site was selected for its proximity to the capital: at 34 miles (55 km) from the centre from where the airport could be reached in twenty-six minutes by high-speed rail. The proposal to build the airport on a platform, like those at Chek Lap Kok in Hong Kong and New Doha International Airport in Qatar, would allow flights to take off and land over water, significantly reducing noise impacts and enabling the airport to operate twenty-four hours daily.

London Britannia Airport's proposal was submitted to the UK's Airports Commission in July 2013 as a proposed solution to the question of how the UK can maintain its global hub status. It was rejected on grounds of cost (possibly as high as £100 billion) and environmental damage by the Airports Commission in an announcement made on 2 September 2014, leaving Gatwick and Heathrow as the remaining options.

* * *

So, who now owns Britain's only aviation hub at Heathrow Airport?

Many think of Heathrow as a thoroughly British institution made up of British investors and quoted on the UK Stock Exchange, but they would be wrong. There are just two British shareholder/investors in Heathrow out of a total of seven other international investment organizations.

Heathrow Airport Holdings Limited (formerly BAA) owns and runs the airport. Heathrow Airport Holdings Limited is in turn owned by FGP Topco Limited, a consortium owned and led by the Spanish-owned infrastructure specialist Ferrovial S.A. (25 per cent) along with Doha-based Qatar Investment Authority (20 per cent); Canadian company Caisse de dépôt et placement du Québec (CDPQ) (12.62 per cent); Singapore-based global long-term investor GIC (11.20 per cent); Greenwich, Connecticut-based infrastructure investment firm Alinda Capital Partners (11.18 per cent); Beijing-based China Investment Corporation (CIC), a wholly state-owned company incorporated in accord with China's Company Law, (10 per cent); and Universities Superannuation Scheme (USS), a Liverpool-based pension scheme with over £50 billion under management (10 per cent).

A joke circulating around Heathrow since 2013 claims that the airport is twice the size in area of Gibraltar. The other difference between the two places? The Brits still own Gibraltar …

Chapter 22

The Airports Commission and the Third Runway

Today Heathrow is one of the biggest and, according to passengers, one of the world's best airports. Over the last fifteen years Heathrow Airport Limited has used over £11 billion of private investment to transform the airport into a national asset of which Britain can be proud. For over 300 years the world's largest port or international airport has been in Britain. Today, that source of competitive advantage is being gradually eroded. The construction of a third runway is the last and best chance for Britain to act to maintain its global connections before it is too late. The UK is in a global competition for trade, jobs and economic growth. Direct flights support the economic growth that Britain needs. They support exports to fast-growing markets, make the UK a more attractive location for business, and bring tourists to Britain.

Connections to long-haul markets are important to Britain's competitiveness. The fastest-growing markets over the next fifty years will be in Asia, Latin America and North America, while traditional European markets face a slower growth future. That is why Heathrow's competitors are investing in their airports and in one type of airport in particular: the hub. Hub airports are the only airports that support frequent and direct long-haul flights. By combining transfer passengers, direct passengers and freight, they are able to fill long-haul aircraft and serve destinations that cannot be served by airports that rely on local demand alone. This is why Heathrow, as the UK's only hub, accounts for only around 20 per cent of flights from the UK but nearly 80 per cent of long-haul services. Having a successful hub airport is uniquely important for reaching the markets critical to Britain's economic future.

The Airports Commission was an independent group established in September 2012 by the UK government to consider how Heathrow could 'maintain its status as an international hub for aviation and take immediate actions to improve the use of existing runway capacity in the next five years.' The question of how to make best use of and expand airport capacity then became the UK's hottest topic, with media stories appearing on an almost daily basis both for and against the plan.

The Airports Commission was an independent group established in September 2012 by the UK government to consider how Heathrow could 'maintain its status as an international hub for aviation and take immediate action to improve the use of existing runway capacity in the next five years.' The five-person commission, chaired by the economist Sir Howard Davies (pictured here), reported to the Department for Transport and produced an interim report in December 2013 and a final report on 1 July 2015. On 25 June 2018 Parliament formally backed Heathrow's expansion. (*Paul Patel*)

The five-person commission, chaired by the economist Sir Howard Davies, reported to the Department for Transport and produced an interim report in December 2013 and a final report on 1 July 2015. On 25 June 2018 Parliament formally backed Heathrow's expansion, with MPs voting in support of the government's Airport National Policy Statement. The next day it was confirmed that the formal government policy for new airport infrastructure included support for a new north-west runway.

The proposal for a new runway will be combined with a package of measures to address its environmental and community impacts, presenting the strongest case and offering the greatest strategic and economic benefits, providing around forty new destinations from the airport and more than 70,000 new jobs by 2050. The Airport Commission had cost taxpayers £20 million and took three years to arrive at its conclusion. As the government gave the green light to the controversial third runway after almost twenty years of wrangling and delays, Heathrow's management team went into top gear.

Strong lobbying teams were created by both sides with 'Back Heathrow' (funded by Heathrow Airport Limited) in favour and former Mayor of London and Foreign Secretary Boris Johnson claiming he would 'lie down in front of bulldozers to prevent the project from going ahead.' Others against the plan included HACAN (Heathrow Association for the Control of Aircraft Noise), SHE (Stop Heathrow Expansion), AirportWatch, the No 3rd Runway Coalition, Slough & District Against Runway 3, and North Surrey Green Party, plus Hillingdon, Richmond, Wandsworth and Windsor & Maidenhead councils who want to launch a judicial review of the decision. The councils have also received backing from Greenpeace, the local authority in Hammersmith & Fulham and Sadiq Khan, the current Labour Mayor of London.

After an announcement that the new runway would go ahead, John Holland-Kaye, chief executive of Heathrow Airport, said:

> Heathrow is a crucial part of the UK economy and its expansion is vital to securing the country's economic future as an outward-looking nation . . . . Heathrow's expansion is about more than just a runway. It is about opportunities for our local community, inside and outside of the airport's boundary. It is about securing the country's economy and connecting the whole of the UK to global growth. And it is about legacy – building the infrastructure today that our children will need for tomorrow.

Heathrow's management began a detailed consultation process presenting the airport's options and proposals to build the new runway. It provided opportunities for people living in the airport zone to have their say to help share emerging proposals. Heathrow stated:

> Heathrow has agreed to meet or exceed a significant package of measures that addresses its environmental and community effects. Detailed expansion plans – which are still subject to change – will be subjected to a public consultation and a future planning inquiry. It hopes to receive final planning permission and begin construction in 2021 with a view to opening the new runway to air traffic in 2026.

The measures include the following:

Night Flights: Heathrow will introduce a ban on scheduled night flights for 6.5 hours between the hours of 11.00 pm and 7.00 am. Around 80 per cent of current night flights at Heathrow are between 4.30 am and 6.00 am, with on average around sixteen aircraft scheduled to arrive each day between these hours.

Noise Envelope 1: The airport promises to consult and establish its plans for a clear, legally binding noise envelope that will provide certainty to local people on how Heathrow addresses noise.

Noise Envelope 2: The airport promises to provide predictable periods of respite so local people will know when no planes will fly over their homes.

Property Compensation: People in danger of losing their homes in order to build the third runway and its surrounding infrastructure will receive compensation at market value plus 25 per cent, all legal fees, stamp duty and removal costs.

Community Compensation: Heathrow will spend over £1bn on community compensation (noise and property) and support the introduction of schemes to ensure airport users pay to compensate local communities for impacts the airport might introduce.

Community Engagement Board: The airport will establish an independent Community Engagement Board which will have influence on how money is spent on compensation and community support.

Independent Aviation Noise Authority: The airport will back such an authority with statutory powers.

Training and Apprenticeships: The airport will create 5,000 additional apprenticeships at Heathrow, bringing the total to 10,000 by 2030. (Presumably this will be in association with airlines and operators already providing training and apprenticeships working in a number of different areas.)

Travel Mode Share: The airport will incentivize and support a shift in transport modes for those working at and travelling through Heathrow.

Air Quality: Heathrow Airport Limited states that new capacity at an extended airport will only be realized when it is clear that the airport's contribution will not delay the UK's compliance with EU air quality limits.

Fourth Runway: Heathrow Airport Limited would accept a commitment from government ruling out construction of any fourth runway, putting a cap on future airfield expansion following the opening of the third runway and possible additional passenger/freight buildings.

Chapter 23

Where Shall We Put the New Runway?

Heathrow's two existing runways are full but the airport that was once the busiest in the world for international traffic and third overall as recently as 2014, has since slipped to seventh in global rankings. Dubai, Tokyo, Los Angeles and Chicago have usurped Heathrow and others – such as Hong Kong, Shanghai and Amsterdam – are closing the gap fast.

So one thing is certain: when Heathrow's plan for a third runway is finally rubber-stamped it will be constructed in the north-west area of the airport which is more or less identical to the same site highlighted for airport expansion back in 1946. Three different options are available, all covering the same site: two of them with a 3,200m-long runway and a third 3,500m in length. Whichever site is chosen, a number of things will be common to all:

- They will all be 1,035m from the existing northern runway
- The new runway will sit between the villages of Sipson, Poyle and Colnbrook
- They will all cross the path of the A4 Colnbrook by-pass
- Option 1 (3,200m long) will be located towards the east; option 2 (also 3,200m long) will be located towards the west while option 3 (3,500m long) will enable the largest commercial aircraft to take off/land and allow an expanded Heathrow to be more resilient and enable aircraft to be higher over local communities on landing/take-off and reduce noise. For obvious reasons this is Heathrow Airport Limited's favoured site for a third runway.
- Whatever site is chosen, the height of the runway will vary over its length. At the eastern end adjacent to Harmondsworth and Sipson it will be at ground level. As it crosses the M25 it will be on an embankment at heights of between 3 to 5 metres. At its western end near Colnbrook it will again be close to ground level.

Heathrow Airport has also put forward new options to re-position the M25 carriageway and tunnel out a section in order to make way for the new runway. Once constructed, the new runway will extend several hundred metres past the current M25, between Junctions 14 and 15. Heathrow plans to move the motorway carriageway 150 metres west of its current site and lower it 7 metres into the tunnel.

Inevitably, the new runway will ultimately need either a new terminal or major expansions to Terminals 2 and 5 to accommodate the additional number of passengers passing through the airport. None of the existing four terminals have the space to service an increased number of travellers, passengers and their luggage. The favoured option is to build a new satellite terminal and apron between the new north-west runway and what will become the central runway. Construction designs and precise locations have yet to be revealed.

Heathrow's expansion will increase demand for airport-related development such as hotels and commercial facilities and generate considerable local employment. Heathrow Airport estimates there will be a demand for an additional 8,300 new rooms in around 20 new hotels by 2140. There will also be demand for more office space of a range of sizes from small local companies to international-scale corporate offices. Demand will also increase for industrial warehousing directly related to airport-based organizations including airline catering and maintenance, cargo-handling, freight-forwarding, warehousing and logistics. Nearly thirty different sites scattered around Heathrow have already been identified as suitable locations for such businesses.

* * *

More than seventy years on since BSAA's Avro Lancastrian left Heathrow on its first long-haul flight to Latin America, the airport has become a way of life for thousands of people, many of whom have been employed there for their entire working lives. In all probability Heathrow has yet to reach its prime. Love it or hate it, Heathrow is likely to be there for at least another eighty years once the third runway is open for business, despite statements of gloom from certain MPs who insist that the airport 'is in the wrong place'.

While politicians, councils, pressure groups and local residents argue, life at Heathrow goes on; the airport, in fact, teems with life morning, noon and often through the night. It currently provides employment for more than 70,000 people and sustains more than 200,000 other jobs across the country. The airport generates £2.5 billion in local wages, acts as a gateway for 77.9 million annual passengers (2017 figures) flying on 474,025 aircraft movements (in 2017) with more than 80 airlines flying to or from around 183 destinations in 82 different countries. It handles over 1.7 million tonnes of air cargo (in 2017), making it one of the world's leading trading ports. Thanks to its fabulous shops, the airport has become one of the country's leading retail centres. The airport is a key economic driver, generating around £6 billion every year for the UK.

By the time Heathrow had celebrated its seventieth anniversary back in 2016, it had handled around 2 billion passengers flying on more than 17 million flights. Not bad for a building site that handled just ten passengers on its first day, and 60,000 passengers, 2,400 tons of cargo and 9,000 movements in its first year more than seven long decades ago.

How time flies ...

Bibliography

Primary Sources:

Balfour, Harold, *Wings Over Westminster* (Hutchinson & Co., London, 1973)

Bate, G.R., *And So Make a City Here* (Thomasons Ltd, Hounslow, Middlesex, 1948)

Bramson, Alan, *Master Airman* (Airlife Publishing, 1985)

Burton, N.J., *The Lost Rivers of London* (Phoenix House Ltd, London/Leicester University Press, Leicester, 1962)

Duffy, Paul, *Russian Airliners* (Osprey Publishing, London, 1993)

Gero, David, *Aviation Disasters (Since 1950)* (Patrick Stephens Ltd, 1993)

Gilchrist, Peter, *Modern Civil Aircraft 4: Boeing 747* (Ian Allan, Shepperton, Surrey, 1985)

Haddon, Richard, Harvey, Charles and Wolff, E.S., *The Modern World Book of Flying* (Sampson, Low, Marston & Co., London, 1957)

Jackson, A.S., *Pathfinder Bennett – Airman Extraordinary* (Terence Dalton, Sudbury, 1991)

London Britannia – Europe's Hub Airport (Thames Estuary Research & Development Company, 2014)

Masefield, Peter and Gunston, Bill, *Flight Path* (Airlife Publishing, 2002)

Maxwell, Gordon, *Highwayman's Heath* (Thomasons Ltd, Hounslow, Middlesex, 1935)

Maynard, John, *Bennett and the Pathfinders* (Arms and Armour Press, London, 1996)

McVeigh, S.A.J., *West Drayton Past and Present* (West Drayton Chamber of Trade, 1950)

Robbins, Michael, *Middlesex* (Collins, 1953)

Stroud, John, *Airports of the World* (Putnam, London, 1980)

Taylor, John, *Fairey Aviation* (Chalford, Stroud, 1997)

Thetford, Owen G., *Fairey Aviation* (Ian Allen's ABC of Airports and Airliners, Ian Allen, Shepperton, 1948)

Thorne, James, *Handbook to the Environs of London* (Adams and Dart, Bath, 1876)

Wright, Alan, *Classic Aircraft 2: Boeing 707* (Ian Allen Ltd, Shepperton, Surrey, 1990)

Secondary Sources

Airport Expansion Consultation Document (Heathrow Airport Limited, January 2018)

Greater London Plan 1944, ed. Patrick Abercrombie (HMSO, 1945)

Heathrow Airport Interim Master Plan (Draft for Consultation) (BAA Heathrow, June 2005)

London Airport Central Terminal Buildings for Ministry of Transport and Civil Aviation (Taylor Woodrow Construction Ltd publication, 1955)

London Airport – Developments in the Central Terminal Area, Ministry of Transport and Civil Aviation (HMSO, 1954)

Taking Britain further – Heathrow's plan for connecting the UK to growth (Heathrow Airport Limited, 2014)

Miscellaneous

Many news items quoted in this book were sourced from Keesing's Contemporary Archives 1944–66 and archives from the British Library Newspaper Library including *Flight International*, *Air Pictorial*, *Aeroplane*, *Middlesex Chronicle*, *Evening Standard*, *The Times*, The *Economist*, The *Loadstar*, *Daily Express*, *Picture Post*, *Sunday Telegraph*, *Skyport*, The *Sun*, *Daily Mail* and *Daily Herald*.

Thanks also to De Havilland Archives, the George Cross Database and various people in possession of material once owned, produced or distributed by Brenard Press Ltd, Heathrow.

Index